LONG LIVES

LONG LIVES

Chinese Elderly and the Communist Revolution

Deborah Davis-Friedmann

Expanded Edition

Stanford University Press
Stanford, California
1991

Stanford University Press
Stanford, California
© 1983, 1991 by the Board of Trustees of the
Leland Stanford Junior University
Original edition published by Harvard
University Press in 1983
Expanded edition published by Stanford
University Press in 1991

Printed in the United States of America

cloth ISBN 0-8047-1806-7
paper ISBN 0-8047-1808-3
LC 89-64240

Last figure below indicates year of this printing:

00 99 98 97 96 95 94 93 92 91

To Michael, again

Completed 5-18-96

CONTENTS

Eight pages of photographs follow p. 50 —

PREFACE TO THE EXPANDED EDITION

THIS SECOND EDITION of *Long Lives* is a book of two voices, and of two eras. Chapters One through Seven, completed in 1982, were written in the present tense just as the post-Mao economic reforms were gaining momentum, and they emphasize the contemporary and current character of the conclusions. Chapter 8, completed following the Tiananmen massacre of 1989, was written in the past tense in recognition of how very imperfectly I had judged the durability of contemporary institutional arrangements. The shift in tense, however, indicates more than a failure to predict one tragic historical event; it also reflects an altered relationship to my subject.

The first edition of *Long Lives* was a doctoral dissertation, begun when Chinese society was accessible to American scholars primarily through close reading of the official press and debriefings of recent travelers and émigrés. Sociologists who wrote about China could rarely rely on the usual quantitative methodologies, which require random samples of populations with known parameters; nor could we replicate the ethnographic tradition that requires participant observation. Nevertheless, as I noted in Chapter One, comparative reading of multiple sources and extended conversations with recent refugees eager to discuss their past did produce factual descriptions that have stood up well to subsequent field observations made in China after 1978. Even though factual accuracy was possible, one could not grapple as successfully with the simultaneity and contradictions of ongoing social relations. People too easily became subjects, and Chinese society an abstract puzzle to be solved piece by piece.

Since 1982, however, a new research environment has transformed the relationship between researchers writing about contemporary China and their subject. In the past six years, I have made six separate field trips to China. Most visits have involved a return to a city where I had stayed before, and in several instances my hosts were colleagues whom I earlier had sponsored in the United States. As a result of this increased involvement with the reality of Chinese society, I am even more aware of the transitory nature of contemporary outcomes. Repeated visits and deepening personal relations also created the potential for greater intimacy, and on each visit respondents became more expansive. The metaphor that first comes to mind to describe this experience is the peeling of an onion. As one removes one layer, another appears beneath it. The onion metaphor is misleading, however, because with each new revelation about China and my subjects' past, the "object" of study does not become smaller and simpler, but larger and more complex. Thus the experience of greater involvement in Chinese society can better be captured by considering a parallel with biologists who with every technological and theoretical breakthrough find themselves further and further from the total organism and deeper into the outwardly invisible core. Needless to say, I have hardly penetrated to the core of Chinese society. In fact, I do not believe that there is any one core to be uncovered. Instead, increasingly sustained involvement with Chinese society has reaffirmed a belief that societies are multi-centered and that observations by any one person are but single snapshots, which become history the moment they are "developed." As a result, the past rather than the present tense is the more appropriate voice for writing about contemporary society.

Despite this substantial change in my relationship to Chinese society after 1979, there is one important continuity in the research environment that still shapes my writing. In 1990 as in 1982 I must use pseudonyms to guarantee my respondents' anonymity. As we saw so dramatically in June 1989, contact with foreigners may be interpreted as an exchange of state secrets, just as it was during the 1979 crackdown on the Democracy Wall Movement, the 1966–72 witch hunts of the Cultural Revolution, or the 1955 and 1957 searches for rightists among those who had worked with foreign companies or mission hospitals. Thus—as in the first edition—I have not identified my respondents in ways that would enable them to be traced easily. Individuals are described only by their home towns and occupations. In any study where subjects provide information in confidence, authors use pseudonyms, and thus even had CCP policy on scholarly work not dramatically shifted after June 1989, I still might have taken steps to safeguard my respondents' privacy. I hope, however, that in the future this step will be taken in keeping with the universal scholarly convention of protecting confidentiality rather than as a measure to protect my subjects from charges that they revealed state secrets.

The first edition of this book was designed to explore the impact of the communist revolution on the everyday lives of Chinese elderly. There were neither pre-existing classics in the field nor raging scholarly debates with which to compare my findings. The task therefore was first to provide an overview of the lives of Chinese elderly after 1949, and then to examine whether or not CCP collectivization and political mobilizations had altered the position of the elderly and the process of growing old. Chapters One through Seven, retained here in their original form, present those empirical results.

Chapter One explores expectations about the old. The initial focus is a comparison between the ideologically correct views of the didactic press and the personal opinions of individual respondents. Not surprisingly, the two sources did not produce identical observations; neither, however, did they lead to contradictions. The official media presented the elderly as valuable witnesses to past suffering. Individual respondents also appreciated the old in terms of their position in the past, grounding their definition of a successful old age in traditional ideals of parent-child reciprocity and familial interdependence. The two views complemented each other because in both perspectives the elderly were appreciated for who they had been, and what they had experienced. Such a viewpoint supported the claims of the old on the resources of the present, and thereby strengthened the overall security and status of the elderly in the contemporary period.

Chapter Two examines economic dimensions of old age. Drawing on an overview of CCP wage and pension policies, as well as case materials gathered during interviews with Hong Kong refugees in 1976 and with PRC citizens in 1979, this chapter assesses the extent to which collectivization, the disappearance of private property, and the development of a national pension program influenced the strategies rural and urban residents adopted to maximize financial security in old age. As one would expect in a country governed by a communist party committed to egalitarian welfare ideals, state actions after 1949 generally helped the old. The allocation of benefits was irregular, however, and not necessarily along the lines one might first have predicted. For example, the elimination of private ownership and egalitarian distribution of collective income guaranteed subsistence to virtually the entire population over age sixty, and also narrowed the gap between rich and poor elderly. But in the urban areas, where collectivization of industry, commerce, and the service sector was most complete, certain key welfare programs, notably pensions and medical care, were offered incrementally to subgroups within the elderly population. This incremental expansion of pensions and medical coverage created distinct cohorts of opportunity, so that even in the late 1970s only a minority of the urban population over sixty had actually received the full benefits of socialism.

In rural areas, the government also could not fully realize the socialist blueprint, and small pockets of private enterprise persisted even during the

Mao years. But in contrast to urban areas, the incompleteness of communization worked to the advantage of the rural elderly because it permitted the old to devote themselves full time to private plots and family sidelines. Because most rural elderly pursued these private endeavors within the context of a multigeneration household, the employment of the old outside the collective also worked to the advantage of the young, and thereby cemented the generations ever more tightly into one cohesive economic and social unit.

Chapters Three through Six, which examine housing arrangements, relations with children, funerals, and the fate of filial piety, shift to a more exclusive focus on private rather than public life. Again the central question is how the communist revolution changed the precommunist situation. Were elderly as likely to live with adult children as they had before 1949? To what extent did the communists' commitment to female equality eliminate preference for patrilocal households? Had the attack on religion in general, and on ancestor worship in particular, undermined respect for the elderly? What were the most common causes of family disputes, and how dominant were the old in the household?

In terms of household composition and flow of aid between parents and children, it became clear that the redistributive income policies and post-1949 reward structure greatly improved the overall security of the elderly. The primary reason, however, was not that the CCP had explicitly targeted the old for special attention. Instead the communist revolution greatly reduced the insecurities that had dominated the family life of elderly before 1949 because core economic policies stabilized family life in general. After 1949, and particularly after 1955, migration restrictions immobilized young and old, and development policies promoted aggressive investment in industry. As a result of these official priorities, adult children and their elderly parents found it difficult to establish independent households. Multigeneration living persisted as the norm, and elderly benefited greatly from dense, stable networks of close kin that reinforced the norms of intergenerational solidarity.

Other policies pursued after 1949 had less benign effects on the family lives of the old. For example, the CCP clearly distinguished between families of "good"—i.e., proletarian or poor peasant backgrounds—and those of "bad"—i.e., capitalist or rich peasant heritage—and these distinctions played a major role in every political campaign and mobilization after 1949. As a result of the emphasis on good political pedigrees, elderly who were from the formerly advantaged classes, or who had worked with the Nationalist government or foreigners were penalized. Strong ties with children were threatened when an unfavorable class label presented a liability to the younger generation, and in many of these families obligations to parents were shallow and relations tense.

Chapter Seven looks briefly at the success of the CCP in developing a comprehensive safety net for the small minority of elderly who had no surviving children. By the late 1970s, childless elderly represented less than 5 percent of the population over sixty, and as a result of improved public health after 1950, the absolute number was slowly declining as fewer people reached middle age unmarried or without surviving children. Nevertheless, the ability to provide basic subsistence to this most needy population shows that CCP organizational skills and socialist ideals met the needs of the most vulnerable elderly more successfully than any other twentieth-century Chinese government.

Chapter Eight, written in early 1990, replaces the original concluding chapter. As in the first edition, this new conclusion summarizes the major findings of the preceding chapters and responds to the overarching question about the impact of the communist revolution on the lives of ordinary elderly, focusing in particular on how CCP policies shaped family obligations and the evolving boundaries between public and private responsibilities. The chapter updates the information on housing, retirement, and welfare policies and also examines how the post-Mao economic and political reforms have affected the old.

On balance, despite a significant decline in collective economic and political power, the 1980s represented continuity with the late 1970s. However, the reduced role of the CCP in direct supervision of private life after 1980, as well as the expanded role for entrepreneurial and individual endeavors, created conditions for change. There was more regional and individual variation, and in rural areas the withdrawal of state resources had begun to weaken collective welfare programs. As a result, there is a definite possibility that within the near future, the elderly might emerge as a more vulnerable group than they were in the Maoist era.

Chapter Eight of the expanded edition also differs in the quality of documentation. Beginning with the publication of the 1982 census, Western scholars have had much easier access to statistical materials than ever before. In addition, our Chinese colleagues—particularly in demography and gerontology—have published reports on a vast array of field projects that are generally of very high quality. Chapter Eight takes advantage of these new sources, and has more extensive quantitative and longitudinal measurements than were feasible in earlier chapters. For example, in 1982 to answer questions about the most basic demographic or financial trends, I had to piece together estimates for the population over sixty from a variety of sources, and often it was impossible to make matched comparisons with earlier decades. By 1990 I had copies of the 1982 and 1987 censuses, as well as annual editions (1981–88) of national and municipal statistical yearbooks in my office. No longer was it necessary to estimate how

Preface

average pensions varied by gender or age, or how dependency ratios would shift under different fertility rates based on a small sample of one hundred interviews. I could instead consult directly the relevant publications.

The concluding chapter also benefited from several opportunities to return to China and interview recent retirees about the ways the post-Mao reforms were changing their lives. In 1986 and 1987 I spent three months in Shanghai interviewing 130 women born between 1925 and 1935 about their work and family experiences. In 1988 I followed the same interview schedule in meetings with one hundred of their peers in Wuhan. The result is an update that confirms the original conclusions, but also strengthens and extends them.

When a seminar paper written in Boston expands into a dissertation completed in Pittsburgh and then into two editions of a book written in New Haven, the list of individuals who have provided essential support is almost as long as the book itself. Thus in deference to my subject matter and the reader's patience, I will explicitly thank only those who have most directly contributed to the project since the completion of the first edition, but with the recognition that this most recent effort would have been impossible without the support of those acknowledged previously.

Most documentary materials used in Chapter Eight were collected during two summers spent at the University Service Center in Hong Kong. For their excellent administrative help and support at the Center, I would like to thank the directors, John Dolfin and Jean Xiong, and my research assistant, Hung Chiu-kong. For facilitating and supporting my interviews in Shanghai and Wuhan, I am indebted especially to the staff of the Shanghai General Union, Putuo District government, the Hubei Academy of Social Sciences, and the General Welfare Committee of Wuhan General Union. Funds for the several research trips came from the American Council of Learned Societies, the Committee for Scholarly Exchange with the People's Republic of China, and Yale University. And finally I owe special thanks to Muriel Bell at Stanford University Press, who made it possible for *Long Lives* to have a second life, and to my friend and colleague Helen Siu, who made the critical introductions.

D.D-F.

LONG LIVES

INTRODUCTION

STUDIES OF THE ELDERLY in the twentieth century consistently document a decline in the economic and social status of old people during periods of rapid change.[1] Explanations for the reduced status of the old stress their lack of formal education, their commitment to the status quo, and their inability to retrain for new types of jobs. But the usual context in which these observations are verified is a society where land and capital are privately owned, the market distributes income and wealth, and the state fails to take any significant responsibility for the destitute or disabled. It has yet to be shown whether rapid change within a state socialist economy has equally negative consequences for the old.

In view of the socialist commitment to public ownership, egalitarian distribution of wealth, and collective responsibility for the material welfare of all citizens, the elderly in socialist countries would not be expected to suffer the same hardships experienced by the elderly in market economies. Theoretically, the ideals of socialism should protect the old from direct competition with the young and distribute the responsibility of caring for the old among all citizens. Thus, to the extent that the socialist ideology of the Chinese Communist Party (CCP) has dominated Chinese government policies since 1949, it would be logical to presume that the Chinese elderly are protected from the vicissitudes of aging experienced by the elderly in rapidly changing market economies.

In addition, the Chinese elderly live in a society where until 1949 the government officially endorsed the practice of ancestor worship, and the Confucian values of filial piety dictated deference and respect for the old in both public and private relationships. Thus, most citizens over age forty carry with them vestiges of their childhood training and early religious instruction. Among the middle-aged and the old are many who were taught that the oldest generation merits special treatment as the closest link to the deceased ancestors.

The priorities of communism and the tradition of Confucianism would therefore appear to reinforce one another in providing a secure place for the old in years of rapid change. But there are tensions between the Confucian and socialist ideologies. The CCP propagates atheism and explicitly attacks Confucianism as a feudal superstition. By concentrating their social welfare spending on primary school education and preventive medicine, the CCP gives priority to the young. The elimination of ownership of private land and capital and the total ban on buying and selling of children have weakened the hold that elderly parents exercised over the young in the pre-1949 decades. Fathers cannot now tame a rebellious son with threats to disinherit, and daughters do not live in fear of being sold as a servant, mill hand, or prostitute. The official curb on ancestor worship has further reduced the pre-1949 prerogatives of the old. Without state support for the cult of the ancestor, parents cannot as effectively invoke the threat of supernatural punishment against those children who desert them or fail to provide adequate support.

The tensions between the ideals of the Confucian past and the communist present shape the material environment and the social relationships of the elderly in contemporary China. Two of the best locations in which to observe the positions of the old are the workplace and the family. The family is especially important, because it is here that the Confucian ideals of filial piety are fully elaborated, and it is within the family that conflicts over housing, exchange of aid, and the central rituals of marriage and burial occur. In the larger community, and even in the workplace, the different generations can avoid one another. In the family, particularly in the multigeneration households that prevail among rural and urban elderly, the young and the old are thrown together in daily contact. Since the 1970s intergenerational relations have had particular significance, because elderly parents raised under pre-1949 Confucian precepts and children who matured under the CCP must agree upon a viable mode of exchange.

Aging is a universal process, but identifying the chronological threshold to old age is difficult. Those who perform heavy manual labor age faster than those with white-collar or professional jobs. In some societies the end of the reproductive life marks the onset of old age, so that women are perceived as aging faster than men. The most general criterion in the contemporary world, however, is job-related, with permanent withdrawal from the full-time work force being seen as synonymous with growing old. In the west, sixty-five most often marks the onset of old age. In China, however, withdrawal from the full-time work force usually comes well before age sixty-five. In urban China, women workers may retire at age fifty and men at age sixty.[2] In rural areas, where over 80 percent of the population lives, there is no legislated retirement age, but as workers enter their fifties, they pass their prime earning years as field hands and are designated older workers.[3]

The arrival of grandchildren is also strongly associated with the on-set of old age. For many Chinese, the birth of a first grandchild encour-ages self-identification as an old person. For those people who have their first child at age eighteen and whose firstborn also has a first child at eigh-teen, grandparenthood can come as early as age thirty-six. In these cases, most of the new grandparents have other children under age ten and con-tinue to be prime agricultural workers. Neither they nor anyone else views them as old. But in most other cases, the first grandchildren arrive when the parents are in their late forties or early fifties. For women, this family event tends to coincide with retirement from the work force, and therefore the arrival of grandchildren is a significant indicator of the transition into old age. Because the legislated retirement age for women workers and the approximate age at the birth of first grandchildren are both fifty, that year, rather than sixty or sixty-five, is the minimum age for the onset of old age in contemporary China. Age sixty, however, marks a more universally accepted point in time for entry into the oldest generation, and among those who have celebrated this birthday there are few who still identify themselves as middle-aged. Consequently, in terms of social functioning, the years between fifty and sixty are a transition period in which Chinese men and women come increasingly to be seen by others and by themselves as old, while the years after sixty mark a clear-cut turning point and are virtually always designated as the years of old age.[4]

Whether the chronological boundary for the onset of old age is fifty, sixty, or sixty-five, the elderly population of China is enormous. A con-servative estimate for 1980 is 138 million Chinese fifty and older, 68 mil-lion sixty and older, and 43 million sixty-five and older.[5] In the first decade of CCP rule, China averaged 20 million births each year, and in the second decade yearly averages exceeded 25 million.[6] These enormous increases in the size of the population under the age of twenty completely overshadowed the gains in the elderly population and kept most govern-ment officials from giving special attention to the needs of the old. But after the annual number of births stabilized at 21 million per year in 1976, it became obvious that not only is the absolute number of Chinese elderly large, but the percentage of elderly in the total population is higher than in any other developing Asian, African, or Latin American nation. Moreover, by the end of the twentieth century these already high percentages will nearly double.[7] Under these demographic conditions, the changing position of the elderly in the 1970s indicates not only whether the Confucian heritage complements socialism to the advantage of the old, but also whether a poor country like China can be expected to deal successfully with the still greater increases in the percentage of el-derly predicted for the future.

When the total population under study exceeds 100 million, the range of significant experiences is enormous. To generalize about the overall impact of the communist revolution on the Chinese elderly would ideally combine extensive statistical surveys with intensive case histories and participant observation. Unfortunately, such comprehensive and reliable data are unavailable to foreign researchers working on contemporary China. As a result, it is necessary to develop as diverse a data base as possible, and to increase the reliability of conclusions through observations drawn from a variety of independent sources.

This study relies primarily on three different sources: news reports and literature published by the Chinese government between 1949 and 1982, interviews with emigrants from China to Hong Kong in 1976, and interviews with Chinese citizens in the People's Republic of China (PRC) in 1979.[8] The news media reveal shifts in government policy affecting the jobs, housing, and welfare conditions confronted by the old, while the literary sources identify official criteria for good behavior among the old and suggest the officially approved strategies for survival and success in old age. Government publications since 1949 vary in usefulness as data sources. As a rule, sources published in the years before 1958 and after the death of Mao in 1976 give the greatest depth and range of opinion. In the intervening years, most scholarly journals in the social sciences either ceased publication or retreated into ideological debates that provided only indirect access to official strategy and policy.

The two sets of interviews are uneven in a different way. The Hong Kong residents, who had left the PRC to start new lives outside of China, were predominantly urban men from Guangdong Province between the ages of twenty-five and fifty. The residents of the PRC were primarily retired urbanites between the ages of fifty-five and seventy. The Hong Kong interviews lasted a minimum of two-and-a-half hours, with all but four people returning for at least one follow-up session, and on only four occasions was a translator present. In contrast, the PRC interviews typically involved one thirty-minute session, which was observed and recorded by at least one official government representative. There were also more extended interviews with 17 individuals contacted outside of the official briefings which were not transcribed by government officials.

With both the Hong Kong and PRC residents, the interviews focused on household composition and work histories of elderly family members. Because of the multiple sessions, most of the Hong Kong emigrants were able to discuss more people than their own immediate family and provided extensive data on close relatives and neighbors. As a result, the 29 Hong Kong residents gave detailed work histories of 164 rural elderly living in 116 households and 85 urban residents in 53 households. The 88 PRC residents, restricted to speaking about themselves and their closest family members, provided comparable detail about only 114 individuals in 74 households. In addition, the more intense questioning and the privacy of the Hong Kong interviews allowed these emigrants to speak extensively about personal problems at home or at work. As a result, they gave more insights into the conflicts and anxieties of the elderly than did people in the PRC.

The interviews in China, however, both formal and informal, had other strong points. The formal briefings, which took place at four villages, eight factories, three hospitals, and seven old-age or convalescent homes, gave far more comprehensive explanations of institutional resources and priorities than the Hong Kong residents were able to reconstruct from memory.[9] The informal interviews, which took place in parks, restaurants, and homes, permitted direct observation of the interaction between the old and the young. The immediacy and the intensity of such first-hand experience greatly enhanced the human dimension of the study and identified subjective elements only hinted at by the Hong Kong emigrants.

Surprisingly, the Hong Kong and PRC interviews do not contradict each other. Nor do they polarize, with the emigrants focusing on the hardships of their lives and the shortcomings of communism, and the PRC residents painting a rosy picture of their security and high social prestige. In fact, the two sets of interviews consistently corroborate one another. They outline identical patterns of household composition, adjustment to retirement, and intergenerational solidarity. At no point do they lead to mutually exclusive conclusions about the impact of the revolution on the old.

The Chinese elderly, whether known only indirectly through emigrants or directly through citizens, confront the two halves of their lives in a comparable fashion. The socialist transformation of Chinese politics and society forces them to spend their old age in a setting radically altered from the one they knew as children and young adults. Nevertheless, they rely heavily on attitudes and values originating in precommunist Chinese society to explain their experiences within these new socialist institutions. In coming years, the legacy of the precommunist past may steadily weaken, and refugees may come to articulate views that are totally out of step with majority views in China. But today, continuities with traditional values are important for broad segments of Chinese society, and connections with the past create a unifying body of experience against which the fluctuations of the present can be perceived and understood.

1

ATTITUDES TOWARD
THE ELDERLY

This year I'll be sixty-eight.
I remember well what our village used to be like.
Before Liberation we tenants all worked for the landlord.
The scars of past suffering we have on our backs.

But since the CCP came to our village,
Bitter gourds have become honey-sweet melons.
Beginning with land reform, then the coops and communes,
It was like the sesame, flowering all the way up.[1]

BEFORE AND SINCE the death of Mao, the Chinese government has consistently found occasion to feature elderly heroes and heroines.[2] At first glance, the official CCP presentation of the old suggests unadulterated respect and appreciation. Old heroes are invariably strong, loyal, and politically trustworthy, standing as models of orthodoxy for citizens of all ages to emulate. A closer examination of these elderly paragons of virtue and fortitude, however, reveals that the old function primarily as foils for the major protagonist, who in most cases is a party member in the prime of life. Thus, within the official portrait of the exemplary old person is an unarticulated assumption that elderly heroes, while extraordinarily brave and loyal, are not quite the equals of the young.[3]

A typical vignette to teach preschoolers generosity, politeness, and zeal for work presents the elderly as handicapped, needing a small child to fetch a sweater or support them as they cross the road.[4] In stories for grade school, the elderly person is given a history of past heroism or suffering that justifies the child's sympathy and respect.[5] Short stories for adolescents begin to deal explicitly with the issues of weakness, and it is here that the CCP ranks the old most clearly in relation to the young. One such story illustrates the official resolution of the apparently contradictory evaluation of the old as exemplary but secondary:[6]

Lao Die is an old peasant who wants to become a village cadre. But he is illiterate and is therefore passed over in favor of younger men who can read and use the abacus. Lao Die then leaves his village in search of a school where he can learn to read and write. He walks several miles before finding a school, only to discover he is too old to enroll. The headmaster takes pity on the sincere old fellow and offers him a job ringing the bell between classes. Lao Die is delighted with his new responsibilities and settles in as a full-time resident watchman.

Several boys at the school find Lao Die's enthusiasm comical, and they ceaselessly ridicule the foolish old man. Their teasing comes to the attention of the headmaster, who pulls the ringleader aside and lectures him: "Because Lao Die is just an old peasant, you boys look down upon him. If he were an old teacher or an old engineer, you wouldn't. But he never had that opportunity, did he? So from now on I want you to make him an egg soup and take it to him every day. If he asks you why you do it, then tell him it is from the CCP."

The boy brings the egg soup to Lao Die the next morning, but Lao Die is completely confused. He thinks the boy has been to Beijing and that there the CCP leaders have told him to give the old man the eggs. Then he reasons that if the boy has already been to Beijing, he must be headed for a university education and then study overseas. And if this is the case, concludes Lao Die, then the school will need to prepare him better and the headmaster will need more supplies. To help contribute to this effort, Lao Die becomes a zealous scavenger, and in particular he saves every scrap of paper with writing on it, sure that it must contain important instructions from the CCP.

A few months later, the struggles of the Cultural Revolution reach the school. The boy who had led the ridicule of Lao Die spearheads a violent struggle against the headmaster. Lao Die steps in to protect the headmaster, urging the boys to return to their books. He is struck by a stone and killed. The boys overwhelm the headmaster and bring him to his supervisors at the county seat. The ringleader, recounting the story several years later after the verdict against the headmaster has been reversed, concludes his description of Lao Die's naive loyalty and simple honesty in tears of remorse.

In the story of Lao Die and others of its genre, the elderly are often portrayed as weak, pitiful individuals sadly out of step with the modern, socialist world, yet at the same time, these frail and marginal people exhibit the essential virtues of honest, loyal subordinates who are the worthy beneficiaries of the revolution's success. In other moral tales, the connection of the old to the past society is less sympathetic, and here the old, unable to forget evil habits learned in pre-1949 China, emerge as vile and untrustworthy. In the literature of the 1970s such elderly villains often appear in a central dramatic episode where class enemies try to subvert the revolution. Usually these villains are unreformed landlords, rich peasants, or successful merchants who survived the collectivization of the economy in the early 1950s but continued to work for the defeat of the CCP.[7]

Elderly men of this genre generally commit economic crimes, acting as saboteurs of new government investment or as speculators undermining the collective economy. Typical female villains resort to sorcery and exorcism, keeping alive superstitions and religious beliefs that corrupt the young. Because the collectivization of agriculture and industry dating from 1949 prevents the emergence of new landlords and capitalists, these villains are by necessity drawn from among the old, and the association between old age and this type of corrupt behavior grows stronger each year.

On balance, however, the official press systematically encourages a positive image of old age, suggesting that the elderly are to be treasured because of their steadfast character and protected because of their past suffering. The immediate explanation for this favorable assessment is the twofold decision of government editors to present the elderly as victims rather than perpetrators of the pre-1949 injustices and to use the elderly as witnesses to the accomplishments of the communist revolution. Since 1949, official judgments of historical events and personalities have shifted drastically from one year to the next. Leaders who were condemned as reactionary emerge later as true friends of the revolution. Conversely, some who first appear as close comrades in arms subsequently become traitors secretly plotting against the revolution for decades. Yet while the specific interpretations fluctuate, the need of the CCP to justify current choices in light of favorable comparisons with the precommunist past persists.

For the elderly this emphasis on the past means that their ability to recall the past has been more important than any possible contamination resulting from living in the decadent, bourgeois pre-1949 society. By repeatedly turning to the old as key links to the nation's collective past, the CCP strengthens the social prestige of the old and cultivates admiration for their long experience.

One example of how the elderly have benefited from their experience in precommunist society appears in documents from the 1973–1974 Anti-Lin Biao/Anti-Confucius (Pi-Lin Pi-Kong) Campaign.[8] As in earlier ideological campaigns, during this one the CCP attacked the decadent morality of traditional Confucian ideals. Yet the old themselves rarely became the direct targets of criticism. Instead, as the campaign developed in the national press, the primary role of the elderly was to recount tales of past suffering.[9]

During this campaign veteran workers and village elders were asked to share stories of bitterness with younger family members and neighbors. The elderly were cited for recognizing, better than any other age group, the hypocrisy of the old Confucian morality and therefore seeing more quickly than the young how the efforts of Lin Biao and his local followers could restore the evils of the old society. Thus the elderly's ambiguous connection to the old society is resolved to their advantage by portraying them as repositories for stories of CCP heroism. Throughout the post-1949 era this selective interpretation of the elderly's connection to the "old" China has usually prevailed. As a result, the old are absolved from taking responsibility for the pre-1949 evils, and official stereotypes generally project sympathetic images of the elderly.

Unofficial Stereotypes and Popular Attitudes

Outside the classroom, personal experience and general custom shape predominant stereotypes and general attitudes more decisively than officially fabricated models. As a rule, in everyday life, old age or "the evening years" *(wan nian)* are associated with physical degeneration and social and political conservatism. The old are perceived as dependents in need of help and support. Thus theirs is a position of considerable weakness and vulnerability that could easily generate attitudes of fear and disdain. In fact, however, the prevailing attitudes toward the old are characterized by tolerance and sympathy.

The response of the elderly to old age also appears to be one of acceptance. The elderly exhibit high self-esteem. They speak of their advanced years with pride and enjoy an easy familiarity with the younger people who surround them. The elderly are openly affectionate toward their family members or younger neighbors and spontaneously reach out to touch those with whom they are speaking. The young frequently offer a supporting arm, and the old accept the aid without embarrassment.

The easy rapport between young and old and the general acceptance of the frailty of the old became especially clear to me one night when I visited friends in a new high-rise apartment building in Beijing. The building faces onto a main commercial street. Stores and offices occupy the two lower floors, and residents reach their homes by an external staircase that enters the building at the third floor. On the night of the visit it was especially hot, and many people had come down from the upper floors to sit on the stairs and catch a bit of breeze. My hosts and I stopped on the landing before their apartment to let several boys race past in a game of tag. Looking up, I saw an old lady with tiny bound feet, slowly making her way down to the outside staircase. One hand gripped the railing tightly, the other held a small wooden stool. Suddenly my hostess called to her twelve-year-old son. As she offered her arm to the old woman, the boy took the small stool, jumped down the steps to the next landing, dropped the stool to the ground, and quickly rejoined the game of tag. When the old lady reached the landing, she drew the stool closer to the railing and slowly bent down to sit, alone and undisturbed. During the few minutes I watched, no one spoke more than two or three words. No pleasantries were exchanged, and neither the young nor the old started a conversation. As we entered the apartment, I turned to see the old lady, still alone and staring out through the dusk at the deserted construction site that filled the adjacent back alley.

What explains the apparently effortless acceptance of the old and their frailties? What are the roots of this pervasive sympathy, and why does there appear to be so little variation between official ideology and private expectations? Conscious efforts by the communist leaders to develop appreciation for the past sufferings of this generation of old people provide a partial explanation, and use of the elderly as witnesses to the success of the communist revolution bolsters the positive, official image. The primary supports, however, come not from any ideological or political decision of CCP leaders but from expectations rooted in precommunist culture and society that good human relations should be asexual and reciprocal. This definition of appropriate interpersonal behavior shapes daily interactions for Chinese of all ages, but it is especially important and favorable to the old.

As a rule, Chinese society does not encourage exclusive male-female couples as the primary focus of adult social life. In pre-1949 families, parent-child loyalties took precedence over those between husband and wife, and sexual relationships between men and women were valued primarily for the contribution of children.[10] Since 1949, these traditional mores have continued to influence contemporary behavior. Women's clothing is still designed to hide rather than enhance female sensuality. Married couples rarely show physical affection for one another in public, and overt appeals to sex drives are absent in advertising and entertainment. Sexual relations are expected to be confined to a limited, private sphere and are not permitted to dominate most formal or informal social relations.

This perspective on sexuality favors positive attitudes toward the elderly in several ways. The most obvious consequence is that youthful, physical attractiveness and sexual activity are not essential to a positive self-image. Because overt appeals to sex drives are muted or even absent, in most public situations elderly widows and widowers are also not repeatedly reminded of their loss as they pass through their daily routines. Nor are they excluded from the ordinary round of social life inside or outside the family. When such sexual mores prevail, sexually inactive elderly can view themselves as complete adults and continue to participate fully in social activities with younger friends and relatives.

Chinese personal relationships are saturated with the obligation to reciprocate. In fact, so great is the demand for high levels of mutual exchange that some people prefer to curtail meaningful social contacts for fear that participation in joint activity will eventually impose obligations that they are unable or unwilling to repay. The experience of one urban man sent to resettle in the countryside illustrates how the expectation of reciprocity shapes relations between old and young neighbors:[11]

Chen Ximing is a married man of thirty who lived for six years in a village in central Guangdong with his wife and three small children. Gregarious and ambitious, Chen Ximing quickly made new friends when he settled in the village, becoming especially close to the invalid brother of the local CCP secretary. After his friend's father died, Chen helped with the funeral arrangements.

He went to the commune center to register the death, and at the funeral he was one of the pallbearers. Despite his closeness to the family and his participation in the funeral rites, his friend's elderly mother has repeatedly rebuffed any offer of help. During the entire time Chen Ximing and his family lived in the village, the old lady refused all gifts from the city and even preferred to let her private plot go untilled rather than permit the young couple to share the work.

When asked if he thinks the old lady spurned him out of a fear that contact with a resettled urban youth would damage the political career of her oldest son, Chen rejects the explanation, citing the absence of any overt hostilities. He emphasizes that her attitudes are typical of many old mountain women of her generation for whom the necessity of exchange is an over-riding concern in establishing new relationships outside the family. By refusing Chen Ximing's help, she denies the existence of any mutual responsibility between the two. In this way she forfeits the immediate support that she could have used, but at the same time she eliminates the threat of unspecified claims against herself or her sons at a later date.

Obligations to reciprocate imposed in the public sphere are generally subject to more negotiation than are those within the family, and the elderly cannot rely on sympathy and support from neighbors and friends with the same certainty as from relatives. Yet both official and unofficial sources report many instances where the elderly have successfully relied upon nonkin for survival in old age.[12]

One of the best-known fictional accounts within China of the strength of nonkin reciprocity is depicted in the *Red Lantern*, one of the eight operas chosen by Mao's wife, Jiang Qing, to monopolize Chinese stage and screen in the late 1960s and early 1970s.[13] In this story of revolutionary heroism and triumph, the denouement is the revelation that in this ideal family the son, the grandmother, and the grandchild are not really blood relations. Inspired by the ideals of communism, these three have forged loyalties as strong as those between real family members and have thereby triumphed against insuperable odds.

But it is not necessary to limit oneself to ideal types in the official media to find approval of long-term reciprocity. The case of Wu Ruiqing is typical of how ordinary people also rely on deliberate calculations of reciprocal exchanges between young and old:[14]

Wu Ruiqing is a widow in her sixties who lives in a prosperous suburban village just outside of Guangzhou (Canton). Forty years ago she and her husband were tenant farmers. Later they moved to the city where her husband became a wine maker. Eventually the two saved enough money to buy some land in the countryside. By the time land reform was completed in 1952, Wu Ruiqing's husband was dead. Nevertheless, she and her two daughters returned to her husband's village as "former landlords."

Both daughters married within a few years of their move from the city, and Wu Ruiqing was left alone to support herself. After the collectivization of village land in 1955, she survived by working as a laborer in the vegetable fields and raising chickens at home. But by 1968 she had become too weak to do even the easiest field work. She lost her grain ration and has to depend on her two daughters to buy her rice. To supplement this meager diet, she relies on homegrown vegetables and sales of her poultry.

Wu Ruiqing lives near a subsistence level, in a small windowless house that was previously a woodshed. She has only three or four hens, and she seems to have little talent for raising baby chicks. Yet she has not withdrawn into isolation. Within the village, she has many acquaintances among elderly widows of her generation. They share a long communal past, and they talk incessantly about the many families of the village. Even more important than her peers is her relationship with the local CCP party secretary. The secretary is a distant relative, the son of a gambler who deserted his family when the party secretary was in his teens. Wu's husband, who had no male heir, helped the family, and even though the boy is now a grown man and a CCP official, he is still known as the foster son of Wu Ruiqing.

After Wu's poor health forced her to leave the work force, her foster son helped her by tending her private garden plot and by sending his eldest daughter to wash her clothes and draw water from the river. During one political campaign to eliminate antisocialist elements, some villagers criticized the party secretary for helping an old landlord, and a few women urged his wife to stop their daughter from visiting the old lady's house. The criticism came to nothing, and throughout the campaign Wu Ruiqing continued to receive help from her foster son and his daughter.

Nevertheless, Wu Ruiqing's relationship to her foster son has its limits. She does not go to him for help when she is sick or when she needs grain for her chickens. For these types of aid she goes to a group of Guangzhou teenagers who, like Chen Ximing, were sent to resettle in the countryside in 1968. At the outset it was Wu Ruiqing who sought out the youths, but over time the young people came to her. She knows folk remedies for common illnesses; she sells her eggs at a lower price than the other villagers; and she willingly lends out her few possessions as the youths need them. It is, however, an uneasy exchange. Some of the boys take advantage of Wu, stealing her eggs or raiding her garden and fruit trees. Yet Wu doggedly continues to extend, and to accept, overtures for reciprocal exchange, ever hopeful that her repeated efforts to please the young people will strengthen their obligations to repay.

The way in which Wu Ruiqing defines and realizes the norm of reciprocity is typical of elderly men and women. Just as before 1949, today it is older or richer persons who usually initiate the exchange, extending protection or giving help with the expectation of repayment at a later date when they are weaker and poorer than those they first helped. In the precommunist era when Wu Ruiqing and her husband established the foster son relationship, fictive kinship relationships such as these were common, and the obligations of both parties were specifically defined. Since 1949 such arrangements have become less frequent and more informal. Nevertheless, old obligations contracted in the pre-1949 years are still honored, and the underlying assumption of long-term reciprocity continues to guide relationships between individuals of all ages.

CCP leaders have not eliminated the traditional attitudes of respect and concern for the elderly based on Confucian ideals, nor have they established an entirely new socialist ethic grounded in the ideology of communism. Instead of a rejection and dismissal of the old, there is a generally sympathetic and accepting attitude toward them that has definite continuities with precommunist values. Even in the most secular and modern sector, sympathetic attitudes toward the elderly exist, and old age signifies far more than mere survival. Despite this generally positive outlook on old age, no one looks forward to being old. On the contrary, people of all ages express fear of the physical decline and dependency of old age, and most hope to maintain the status and obligations of middle age as long as possible.

Acceptance of dependency within a society that observes the norm of reciprocity creates the most decisive support for the favorable attitudes toward the elderly. The emphasis on mutual obligations throughout the life cycle coupled with the necessity of repayment eliminate the need for the elderly to justify their need for care and respect on an individual basis. As a result, dependency in old age is viewed as unpleasant but inevitable, and few people envision an extended period of complete independence from those of other ages. The elderly do not view their dependency as a fatal attack on their self-esteem, and the young and middle-aged do not entertain illusions of perpetual self-sufficiency or disengagement from the old.

In general, this acceptance of dependency and old age exists independently from government efforts. But through the didactic press and through their reliance on the old as witnesses to pre-1949 suffering, the CCP actively fosters positive and sympathetic attitudes toward the old. Overall, the communist revolution has thus strengthened rather than weakened traditional views of old age, and the elderly have benefited from government support. By repeatedly calling on the old to compare China before and after 1949, the CCP reminds the young and middle-aged of the importance of the past for the present and thereby links the different generations into one common history. And by asking the old to recount their previous hardships and sacrifices, the CCP explains how the young are obligated to the old and in this way actually reinforces the precommunist norm of reciprocity. As a result, the Chinese elderly do not need continually to prove their values as exemplary individuals in order to merit a modicum of respect. Instead, individuals grow old in an accepting environment where dependent elderly are incorporated into ongoing routines of everyday life and the past continues to shape the future.

2

WORK AND RETIREMENT

IN 1949 THE CHINESE communist leadership outlined an economic program to redistribute wealth and increase output. Within one generation this dual strategy was highly successful. Productivity gains in agriculture and industry outstripped population growth rates, and the worst poverty disappeared.[1] Rationing and price controls ensured the even distribution of basic necessities, and no new class of concentrated wealth emerged.[2] But despite the CCP's commitment to the twin goals of equity and growth, the economic gains of the communist revolution have not been equally distributed. Regardless of age, urban residents enjoy the greatest rewards, and rural residents are consistently asked to accept a distinctly inferior standard of living.[3] After thirty years of CCP leadership, the average return for ten hours of agricultural labor rarely exceeds 50 percent of the wage for an eight-hour shift in a factory or store.[4] Yet farm jobs continue to be more exhausting and less secure than jobs in industry and commerce.

A vast difference in the degree of government responsibility for worker salaries and benefits accounts for most of the rural-urban inequalities. Since the full collectivization of agriculture in 1956, rural residents have worked in small cooperatives where the members, not the national or local governments, collectively own the land. These cooperatives, known as production teams (sheng chan dui), use the household as the basic unit of membership.[5] Usually a team includes less than forty families and controls a labor force of sixty to eighty workers. Team members select their foremen from among their own ranks, and once production quotas have been received from the national Ministry of Food, farmers work with little outside supervision.[6] Wages fluctuate with the profitability of each local harvest and are paid largely in kind. Although prohibited from selling their land, each team bears full responsibility for all losses, and only in years when the harvest cannot provide members with a minimum diet does the state subsidize team production.

In urban areas, the post-1949 reorganization of the economy instituted a very different employment system. Urban workers generally work in large enterprises owned by the nation or the city.[7] Neither individuals nor small work groups assume major responsibility for production planning or short-term profitability. A national wage scale guarantees a monthly wage based on job category and individual seniority. Once employed, workers enjoy almost total job security.

Fringe benefits also differ between rural and urban workers. As early as 1951 the National Labor Insurance Regulations provided most urban workers with free medical care, disability pay, and pensions.[8] Farm workers are explicitly excluded from this legislation and in times of need must rely entirely on their families or fellow villagers.[9] Thus in terms of salary, job security, and welfare support the Chinese communist revolution has created one employment structure in the countryside and quite another in the cities. So distinct are these two subsystems and so great is the disparity in financial outcomes, that it is necessary to evaluate the economic consequences of the communist revolution for rural elderly separately from those for urban elderly.

The Rural Elderly

In the decades immediately preceding 1949, the rural elderly worked on the margins of the agricultural economy. Except for a tiny minority who held deeds to large tracts of land or controlled commerce, the rural elderly toiled ceaselessly either in the poorly paid jobs of scavenger or watchman or in unpaid housework.[10] Because these jobs supported only a minimal existence, the commonest strategy for daily survival in old age was a combination of irregular employment and increasing dependency on adult children.

Since 1949 most rural elderly have continued to follow the precommunist pattern.[11] In the team labor force, the elderly take on the auxiliary jobs of orchard watchmen, stockmen, and scavengers of dung and manure. In the households they assume primary responsibility for children, cooking, and domestic animals. Although frequently honored for hard work, frugality, and perseverance, elderly team members are rarely assigned roles of economic leadership or allowed to perform skilled jobs.[12] Elderly women take an especially small role in the collective work force, and if they have grandchildren at home, they are rarely expected to contribute regularly to the labor power of the production team.[13]

The timing of retirement also closely resembles the pre-1949 conditions. The usual pattern is for elderly men to work full time outside their homes, gradually taking on less strenuous jobs as their physical strength noticeably declines or until family fortunes permit them to pass on primary financial responsibilities to their sons. Elderly women, in contrast, withdraw from the team jobs precipitously. After the birth of their first grandchild they usually leave the full-time collective labor force completely and focus all their energies on household tasks.

These clear-cut differences between the work and retirement of elderly men and women create different patterns of leisure in advanced old age. Elderly men often continue to work outside their homes, even into their seventies. But when they finally retire, they drastically reduce their overall work load and often have time to socialize and relax with friends away from home. Women, who withdraw from the production team at a much earlier age, actually continue to be economically active as long as their health allows and almost never can rationalize, or accept, a life without ceaseless toil. As a result, elderly women remain economically active longer than elderly men, although their work is often invisible to outside observers because of its intense focus on family enterprises and housework. The working conditions of one elderly couple illustrate these pervasive patterns among elderly men and women in contemporary rural China:[14]

Li Hoizhong was born in the first decade of the twentieth century. He is the third and youngest son of a man who farmed his own land in a small backwater of eastern Guangdong Province. The land there is poor, and as late as 1970 it was a half-day's walk to the nearest market town. Before 1949, rents were lower there than in the prosperous Pearl River delta, and even the landlords had meager lives.

During the Japanese occupation, the village suffered several air attacks, but no troops were billeted in the area. Although five men from the village joined the communist guerillas, most villagers cut themselves off from the outside world. Commerce dwindled, and families subsisted on sweet potatoes and boiled vegetables.

The times were inauspicious for marriage. But Li Hoizhong, who was then almost forty, could no longer afford to postpone his wedding. He sold a portion of the family land and "bought" a wife fifteen years his junior. Li Hoizhong and his young wife, Chen Pingfong, lived frugally and prayed for a son. After one year of marriage they had a girl. Five years later their first and only son was born. They named him Li Saikwok. Li Saikwok arrived at a propitious moment just prior to the Communist victory in 1949, and he profited from each advance of the CCP revolution. When he was eight, the village opened its first primary school, and when he was fourteen, the commune started a secondary school. In his early teens he stood several inches taller than his father, and by 1964, as one of the few junior high graduates, he was regarded as the most promising teenager in the village. He first served as team accountant and then during the Cultural Revolution rose to a position of village leadership. But his greatest opportunity came in 1968 when, after the army dropped its earlier restriction against recruiting only sons, he was accepted for a five-year tour of duty. During his years of service he drilled as a foot soldier, worked in construction, and traveled, first beyond his county and then beyond Guangdong.

When he returned in 1973, at age twenty-nine, he immediately married and took over the position of production team head.

In contrast to most rural men, Li Saikwok married a woman he had known since childhood. The couple had announced their engagement even before he left for the army, and during the five years Li Saikwok was absent, his fiancée conscientiously helped her future in-laws with all their heavy housework. For their basic livelihood, however, the old couple relied on employment in the collective labor force. Li Hoizhong, who was over sixty, was crippled with arthritis and totally unable to work in the rice paddies or vegetable plots. He was assigned to be the watchman in the village orchards, where he earned a minimum income. Chen Pingfong, not yet fifty, enjoyed excellent health, and through her job as head of the village piggery she became the financial mainstay of the household.

After Li Saikwok's return from the army, Li Hoizhong retired from his job in the orchard and now spends most of his time scavenging animal droppings, which he sells to the team. His contribution to the family income is negligible. Li Saikwok is recognized as the family head, and the transfer of power from father to son is complete.

Two years after her son's marriage, Chen Pingfong still has not achieved a satisfactory retirement. She has left the collective work force but is heavily burdened with the primary responsibility for housework, the family pigs, and her infant granddaughter. Her daughter-in-law seeks to placate the older woman but can do little to reduce Chen Pingfong's work load. Within the family Chen Pingfong is recognized as an important worker who makes essential contributions to the family income, but she is dissatisfied with her work load and experiences tension and conflict from which her husband is spared.

This pattern of ceaseless toil combined with a high level of dependency on married sons continues to predominate among the elderly throughout rural China. Starting in 1978, however, a few wealthy villages and communes inaugurated pension systems to reduce the financial burdens on individual elderly and their families.[15] Such pensions (*yang lao jin*) are funded locally, and eligibility varies from one village to the next. In some villages, all members who have reached their sixtieth birthday and have worked for twenty consecutive years in the collective labor force are eligible. In others, women first qualify at age fifty, while men have to wait until age sixty-five.

The value of these experimental pensions varies according to the prosperity of the village. In some communities the pensions guarantee 40 percent of the average male income from collective sources. Such a replacement rate, while much below the 75 percent standard provided urban workers covered by the Labor Insurance Regulations, is well above the subsistence standards set for the rural destitute or disabled.[16] Furthermore, when combined with outside earnings, pensions theoretically make rural elderly financially independent of their children.

There is nevertheless little evidence that rural pensions will precipitate significant changes in employment rates of rural elderly. The pensions by no means replace preretirement earnings, and very few rural families can afford to forgo even a few dollars of additional income. In the decades since 1949, rural per capita income has risen substantially, but only in the wealthiest areas has it become so high that families can consider the economic contribution of the elderly to be negligible. In 1949, leisure among the rural elderly was a privilege reserved for a tiny minority. Today the situation remains basically unchanged.

Despite the similarities between the work routines of the elderly before 1949 and today, the collectivization of agriculture has significantly increased the financial return for agricultural labor by elderly workers. As a result, although the elderly continue to work in the same jobs, they earn greater rewards and thereby have noticeably increased their economic security. This is not to say that the rural elderly earn more than the young and middle-aged or that the CCP deliberately set out to give special benefits to the old. On the contrary, while the income gap between young and old has narrowed, the elderly still earn less than the young, and some of the most important gains have come as unplanned rather than planned consequences of the restructuring of the rural economy. Through both the payment system for collective work and the price structure for different agriculture goods the elderly have benefited economically from the communist revolution.

Since 1956 payment for work done in the production team has followed several different schemes.[17] During the "high tides of socialism," such as the Great Leap Forward (1958–1959) and the Learn from Dazhai Campaign during the Cultural Revolution (1968–1970), production teams divide the collective harvest primarily in proportion to the number of hours worked.[18] Thus if the elderly work as many hours as the young, they get roughly the same payment. In periods when a less egalitarian ideology holds sway or when there is greater concern with incentives and labor productivity, the time-rate payments are replaced by piece-rate or skill-level payments. When time rates prevail, the elderly earn between 70 and 80 percent of what the young earn. When the more differentiated systems hold sway, the elderly earn 50 to 70 percent of what the young earn.[19]

The very old or the disabled, like Li Hoizhong, who work on the margins of the collective labor force as watchmen or scavengers fare less well, gaining only 30 to 50 percent of what younger workers earn. However, even in cases of the weakest workers or in periods when piece-rate or skill-rate payments prevail, collectivization continues to benefit the old because collectivization guarantees a job to all team members who need work and who can still contribute some minimal labor. For the elderly, who in the precommunist years were the first to lose their jobs in each economic downswing, this guarantee of even minimal employment provides a significant increase in economic security.

The second major gain from collectivization comes as a result of the payment system, which distributes a fixed portion of each harvest in terms of family need, not worker productivity. Most teams distribute income in two phases. In the first phase, 30 to 40 percent of the harvest is distributed to provide subsistence grain to all team members. In the second phase, the remaining 60 to 70 percent is distributed according to the proportional number of workdays, in the form of either additional grain or cash. The cost of the grain distributed according to need is charged against the number of workdays earned by each household, but if a family is unable to pay for the grain they need for survival, the charge is carried over to the next year or until such time as they can repay. In many teams, 10 to 20 percent of households regularly eat more grain than they earn.[20] Because the debts carry over from year to year and are canceled at death, the elderly derive special benefit from this form of collective welfare.

Overall, the CCP labor and wage policies implemented during collectivization have created structural changes that greatly reduce the incidence of starvation, destitution, and long-term unemployment among rural elderly. But equally important gains have come for the elderly and their family members as a result of specific, short-term policies that stand directly opposed to the general, long-term commitment to socialist transformation.

In most rural households, income earned in the collective sector supplies the main portion of family income, while profits from the private household sidelines provide between 20 and 30 percent.[21] However, this 80:20 or 70:30 ratio between collectively and privately earned incomes does not apply equally to the incomes of all family members. Typically, the younger members of a household earn 80 to 90 percent of their incomes from work in the collective labor force, while the elderly members, like Chen Pingfong, earn all of their income from profits on private sidelines. The key to this large difference in activity in the private sector lies in the specific way in which the CCP guidelines on rural employment restrict access to the private sector in favor of the old.

The prices paid for grain, the main cash crop for most production teams, are kept low in order to hold down the basic cost of living for urban workers. As a result, profits for grain growers are also kept low, and labor spent on the collective grain harvest brings a far lower return than labor spent on raising eggs or perishable vegetables whose prices are allowed to rise roughly in response to demand. In order to guarantee that the best agricultural workers give maximum effort to the grain crops, teams require all able-bodied adults to work full time in the collective fields and to use only their leisure time for work on private endeavors. The elderly are the one exception to this rule. Women over the age of fifty and men over sixty are permitted to work entirely in their households on private tasks if at least two other adult members of their household continue to work full time for the collective.[22]

Two activities that frequently occupy the elderly who work outside of the collective labor force illustrate how this special permission to leave the team work brings gains to the rural elderly. One of the most profitable cash sidelines is pigs. Pigs raised for meat take seven months to bring to market, and each pig earns between sixty and eighty yuan profit.[23] Although direct costs to the producers are low, pigs demand considerable labor time. It takes hours to prepare the food and to guard against the many infectious diseases to which pigs are susceptible. As a result, only families with elderly members working full time at home have the labor power to raise more than one pig per year.[24] And because the pigs bring such high profits, the elderly working full time at home often are able to make twice as large a contribution to household income as they can by continuing in the collective workforce.[25]

Another way in which release from the team work force benefits the elderly and their families is the contribution the elderly make to household income through their replacement of younger members as the main household workers. The most common replacement, as in the case of Chen Pingfong, is the substitution of an elderly mother-in-law for a young wife as the primary housekeeper. When young women are able to pass on most of their responsibility for children, cooking, and sewing to their mothers-in-law, they can usually double their wages from the collective labor force and still have time to contribute additional income working in the household.[26]

Elderly fathers also make economically valuable contributions in the home, tending the family vegetable garden and collecting firewood and kindling. In general, however, elderly women assume the bulk of the housework, and their shift out of the collective work force and into the household economy is particularly important for improving the family's overall levels of prosperity and security. As a result, elderly women seek to leave the team labor force as soon as possible, and both they and their families consider housework to be a legitimate and remunerative form of employment.

The early CCP outline for socialist development of the Chinese countryside envisioned technological as well as organizational changes.[27] Tractors, electric pumps, and chemical fertilizer were as important to socialist transformation as the abolition of private land ownership, private money lending, and contract labor. The peasants were to become workers, a rural proletariat, and mechanization was dramatically to increase labor productivity. In practice, however, the CCP has done little to modernize agriculture. Almost all jobs from planting to harvesting still rely heavily on manual labor and traditional tools. Persistence of traditional technologies depresses economic gains for young and old, but the old derive some protection from this backwardness. Their skills and knowledge have not become obsolete, and even when their physical strength begins to fail, they can still earn a decent wage laboriously patching an irrigation channel or carefully transplanting seedlings too delicate to be handled by machine into a small patch of soil too small for any mechanical cultivator.

But the failure to modernize agriculture only partially explains the economic security of the old. The ideological commitment to socialist redistribution has also brought gains to the old, particularly to those who have lost the protection of younger family members and would otherwise be forced to compete directly with the youngest and strongest. Joint ownership of the land, the work point system, and the CCP system of distribution according to need have all bound the old to the young through new ties of economic cooperation and thereby created a safety net which guarantees survival to an age group for whom survival has not always been guaranteed.

The Urban Elderly

In the decades just before 1949, elderly urban workers suffered a tenuous existence. Virtually no employers provided pensions, and high rates of inflation and low wages made saving for a secure old age impossible. Nor could the urban elderly routinely turn to their extended family or to local benevolent associations. Years of war and migration from the villages to the city had split families apart and undermined the social cohesion necessary for the functioning of community welfare supports. As a result, the urban elderly worked as long as their health permitted and turned to their adult children or charity only when they were totally unemployable. Except for a minority of professionals and owners of successful shops and factories, elderly workers earned less than they had in middle age, and old age was synonymous with poverty or financial dependency.

The victory of the CCP brought immediate improvement. Elderly workers in industry became part of the politically advanced and economically favored proletariat, eligible for rewards and protection unknown in the precommunist years. Of greatest consequence for the elderly was the CCP commitment to the perquisites of seniority, lifetime job security, and on-the-job fringe benfits. Among the benefits, pensions that provide 70 to 80 percent of the last wage brought the most radical change.[28] In contrast to the dominant pattern of reduced or negligible income in advanced old age that had prevailed before 1949, urban workers were promised a lifetime annuity nearly identical to the wages earned in the prime of life.

In contrast to the rural situation, where the communist priorities aided all elderly in comparable fashion, the gains for urban elderly were distributed through entitlement clauses that favored some segments of the labor force over others. As a result, in the early years retirement benefits often bypassed a large proportion of the elderly population.

When the CCP took over the urban economy, it hoped to make all workers state employees and to guarantee full employment to all able-bodied adults. Material shortages and the necessity of quickly expanding the existing supply of goods and services, however, forced it to compromise. Jobs had to be distributed according to a two-tier system whereby those working in areas deemed most essential for rapid industrialization and government administration were classified as state workers and given the highest wages and fringe benefits, while those working in the less critical areas of commerce and consumer services were classified as collective workers and given lower wages and benefits. For collective workers, wages fluctuated according to monthly or annual productivity, and they received no pension or medical benefits.

In the mid-1950s the CCP rapidly expanded state ownership to include many small factories and most commercial establishments, so that since 1958 approximately 80 percent of urban workers have been employed in the state sector.[29] Yet because few elderly or middle-aged women initially worked outside of their homes and because elderly men were disproportionately employed as artisans and craftsmen — jobs that even then often remained outside the state sector — the elderly as a group did not benefit from the expansion of the state sector as soon as the young. Thus, although pensions had been guaranteed for all eligible state workers since soon after Liberation, relatively few elderly qualified and most elderly urbanites survived as the elderly had before 1949: they worked as long as possible and, when failing strength or illness forced them out of their original positions, moved to less demanding jobs or to temporary positions at salaries far below their previous ones. When they could no longer hold any steady job, they were left with nothing more than their last day's pay.

In some of the larger or more prosperous collectives, elderly workers were granted severance pay (tui zhi jin) which amounted to one month's wage for each year of work.[30] These pensions provided a small cushion of security, usually for less than three years, and were generally given only when illness or extreme frailty forced workers to leave the work place totally unable to find other employment. In 1964, however, conditions for elderly workers in the collective enterprises greatly improved when the largest collectives began to provide disability coverage and a modified pension *(tui xiu bu zhu fei)*. Such pensions require more years of continuous employment than the Labor Insurance Regulations do and replace a lower percentage, or 40 to 60 percent, of the last wage.[31] Nevertheless, they are an enormous improvement over the earlier lump-sum arrangements, providing a steady income for the rest of the individual's life.

Differential access to jobs in the state sector creates the primary economic cleavage among the urban elderly. The specific steps by which the CCP has implemented the Labor Insurance Regulations have created additional inequalities. Between 1951 and 1978 the Labor Insurance Regulations were revised at least six times.[32] Each version increased the size of the benefits and reduced eligibility requirements.[33] Yet because new benefits were rarely retroactive and because pensions, even in the most liberal legislation, continued to be implemented as a privilege and not a routine entitlement, the steady improvement in terms of retirement did not produce sustained growth in the total number of urban pensioners. Instead, policy changes further subdivided the urban elderly into several "cohorts of opportunity," whereby those able to postpone retirement until a major expansion of benefits draw far higher rewards than age mates forced or electing to retire only a few years, or even months, earlier.

In most Chinese enterprises, retirement is not mandatory and pensions are not routinely guaranteed. The ages of fifty for women and sixty for men establish a general minimum age of eligibility, and the actual day of retirement varies according to occupational status, health, and family need. In principle and practice, pensions are granted only after a case-by-case review. First, the person approaches the union official or personnel officer in charge of pensions in that enterprise no sooner than three months prior to the minimum age of eligibility. If the supervisor agrees with the request, the person files a formal application with the enterprise finance committee. Then the finance committee assigns someone to investigate the applicant in terms of quality of past contributions on the job, current health status, incidence of past sick leaves, current financial situation of the worker's family (parents, spouse, and children), financial cost incurred by the unit for the retirement, and past political record. After this assessment is made, the union or personnel committee accepts or rejects the request for a pension. If the person is a CCP member, holds a position of authority, or works in a unit without the financial authority to grant a pension, the recommendation of the investigation committee is only provisional, and the final decision is made by the next higher administrative level.

In the first six years after the implementation of the Labor Insurance Regulations in 1951, benefits were concentrated in payments for disability, maternity leave, and job-related death provisions, which addressed the immediate needs of the predominantly young state labor force.[34] During this phase, retirement issues were a secondary concern, affecting only a small percentage of the state employees. In the few cases where pensions were awarded, the total monthly payments, even in model cases, were only 50 percent of the last wage and rarely exceeded 25 yuan.[35] In recognition of the small size of the pensions, workers who stayed on their jobs were given a bonus, and those who were forced to retire owing to health problems were encouraged to move to the countryside, where their pension would provide a higher standard of living than it could in the cities.[36] Given the young age of the industrial and government work force and the small size of the actual pensions granted during this first phase of implementation, very few elderly urban workers retired with a lifetime pension. One government source estimated that in 1957 out of a total population of 632 million, there were only 67,000 workers nationwide who had retired with a guaranteed lifetime pension.[37]

Just prior to the Great Leap Forward in 1958, some economists argued for the mandatory retirement of women at age fifty and men at age sixty. They contended that China suffered from a labor surplus and that only the forced retirement of elderly workers would permit employment of the large number of recent high school graduates. According to one estimate, an annual rate of 100,000 retirements would automatically create 100,000 to 200,000 new openings.[38] Six months later, however, officials denied the existence of any labor surpluses and predicted labor shortages. Retirement policy shifted to accommodate this new economic orthodoxy. Pensioned retirees were urged to return to work, and all those who would have soon been eligible for pensions were encouraged to remain on the job as long as their health permitted.[39] In accord with this new emphasis on labor shortages, the 1958 revision of the Labor Insurance Regulations dropped the bonus system.[40]

In the short term the retirement policy of the Great Leap Forward slowed the expansion of pensions. During these years few elderly who technically were eligible for pensions exercised their options, and those pensions that were granted were small, reflecting the desperate conditions necessary to force an older worker to leave the paid work force.[41] But in the long run, the Great Leap priorities produced a significant upsurge in retirements because the 1958 revisions permitted a minimum pension after ten rather than twenty years of continuous employment. Although pensions after ten years of employment were 50 rather than 70 percent of the last salary, such a pension usually provided an adequate standard for a single person. The result was a noticeable increase in the number of pensioners in the mid-1960s when a large number of those who had entered state sector jobs between 1951 and 1956 satisfied both the age and the employment criteria.

In the years immediately preceding the Cultural Revolution, government attitudes toward pensions again radically shifted as the material shortages of the 1958–1962 period were redressed and the economy entered a period of growth. At the same time, the number of men and women reaching retirement age rose by approximately 15 percent.[42] When this population expansion coincided with the implementation of the 1958 revisions of the retirement regulations, the number of urban workers who qualified for pensions rose dramatically, and an enlarged network of municipal agencies was created to supervise the well-being and spare time of the growing population of pensioners.[43]

The onset of the Cultural Revolution in 1966 marked another significant policy shift as retirement benefits like day care and housing subsidies were criticized as "bourgeois" material incentives that reduced workers' class consciousness and created inequalities within the proletariat.[44] Pensions were also difficult to implement because the organizations that administered retirement programs, such as municipal party organizations, citywide unions, and municipal civil affairs bureaus, had been disbanded, and the revolutionary committees that replaced them were both unwilling and unable to implement the regulations consistently. Thus bureaucratic disarray was at least as responsible for cutbacks in retirement programs as was ideological dispute. However, the degree of breakdown in the pension benefits varied from one city to another and even between enterprises within the same city. This variation stemmed from the fact that although most unions were inactive, some of them continued to function. Moreover, individual enterprises could occasionally cover the cost of pensions from their own wage bill.[45]

Yet even in factories where the struggles of the Cultural Revolution were minimal, workers fearful of the general climate of economic and political instability voluntarily postponed their retirement and continued to work well beyond the minimum ages of eligibility. Some of the elderly, particularly those with a past political problem or questionable social status as technicians or intellectuals, declined to apply for pensions for fear that they would be criticized for lack of revolutionary ardor. Others feared for the economic welfare of their families. Even though the pension guaranteed 70 percent of the last wage, in many of these families the careers of the young adults were not well established. Thus, elderly parents carried the major responsibility for family finances, and they felt unable to meet their current obligations with a pension that would bring a 30 percent cut in monthly income.

Moreover, between 1966 and 1976 benefits rightfully earned were frequently withheld when the individual had been designated a "bad element."[46] The number of potential retirees who were penalized in this way was probably small, but their experiences were well known, and their example served to dissuade others from routinely applying for retirement.

In 1978, after the death of Mao Zedong and the subsequent return of Deng Xiaoping, the CCP leadership significantly revised the pension programs.[47] The new legislation has relaxed eligibility requirements and made benefits more generous. Age requirements are the same as first stipulated in 1951, namely a minimum age of fifty for women and sixty for men. But in terms of employment history, the revised pension legislation permits those with only ten years' employment in the state sector to collect pensions of 60 percent of their last wage. Those who have worked between fifteen and nineteen years receive 70 percent, and those with twenty years or more received 75 percent.[48] If members of this last group also participated in CCP revolutionary work during the civil war against the Kuomintang (KMT), they are eligible for pensions of 80 percent, and if they joined the revolution during the Japanese war before 1937, they receive 100 percent of their last salary. In general, these upward revisions increase the minimum pension by 10 percent and the maximum by 20 percent. In addition, the raising of existing monthly pensions to a minimum of 25 yuan, regardless of the length of service prior to retirement, significantly improves the economic position of the oldest retirees whom ill health had previously forced to retire on inadequate pensions.[49]

The single most critical revision in the 1978 pension reforms, however, does not concern the retirees but their children. Since 1978, pension regulations permit one child of each retiree to enter the parent's former place of employment as a full-time state worker. This option of replacement *(ding-ti)* or succession *(jie-ban)*, was used before 1966 by families in which the loss of the principal breadwinner had created financial hardship.[50] The new regulations, however, make the option of the replacement an ordinary procedure.[51]

Workers eligible for retirement since 1978 have responded to the new provision enthusiastically. Those who were postponing retirement for several years applied immediately, and many have exercised the replacement option. In eight factories where union officials gave me complete numerical breakdowns, an average of 80 percent of new retirees had been replaced by a child.[52] Individual retirees report that the replacement option has been the single most important consideration behind their decision to retire.

These swings in policy and the changing content of the pension benefits since 1951 mean that the conditions of retirement vary significantly

from one year to the next. In addition, age, work history, and health
determine which of the elderly will benefit from the specific options
available at the time they choose, or are forced, to retire. Often a ten-
year age difference effectively excludes an entire cohort from new financial opportunities and creates economic inequalities completely out of
proportion to individual differences in education, health, or work history. The way in which these policies have brought particular gains to
certain segments of the urban elderly population is illustrated by comparing two generations in one family:[53]

Chen Youli retired in 1979 after twenty-three years on the janitorial and
kitchen staff of a Beijing machine tool factory. Before 1958 the factory was a
large workshop, but during the Great Leap Forward it had been upgraded to a
state factory and relocated on the western outskirts of the city. In 1968 the
plant was again expanded. The work force increased from 900 to 2,300
workers, and new buildings were added. Although representative of the modern industrial sector, this factory is by no means extraordinary. For hauling,
maintenance, and packaging, it relies heavily on manual labor. New workers
are trained in a traditional three-year apprenticeship, and veteran workers
practice and teach the skills they learned from earlier generations of craftsmen.

In 1979 the monthly wage packet averaged 60 yuan. Jobs were ranked
according to an eight-grade wage scale, and monthly salaries ranged from 34
yuan for workers just completing their apprenticeship to 100 yuan for the most
senior technicians. After ten years' experience workers usually achieved a
grade three job with an average pay of 47 yuan. When Chen Youli retired, she
was a grade five worker earning 64 yuan per month.

Even though Chen Youli was three years short of the usual retirement age of
fifty, she was granted a full pension of 75 percent of her last wage because of
her many years of service and her chronically high blood pressure. When
Chen's pension is combined with the salaries of her husband and three adult
children, the family enjoys an extremely comfortable economic position. Their
financial security and the importance of Chen Youli's financial contribution
stand in stark contrast to the position of Chen Pingfong in a rural setting. They
also contrast sharply with the economic position of Chen Youli's mother-in-
law during the 1950s and 1960s.

Chen Youli's mother-in-law, Li Qiuwen, was widowed in 1941 at the age of
fifty-two. She lived with her four children in Beijing. The eldest son, who was
already fully employed at the time of his fathers death, was her main source of
support. Li Qiuwen worked at home, sewing and occasionally taking in wash
or mending. Her youngest son discontinued primary school after his father's
death and, through a friend of his eldest brother, was apprenticed to the owner
of a machine repair shop.

By 1949, the three oldest children had married and left home. Li Qiuwen
lived with her youngest son, supported by his wages and small gifts from the
other children. In comparison to many of her contemporaries, Li Qiuwen had
achieved a considerable degree of economic security. After her youngest son's

marriage to Chen Youli, her situation further improved. Her son was promoted to foreman. His wages increased, his family qualified for subsidized medical care, and his young and energetic wife took over most of the housework. Between 1958 and 1964, life became more difficult. Chen Youli went to work in the factory, and most of the burden of child care and housework fell to Li Qiuwen.

At the time of her death in 1969, Li Qiuwen was financially secure, but her good fortune depended entirely on the economic success of her children and on the quality of her relationships with younger family members. In contrast, at the time of her retirement Chen Youli drew a pension even larger than the wages of her working children, was financially independent, and could pass on housework and child care to others. Her working children helped prepare meals and took care of their own washing. When asked whether her poor health prevented her from caring for her daughter's children who had become the responsibility of their paternal grandmother, Chen Youli explained that it did not, because her blood pressure was now controlled by medication. Rather, the grandchildren were not her responsibility because the other grandmother was a housewife who had never worked outside her home. Chen, in contrast, was a pensioner who had fulfilled her responsibilities to her children and was entitled to leisure after retirement. Because of her favorable job placement in the late 1950s, Chen Youli was thus freed of the obligations that bound her mother-in-law to her home and to her grandchildren. Consequently, Chen Youli's old age would be of a fundamentally different character than that of Li Qiuwen.

Unequal access to state sector jobs and changing pension provisions have stratified the population of urban elderly so that the youngest cohorts of elderly fare far better than the oldest. But other wage policies have reversed this relationship between increasing age and declining economic power, permitting older workers to surpass the earning power of the young.[54] In part, this strong position of veteran workers in their fifties and sixties is a consequence of the younger worker's shorter employment record in a wage system where most promotions strictly follow the criteria of seniority. Often when the incomes of working parents are compared with that of their eldest child, the parents are at the peak of their careers, while the child has been in the labor force for less than a decade. Yet even in cases where the younger person has ten or more years of experience, the older worker continues to command a large financial advantage.[55] Nor is the discrepancy limited to professionals, for the inequality is at least as strong in comparisons among factory workers. Thus, more important than age-specific income inequalities are specific provisions of CCP wage policies. Between 1966 and 1976, wages for most urban workers remained at 1965 levels. This policy did not undercut the earning power of those promoted to upper-level jobs, but it severely limited the ability of younger workers to gain parity with older workers. Wages of younger workers were held near entry-level pay for a decade. And even after five or ten years on the job, workers under thirty-five rarely received promotions comparable to those offered young workers in the 1950s and early 1960s.[56] Because of these wage freezes, workers at age sixty, who at forty-seven had earned 65 yuan per month, maintained a constant financial advantage over younger workers whose wages remained at the lowest pay levels of 30 to 40 yuan per month.

Another wage policy that directly affected pay differentials among the urban work force rested on the Cultural Revolution policy of eliminating salary differences between professionals or skilled workers and manual or semi-skilled workers.[57] To realize this objective, salary differences among entering workers were dramatically narrowed, while differences among established workers continued as before. Over twenty years, the policy might have achieved its objective, but in the short term it produced additional inequalities. While reducing income inequalities between skilled and unskilled workers the policy increased the wage differential between old and young.

Between 1977 and 1979 wages for workers in the state sector were increased nationwide three times.[58] At first it seemed that age-related inequalities, particularly the disparities between the wages of those under thirty-five and those over fifty, would eventually be redressed in favor of the young. But in the short term the differences remain large. Promotions are usually limited to improvements of one grade, and younger workers remain two or three wage grades below veteran workers.

Other basic assumptions of the post-Mao wage policies indirectly but systematically continue to favor veteran workers. Since 1977, for example, the national leadership under Deng Xiaoping has made a strong effort to maximize labor productivity in the most modern enterprises. One means to realize this plan is to curb new hiring and to utilize the most highly paid workers as fully as possible. It is thus not possible to retire the older, highly paid workers and to replace them with younger, lower-wage workers since the high pensions due to the older workers would cancel out any savings made by hiring new workers at lower salaries. Furthermore, the ten-year hiatus in the training of higher-level technicians and engineers means that young workers are not always more skilled than the older workers whom they would replace. Thus many workers over fifty remain in high-level jobs in the state sector, while those under thirty-five have been forced to accept either low-grade jobs in the state sector or poorly paid jobs in the collective sector.[59]

A final wage policy that maintains the favored position of senior workers is the formula for allocating bonuses. Unlike the salary increase that specifically helps workers at the lowest wage levels, bonuses given to spur worker enthusiasm and innovation frequently increase wages among the best paid because bonuses are granted to all workers in a workshop regardless of pay, and sometimes are even calculated as a percentage of monthly wages.

These wage policies explain much of the advantage of the oldest workers, but there is another, less directly measurable ideological support for the elderly. In the 1950s, as the Chinese rapidly expanded employment opportunities in the modernized urban sector, young workers dominated industry. Youthful enthusiasm and energy were extolled for their contributions to the revolution and the establishment of the new republic. Now the People's Republic is itself approaching middle age, and particularly after the Cultural Revolution's divisive battles between veterans and newcomers, youth is no longer the unequivocal hope of the future. Older workers are revered for consistency, loyalty, and steadiness, while younger workers are often presumed to have poor work habits and unreliable ideas.

When China shifted from a decentralized market economy to a centralized planned socialist economy, the national leadership established a wage policy that rewarded seniority and relied heavily on bureaucratic procedures. With each succeeding year, regulations that defined the conditions of entry into the workplace and protected the senior workers proliferated and ossified. Younger workers could not routinely petition to regulators outside the system, and with each passing year it has become harder for young newcomers to alter the conditions of work in their favor.

Economic Consequences for the Old

In many societies the relative status of the old has declined in years of economic growth.[60] Hampered by inferior education and residential immobility, the older worker often has less access than the young to the highest paying jobs in the most modern sectors, and consequently the old as a group fall further behind with each technological or organizational transformation. Without exception, however, these pessimistic conclusions come from market economies where the individual worker bears primary responsibility for securing additional education, promotions, and transfers, and where the employer in turn seeks to minimize labor costs without accepting the obligation to share the profits with anyone but the investors. In a socialist economy, responsibilities and priorities are quite different. The state, not individual entrepreneurs, takes responsibility in redistributing economic gains, and labor, not ownership of capital, is the primary source of income. As a result, manual and illiterate workers in a socialist economy would be expected to command at least as good a return as professionals, and the elderly manual laborer in particular would be expected to gain special consideration.

In both urban and rural China, the CCP plan of economic development in fact supports the elderly in precisely this fashion. Gains made by increased productivity of the youngest and strongest workers are shared with the oldest and weakest, and social welfare programs specifically aid the old. Yet to attribute all the economic gains of the elderly to the income and welfare policies of the CCP is to oversimplify, and even distort, the true meaning of the communist revolution for the elderly. Many of the immediate gains have not been the primary objectives of specific programs but have been the unplanned consequences of adapting the socialist blueprint to the realities of poverty.

In rural areas where physical strength remains a decisive determinant of income, the CCP collectivization of agriculture has softened but not eliminated the negative impact of aging on income. But because China has not yet been able to prosper without a private sector, precommunist economic institutions survive and critically affect the post-1949 strategies for economic security. Most important for the rural elderly is the continued prominence of the family as a unit of production. Because household labor remains highly remunerative, the rural elderly who concentrate their efforts on the private sector maintain a strong financial position relative to the young and middle-aged who must remain in the collective labor force. The original CCP development plans did not expect to benefit the elderly in this way, but in practice this is one means by which the elderly have turned the experience of rural collectivization to their advantage.

In the cities, the socialist transformation is more complete than in the countryside, yet the economic gains for the elderly are less equitably distributed. For the urban elderly the perquisites of seniority and of pensions for individual workers provide the biggest increases in income and security over the pre-1949 era. But because these new rewards have been offered selectively to specific cohorts of urban workers in response to changing labor policy and short-term fluctuations in the urban economy, the improvements for the elderly have expanded unsteadily, and those who became old before meeting the new criteria had to fall back on the precommunist strategies of continued employment and reliance on adult children. As the economy has matured, the percentage of each group eligible for full retirement benefits has increased, and the youngest generation of the elderly—those who entered the state labor force as young workers after 1956—have secured a standard of living far above that of their peers in the rural areas or of earlier generations of urban workers. In the cities, the socialist promises are more generous. But they are also more expensive to fulfill. Therefore, the CCP is forced to reward the elderly in some occupations more than in others, and the urban elderly, as a group, have had to wait longer than the rural elderly to reap the economic rewards initially promised by the leaders of the communist revolution.

3

LIVING ARRANGEMENTS

THE LIVING ARRANGEMENTS of the elderly offer another perspective on the quality of life since 1949. In the decades immediately preceding 1949, the ideal living arrangement for the elderly was a household shared with a married child, preferably a son.[1] Death, poverty, or long-term separation prevented many elderly from realizing the ideal, but with the exception of a minority of intellectuals who protested against the conventional expectations, elderly men and women of all social classes saw no viable alternative to the multigeneration household.[2]

After 1949, however, the CCP took deliberate steps to weaken several of the underlying supports of the existing living arrangements of the elderly. In 1950, through the new marriage law that outlawed the traditional marriage customs of child betrothal, dowry, and bride price, the CCP reduced the parental control over the timing and composition of new households for the young.[3] Between 1950 and 1952, as part of the land reform campaign, the CCP confiscated all lineage temples and thereby systematically suppressed the public rituals of ancestor worship that gave community support and ideological justification to strong exclusive family loyalties.[4] The complete collectivization of agriculture, commerce, and industry in 1956 further threatened parent-child solidarity by eliminating the potentially punitive powers of preferential bequests and inheritance. In addition, throughout these early years of CCP rule, the expansion of low-cost primary education and the creation of new jobs in the military and state sector offered both sons and daughters opportunities for economic advancement independent of their parents' desires or resources. In light of these several attacks on parental prerogatives and the steady economic gains of the young in the first decade after 1949, it seemed possible that three- and four-generation households would disappear and that eventually all elderly parents would live separately from their married children.[5] In fact this has not happened. Few established multigeneration households have dissolved, and new ones have continued to form throughout the post-1949 era. Contrary to expectations, the traditional living arrangements of the elderly are compatible with the communist revolution, and no radically new patterns of household formation have appeared.

In rural areas, where the family continues to be a unit of production and the level of mechanization is low, the persistence of multigeneration households does not come as a complete surprise. But in the cities, where pre-1949 industrialization and post-1949 economic transformations reduced the social welfare functions of large households, the rationale for the continuation of traditional forms is not so obvious. It can be found in the larger context of scarcity and control in which both rural and urban residents, young and old, make their housing choices.

The Typical Household

Throughout China, the ideal arrangement for elderly men and women is a household shared with an adult child. In model families cited by the official press, elderly parents live with a married son, daughter-in-law, and several grandchildren.[6] In fiction and drama, only the extraordinarily deviant or the pitiful live alone; ordinary elderly characters almost all live surrounded by children and grandchildren.[7]

In rural families, the model of an elderly parent living with a married son prevails. In the cities, more options are available, and in this setting the elderly live as often with several unmarried children as with a married son, and some even live with a married daughter. In the didactic press and inspirational literature, the CCP continues to attack abuses of parental authority, such as patriarchal power, arranged marriages, and elaborate funerary rites that were associated with traditional three-generation households. It also actively supports more egalitarian relations between husband and wife and between parents and children, through didactic explanations of divorce legislation, marriage reform, and court proceedings against abusive parents. However, in terms of household composition among the elderly, the party has made no large-scale effort to change the expectation that elderly parents should live with adult children.

When one turns from the ideal families portrayed in the official press to the actual practices described in Hong Kong and PRC interviews, there is surprisingly little deviation from the norm. The majority of the elderly live with at least one child, and the single most likely arrangement is parents living with a married son.[8] The case of parents living with two or more married sons is rare.[9] Of the few families who maintain joint households, most have above-average wealth, which suggests that these arrangements require more resources than most families command. Few families in the two interview groups ever considered this option, because only a minority had two or more married sons.

Households of unrelated individuals are also very unusual among the elderly.[10] In everyday speech and in the registration system maintained by the Bureau of Public Security, the word household (hu) designates the group of people who eat together and draw ration tickets as a single unit. In cities, members of a household almost always share the same residential address. In the country, members may sleep in several locations but eat together and share food rations. In the Hong Kong and PRC groups, the household was also always a family group, usually of lineal descendants. Thus, although there appear to be no legal restrictions on the criteria for membership, household is usually identical with family. In cases where elderly individuals live separately from their kin or have no close living relative, the norm is to live alone rather than to live with unrelated friends or workmates.

Despite the similar incidence of multigeneration households among urban and rural elderly, there is a distinction in terms of preferences. The rural elderly view the multigeneration household as the culmination of several years of joint preparation, and few ever search for an alternative.[11] In urban families, however, living arrangements of the old are primarily a response to immediate necessity and do not form a central part of elderly parents' strategy for economic security in old age. A comparison of two households, one in the countryside and the other in the city, illustrates considerations that differentiate the housing choices of rural and urban elderly:[12]

Li Laoer is a neighbor and distant cousin of Li Hoizhong. In their youths, Li Hoizhong enjoyed more security and status, but in old age, Li Laoer has gained the upper hand. Li Laoer and his elder brother, Li Laoda, were orphaned as teenagers. They remained in the village after their parents' deaths, working as hired hands for the wealthier families in the area. After land reform Li Laoda took his newly acquired land and set up a bachelor household in the old woodshed he had received as his share of the village property. In contrast, Li Laoer married immediately and, by merging his newly acquired land and property with that of his bride, established himself as a man of above-average means.

Li Laoer's wife was the widow of a small landlord who had been killed by the KMT. Consequently, in the post-1949 official history of the village, the family were considered to be the dependents of a revolutionary martyr, and they enjoyed a special honorary status. At the time of her remarriage, the widow had a girl and boy from her first marriage. Within a few years she and Li Laoer added two more boys to the household.

In 1960, one year after the collapse of the Great Leap Forward, Li Laoer's stepson escaped to Hong Kong. For ten years he faithfully remitted money to his mother, which she and Li Laoer saved in preparation for the marriages of Li Laoer's two boys. Li Laoer himself was extremely attentive to family finances. He worked tirelessly and had a reputation in the village as being stubborn, but strong and honest. In 1970 when the village leaders decided to develop several new, collectively owned enterprises, they chose Li Laoer to be the head of the village industries. Two of the new ventures — a brick kiln and an oil press — were immediately profitable. Village incomes rose, and Li Laoer gained a seat on the village Revolutionary Committee.

In 1972, primarily through the initiative of his wife, Li Laoer's first son found a bride. Her family was one of the poorest in the village, but as the eldest of seven children, she had a reputation for being a tireless and obedient worker. Li Laoer's wife felt confident that she knew the girl's character and looked forward to adding another hard worker to the household.

For many years the entire family had saved for this wedding, and as soon as the village brick kiln was in operation, the Lis were among the first to make a big purchase from it to remodel their house. After the 1971 fall harvest, Li Laoer and his sons set to work. The house had once been one of the finest in the village. The foundation was of stone, the roof was of tile, and the location was an excellent one on high dry land. As was the local custom, it had been built directly adjacent to the neighbors' houses, both of which were occupied by descendants of one grandfather. Li Laoer's house stood in the middle of the three adjoining homes. It was fifteen feet wide and thirty feet deep. The front half of the house sheltered the family, their possessions, and a year's supply of grain. In the back of the house was the kitchen, pig sty, and family latrine. At the rear of the property, separated from the house, was the woodshed that Li Laoer had been allocated as his share of village property at the time of land reform.

In 1949 the village had been a rather poor one for the Guangzhou (Canton) delta. Thus, even small landlords built with sun-dried mud bricks, and after fifty years of hard use, typhoon rains, and civil war, the house was continually in need of repair. To the eyes of city visitors, it looked dilapitated and run down.

Before purchasing their bricks, Li Laoer and his sons had patched the front walls and added a new coat of whitewash, but once they acquired real building supplies, they began major renovation. They tore down the existing back wall and knocked out the old kitchen and pig sty to make a new room. They built a new inner wall and extended the sides of the house back twenty feet. Finally, they added a new tile roof and a larger kitchen and pig sty.

For the village, the renovations represented a major improvement in the family's standard of living. But the house was still rather simple. There was only one small window in kitchen, and the only light for the two inside rooms came from the doorways. The floor was packed dirt; there was no running water; and the family still shared the home with their pigs, chickens, and ducks.

In the first few months after the eldest son's marriage, the young bride and groom occupied the new room in the middle of the house, while Laoer, his wife, and youngest son remained in the front room. In the fall of 1973 the family brought another lot of bricks and rebuilt the woodshed by raising the walls and replacing the thatch roof with tile. In 1974 Li Laoer and his unmarried son moved to the refurbished woodshed. Li Laoer's wife and small grandson sleep in the original house, while the first son and his wife have kept the new room.

Despite the separate sleeping arrangements, the villagers still count the household as one because the family eat together and maintain one budget. For the marriage of the second son, they plan to build a new kitchen on the side of the woodshed. After the arrival of the second daughter-in-law the most likely plan is for Li Laoer to rejoin his wife in the original house, leaving the woodshed entirely to the second son and his family. At that time the family will divide into two distinct households. The long history of joint living as well as the short distance between the two houses, however, guarantees that the parents will be intimately involved in the daily lives of both sons.

Li Fulan and her husband Zhang Aiguo share a home with two of their three sons, their daughter-in-law, and their daughter in the industrial city of Shijiachuang. They have both just retired from a large textile mill. Frequent blackouts provoked by chronic high blood pressure forced Zhang Aiguo to retire at age fifty-five. Li Fulan, who also suffers from high blood pressure, retired at the age of forty-seven, after only thirteen years in the mill. She receives a pension of 30 yuan, only 5 yuan less than the wage of her daughter, who has just used the replacement option to follow her mother into the mill.

Zhang Aiguo's pension totals 48 yuan. It is 80 percent of his last wage and exceeds the incomes of his sons by 20 percent. In addition he has a part-time job as a supervisor in a small tool factory in the collective sector, which pays him an additional monthly salary of 35 yuan. Because of these several sources of income, the economic contributions of the two parents dominate the household budget. The parents' superior economic position, however, is also expressed through their control of their children's living arrangements.

The Zhang family of six adults pays a monthly rent of 3.5 yuan for three rooms that total 37 square meters. In addition, they have a makeshift kitchen on an outside balcony that serves as a public corridor and is not included in their officially allocated floor space. Inside the apartment are two small bedrooms and a large sitting room. The bedroom to the left of the entryway was the original kitchen. Now it provides a bedroom for the youngest son, who sleeps in a loft suspended above storage boxes and huge pickle jars. The bedroom to the right is occupied by the second son and his bride of one month. A double bed, a wardrobe, a table, and two stuffed armchairs occupy most of the floor space. Suitcases and large cooking implements, stored on top of the cabinet and hanging from hooks, fill the room to the ceiling. Furniture and other family belongings crowd the large main room that serves as dining area, sitting room, and bedroom for the parents and their twenty-two-year-old daughter. Thus, although the apartment is twice the size of the place they lived in when the children were small and is far above the average urban allocation, the crowding is intense.

The apartment is in a three-story walk-up, built in the early 1950s. After twenty years of hard use, each step slopes downward, and the exterior balconies are packed with household possessions and extended kitchens like the Zhangs'. Despite the dismal exteriors, the dank public latrines on the stair landings, and the obvious crowding, the Zhangs feel fortunate to have such a good apartment, and neither of their two married sons has yet been able to find better arrangements on his own.

After the eldest son married six years earlier, he and his wife, and later their daughter, lived in the bedroom now occupied by the second son and his new wife. Then when the second son reached age twenty-seven and would no longer postpone his marriage, the eldest son moved into the household of his wife's parents, relinquishing the privacy of a separate bedroom to his brother. The parents of the new daughter-in-law live in the same city, but as they already share a home with their second son and his wife, they cannot accomodate another couple. Thus, even as Li Fulan's second son and daughter-in-law settle into their new home, the family continues to look for additional apartments, hoping that eventually both young couples will have their own small households.

As Li Fulan and Li Laoer's housing arrangements suggest, both the immediate and long-range housing objectives of urban and rural elderly differ. In rural families, the elderly actively work to achieve a joint living situation prior to their children's marriages. In urban families, the ideal is for married children and their parents to live separately until the time when the parents are too old to manage on their own. At that time of need, a married child will rejoin the parents or an elderly parent will move to the home of a married child. In practice, however, as in the experience of Li Fulan and the daughter of Chen Youli, often no apartment is available for a newly married couple. Thus many urban families are forced to form three-generation homes earlier than they might prefer, and urban elderly find that they never are permitted a period of years when they can live independently from the younger generations of their families.

Determinants of Household Formation

High building costs and scarce supplies are two housing constraints that discourage the creation of one-generation households, but they are not the only ones. Government controls on migration and the economic efficiency of multigeneration living also prevent both rural and urban elderly from living alone. Thus, although urban residents are more dissatisfied with the necessity to live jointly than rural residents are and actively search for alternatives, urban parents in fact continue to maintain multigeneration homes at least as often rural parents do. Throughout China the same forces of necessity, namely housing shortages, government restrictions on change of residence, and the economic advantages of joint living, consistently limit the housing choices of the old.

In rural and urban China, housing is in short supply, but the degree of the shortage and the strategies necessary to overcome the problem vary between rural and urban areas. In the countryside, where families build and own their own homes, the shortages are the result of inadequate family savings. According to estimates of William Parish for the late 1960s and early 1970s, families in both North and South China needed ten years to accumulate the funds necessary to build a new house.[13] Former residents of Guangdong Province who left China after 1972 give similar reports. A new house in the mid-1970s cost between two and six times the average annual family income; a new room cost approximately half of that.

As in the family of Li Laoer, the usual procedure is for every member of the household to save jointly for many years before beginning construction. Usually the pace of accumulation is irregular, and savings peak after unmarried children leave school and enter the full-time labor force. When the family is financially ready, they build a house to accommodate at least one married son. As there is no long-term housing policy dictated by the higher-level government authorities, the timing, location, and scale of new construction is primarily a local decision. As a result, most rural men live either nearby or with their elderly parents in homes in which both generations have jointly invested and from which neither parents nor adult children can easily withdraw their share.

In urban areas, most housing is rented.[14] Rents in the largest cities range between 5 and 12 yuan and take 3 to 7 percent of a family's income.[15] Therefore, in contrast to food, which often takes 60 percent of monthly expenditures, housing costs do not weigh heavily on family finances.[16] Even in households where the income drops suddenly owing to the loss of a major breadwinner, rents are rarely a major worry. Should a family be unable to pay the rent, their workplace can provide a short-term subsidy, or the housing authority responsible for collecting the rent can lower or even eliminate the rental fee for several months.

While rents are low, housing in the cities is extremely scarce. Workers in the favored state sector average 4.4 square meters per adult family member. However the overall average for all urban residents is only 3.6 square meters, a space allocation that is 20 percent lower than the general standard of 1952.[17] As a result, it is almost impossible for a family like Li Fulan's which is well housed by local standards, to convince anyone that they deserve additional accommodations, or that elderly members need separate apartments. Thus the typical pattern is for younger members to move out of the family home as new space becomes available, but for elderly parents to remain in their own apartment sheltering the children in greatest need. An elderly person does not move to a smaller home after the marriage of a child or the death of a spouse, and only when politically stigmatized does an old person with family remain alone in a room that could have housed additional members.

Another housing constraint that encourages multigeneration households in urban areas is the nearly universal practice among post-1949 architects of planning two-room apartments for a minimum of four adults.[18] Thus in urban areas the very design of new housing dictates against separate residences for the elderly and directly encourages joint living.

The second major determinant of household composition is tight government control over all migration. The 1954 constitution guaranteed citizens of China "freedom to change their residence."[19] One year later the State Council severely restricted this freedom by establishing a system of household registration to increase government control over population shifts and in particular to curb large-scale rural-to-urban migration. Since 1955, all Chinese citizens have been required to register their addresses with the local police station and to obtain prior approval from the public security cadres for any relocation beyond the rural district (xiang) or urban town (chen).[20]

In 1958 the standing committee of the National People's Congress adopted additional regulations further restricting the legitimate criteria for official relocation.[21] During the chaotic years after the Great Leap Forward, the new restrictions were not well enforced, but by the mid-1960s they were again carefully observed and relocation was granted almost exclusively on the basis of a state job transfer or family hardship. Subsequent constitutions have completely omitted the original guarantee of freedom of residence and thereby brought the law into line with actual practice.[22]

The overall impact of these restrictions is to create less household mobility than would have been the case had residents been free to establish new households as often as they wished. In periods of political or economic upheaval, individuals may move around rather easily, but officially their place of residence remains unchanged. When the restrictions on free movement are consistently enforced under conditions of prolonged housing shortage, the elderly and their children remain in the same household, neither generation able to move without considerable effort.

A closer look at individuals who do try to relocate, however, reveals that even in their granting of exceptions to general guidelines, the CCP consistently acts in favor of multigeneration households for the old. Thus, for example, 25 percent of the families described in the Hong Kong interviews and 38 percent of the families visited in China achieved multigeneration status through successful petitions to relocate on the grounds that elderly parents could not live alone.[23] In most of these readjustments the move directly contradicted the official policy of keeping residents from moving from a less densely populated area to a more congested location. Not every person who applies to relocate to care for an elderly parent is given permission. Nor does every child with an ailing parent want to move. But in general adult children accept the responsibility of caring for frail parents and the government permits most of them to fulfill their obligations.

Housing shortages and restrictive migration laws encourage joint living, the economic benefits of large households make multigeneration living desirable on its own terms. In both urban and rural areas, one large household is usually a more efficient unit of consumption than two smaller ones. The larger households use less fuel, need less furniture, and provide better meals at lower cost than the smaller families. In most families these savings do not exceed 5 yuan per month, but because even 5 yuan can cover 30 percent of monthly food costs for city residents and equals the entire monthly cash stipend paid to rural destitute, these small savings are meaningful to the elderly, to their families, and to the Chinese government.[24]

Another economic advantage of the multigeneration household is in the area of social services. In the first years after a three-generation household is formed, the primary need is child care. In rural areas there is little public day-care, and even in urban areas where day care has been widely advocated since the 1950s, only 50 percent of children under six are cared for outside the home.[25] Yet in both urban and rural China most mothers of young children work full time. The rural solution, as in the families of Chen Pingfong and Li Laoer, is for the grandmother to stay at home with the grandchildren, do the housework, and tend the pigs. In the cities, grandmothers are also the primary caretakers. Although retired janitor Chen Youli is happy to pass on child care to her daughter's mother-in-law, Li Fulan, like the majority of grandmothers in the PRC urban interviews, expects to care full time for her grandchildren after her retirement.[26]

Later in the family life-cycle it is the grandparents who need the care, and in rural and urban China such assistance is expensive, or even unavailable, through public agencies. Throughout the post-1949 era the Chinese government has stressed home care as the routine response to short-term medical crises and long-term treatment of chronic illness. Urban old-age homes are reserved for the small minority of elderly who are totally bereft of kin. However, as shown in the case of Chen Youli's mother-in-law, most elderly do in fact care for themselves until a very advanced age, and therefore most parents place substantial burdens on their children only after contributing several decades of support to their children and grandchildren.

Finally, multigeneration households survive and prosper because they are valuable as units of production. This is particularly true in rural areas where pigs, chickens, and produce raised outside of the collective sector account for up to 40 percent of a rural family's total income.[27] In addition, because the work regulations favor the concentration of elderly men and women in these remunerative jobs, the contribution of elderly members is both conspicuous and highly valued. So great, in fact, are the financial gains of three-generation households that rural siblings deprived of parental assistance openly complain about the special advantages of the child living with the parents.[28]

City households, in contrast, are rarely units of production. They do, however, require many hours of onerous housework for which one can calculate a labor replacement value. For example, almost no one has running hot water, and frequently even cold water must be drawn from wells or communal taps. Many people still cook over charcoal braziers, building a fire for each meal. Without refrigeration, families must shop at least once a day, but goods are sold in a variety of shops, and even within one market there are usually separate lines for vegetables, meat, and condiments. The elderly average an hour a day for food shopping, and when they want something special, they frequently spend the better part of a morning just purchasing food for the evening meal. Washing is also time-consuming; clothes have to be soaked for hours in cold water and then beaten against a stone or rubbed on a washboard. If it is sunny and warm, they can be hung out a window or across a courtyard, but if it is rainy and cold, temporary lines are strung up in the already cramped living area.

In families where there is an elderly parent not employed outside the home, most of these household jobs fall to the old. Although very few families pay elderly members for this major contribution to the family welfare, and housework does not bring the direct financial return that pig raising brings to the rural elderly, urban residents consider housework a real job, and young people who live with elderly parents explicitly state that their parents' contribution is essential to maintaining their current standard of living.

Exceptions to the Multigeneration Household

For some families the housing shortages, the migration restrictions, and the economic incentives of joint living do not suffice to produce a multigeneration household, and throughout the country there is a minority of elderly who live independently from their children. The elderly who belong to one-generation households, living either alone or with a spouse, are primarily a rural phenomenon.[29] In the cities, where housing is in such short supply and apartments are not built to individual family specifications, elderly parents do not often move out to live alone in an empty apartment, and almost no city dweller of any age will forgo a room in downtown Beijing or Shanghai in favor of a separate residence on the city outskirts.

The three most common conditions under which the rural elderly choose, or are forced, to live separately from a married child are affluence, rejection, and demographic necessity. The most typical case of affluence is where a rural family has been able to build a second residence in advance of the marriage of a son or grandson, or a married son is temporarily working outside the village.[30] In virtually all these families, the elderly parents are healthy and financially self-sufficient, and the separation of the two generations is not considered a permanent arrangement.

By contrast, the one-generation households created by rejection and necessity are both more permanent and less freely chosen. However, among those living alone because of their children's rejection there are two distinctly separate situations. In one, the remarriage of an elderly widow has provoked irresolvable tensions between her and an adult son.[31] In the other, the children of political outcasts have rejected their parents out of fear of political reprisals.[32]

Legally, since the Marriage Reform Law of 1950, "interference with the remarriage of widows is prohibited," and in areas where the law is fully enforced, the security of remarried widows has improved.[33] Yet prejudice in some areas is still strong, and widows who remarry continue to face special hardships. The elderly couple where the woman is a remarried widow with no children of her own from her second marriage can be scorned both by stepchildren and by children from her first marriage. Sons may deny their usual filial responsibilities, and the local community tolerates a higher level of deprivation before intervening.

The other basis for rural children rejecting shared households dates back to the early 1950s when all rural residents were classified as friends or enemies of the revolution.[34] Among the enemies were former rich peasants and landlords, as well as a residual category of "bad elements," which included bandits, criminals, lackeys of the landlords, and former employees of the Nationalist government. These people were denied full political rights and remained vulnerable to renewed attack in each political rectification movement that followed. Because the class label was applied to all residents according to the political and economic background of the family head of their household, children and grandchildren (through the male line) of landlords and bad elements were also categorized as enemies of the people and excluded from full participation in village society.[35] In some cases, however, children of these political outcasts established separate households from their stigmatized parents and thereby acquired a more favorable class label. Among this group are children who reject their parents out of fear that joint living will bring political reprisals on themselves and their children.

The third group of rural elderly who live alone against their wishes are ordinary people on whom demographic necessity has forced a one-generation household. These are the elderly whose only children surviving to adulthood are daughters. After 1949 most rural communities continued to observe the traditional custom that brides should come from outside the village and grooms should remain in their natal place. The consequences for elderly who only have daughters are clear cut. Barring unusual circumstances, married daughters live far from their parents, and since only a tiny minority of women never marry, elderly parents rarely plan to live with an adult daughter. When only female children survive to marry, the long-run consequence for the parents is a single-generation household independent of any child.

There is, however, a traditional solution to the absence of male progeny. Parents of daughters can adopt a young boy and raise him as their son, or they can adopt a son-in-law at the time of their daughter's marriage. In both cases their living arrangements in old age are identical to those of most elderly. But in the second case, the family integration may be less complete. Sometimes the wife's parents require that the groom take the surname of his father-in-law. In other situations they ask only that one or more of the grandchildren take the grandfather's name and let the son-in-law keep his own. In still other circumstances the new groom never lives jointly but merely promises to support the old couple until their deaths. In parts of China where the adoption of young boys is preferred over the adoption of son-in-laws, such as the Guangzhou delta, there are relatively few examples of a married daughter and her husband living jointly with the wife's parents.[36] But in other parts of China where the prejudice appears to be less strong, the elderly prefer to adopt a son-in-law rather than live alone. Thus the frequency of single-generation households among the elderly with no sons varies according to local attitudes toward adoption and marriage practices.

The single-generation household is one of the two exceptions to the usual pattern of parents living with married sons; the elderly living with married daughters is the other exception. In contrast to the single-generation household, this other atypical arrangement is primarily an urban phenomenon, which directly reflects the greater equality between urban men and women and the weakening of traditional marriage customs in the cities. In contrast to rural parents who almost always express a preference to live with sons, urban parents frequently are willing to live with either a son or a daughter. Nevertheless, the actual arrangements described in the Hong Kong and PRC interviews indicate that when parents have both a married son and a married daughter, they are more likely to live with sons than with daughters.[37] Thus the majority of urban parents living with a married daughter have no sons. But in contrast to rural parents without a son, urban parents in this situation turn happily to daughters and appear to suffer no financial or social disadvantages in comparison to those living with sons.

The greater willingness of urban parents to live with daughters re-emphasizes the basic difference between the housing strategies of urban and rural elderly. Whereas the rural elderly plan their households to maximize their long-term economic security, the urban elderly plan their households primarily in response to the housing opportunities available to their children. As soon as a young urban couple decide to marry, they and their families look for a separate residence. If no housing becomes available before the wedding, the young couple must then choose between living apart or moving in with a set of parents who have an extra room. Most young couples take the second option. Thus, although urban residents express a desire for single-generation households for the young, throughout the post-1949 years it has not been a routine arrangement.[38]

Furthermore, the single-generation household has never been the preferred situation for the elderly. Although eventually many young and middle-aged couples do live separately from their parents, almost no elderly parents ever live alone. Instead, they behave like Li Fulan and Zhang Aiguo and shelter the child in greatest need, until in advanced old age the direction of dependency reverses, and it is the parent who can no longer live without the help and support of adult children.

4

RELATIONS WITH CHILDREN

THE PREVALENCE OF JOINT living among the Chinese elderly and their adult children indicates that for most elderly, family ties are sustained and intense. Few elderly find it possible even to imagine an existence isolated from the younger generations, and they are completely involved in their children's everyday lives. Within this predominant pattern of joint living, however, the intensity of the parent-child relationship varies. Mothers more consciously develop strong emotional loyalties between themselves and their children than fathers do, and in old age mothers reap the benefits of their early attention in terms of especially close ties with adult sons and daughters. Many parents also still cultivate the loyalty of sons more deliberately than that of daughters, and among the elderly, relationships with adult sons are consistently strong. Because parents continue to be more likely to live jointly with sons, it is difficult for married daughters to sustain the same level of daily interaction as their brothers.

But conscious preference and actual patterns of behavior are changing, and elderly parents are increasingly likely to divide their affections between a son and a daughter. Higher age at first marriage and new employment opportunities for women partially explain the shift away from traditional preferences for sons. Deliberate efforts by the CCP to raise the status of women in public and in private life have also been decisive. The way in which the popular acceptance of new economic opportunities coincides with the ideological goals of the CCP illustrates how precommunist family ideals have gradually shifted to accommodate post-1949 political and social reality.

Parent-Child Interdependence

Traditional Confucian ideals for family behavior bound children to obey and serve their parents as long as the child lived.[1] For daughters, daily responsibilities to care for parents ended after they married and joined the households of their husbands. But for sons, particularly eldest sons, the obligations continued throughout their lives, beginning with required household duties in childhood and culminating in the expensive funeral rites and ritual sacrifices of ancestor worship. Parents, in contrast, were required to give little to the child beyond basic sustenance. Yet they were entitled to control the child's education, job placement, and marriage choice.

Thus, when given the most literal interpretation, Confucian orthodoxy systematically favored the rights of the old over those of the young and legitimized concentrated power in the hands of the parents. In actual practice, however, there was a wide range of behavior, and few families were wealthy enough to sacrifice the interests of the economically strongest generation to those of the weakest. In the early decades of the twentieth century only middle-aged parents overtly dominated their adult sons and daughters, and as the parents grew old, the two generations evolved a more interdependent relationship that reflected the increased earning power of the young.[2] But the persistence of classic Confucian texts as a standard means of instruction in primary schools, as well as the KMT's approval of Confucian orthodoxy, maintained the customary right of the old to claim a disproportionate share of family resources and fostered the ideal of the subordination of the young.

In the three decades immediately preceding 1949, the most authoritarian aspects of Confucian family morality came under direct attack. Leading intellectuals attributed China's social and economic "backwardness" to feudal Confucian mores that held the young hostage to the old.[3] The Nationalist government passed legislation that outlawed child betrothal, concubinage, and marriage by force, all practices that strengthened the control of parents over children.[4] In general, however, the criticism by the intellectuals and the new marriage law affected only a minority in the largest cities. Throughout rural China and among most working-class communities, Confucian ideals favoring the privileges of the old persisted, even as most elderly parents accepted in practice a more mutual relationship rooted in economic interdependence.

When the CCP came to power, it promised to alter this fundamental imbalance between young and old within Confucian tradition. Under the CCP, the party and the state were to command the primary loyalties of family members; young men were expected to be dutiful citizens first, filial sons and grandsons second. Marriage was to be an individual, not a family decision. Formal education was to be in state schools with a unified curriculum under the Ministry of Education, not in clan temples or with family tutors educated in the Confucian classics. Government officials, not parents and relatives, were to make job assignments.

If fully implemented, these changes in family and work relationships would have greatly reduced parents' control over the most critical areas of their children's futures. Children would mature less dependent on their parents' help, intergenerational loyalties would weaken, and interdependence would decline. Yet government media and individual reports document a high level of continuity with pre-1949 family values. Lifelong interdependence remains the preferred parent-child relationship among both young and old.[5] And in most urban and rural families, elderly men and women fully realize their desire for high levels of mutual interdependence.[6]

When living jointly, the different generations maintain obviously close ties. Parents and children are in constant contact, share most meals, and usually pool incomes into a common household budget. Contact between parents and children who do not live jointly is more variable, and the contrast between urban and rural families is marked. When parents and children in urban areas live separately, children often journey one or more hours each week to visit the parents' home on their one free day, usually taking a small gift of food. Occasionally the visit centers on a special event, but usually the time together is spent sharing housework or doing family shopping. During the three-day celebration of the Lunar New Year, all the children make a major effort to return to the parents' home. To use this most important holiday of the year to do anything other than visit parents and siblings would be an extraordinary affront to conventional morality which few would risk.

By contrast, rural children who live even less than an hour from their parents rarely visit on a regular basis. Instead, contacts with children living outside the village are limited to special events, such as New Year's, weddings, and funerals. Because rural women usually live outside their natal villages, ties between the rural elderly and their daughters are fragile, and they atrophy steadily with each year that the daughter lives away from the parents' home. Among the oldest generation of rural elderly there are many parents who do not see, or even hear from, their daughters for several years at a time.[7] For the minority of rural women who live in the same villages as their parents, the situation is quite different. These women maintain strong ties with their parents, particularly their mothers, and in times of crisis are an important source of aid.[8]

As rural parents move into advanced old age, they retreat even further into the household that they share with only one child and reduce the scope of exchange with their other offspring. With no private telephones available in rural China, families must rely on face-to-face contact or letters to maintain strong ties. But few rural elderly are literate, and most are unaccustomed to dictating their thoughts for correspondence. As the children living separately enter middle age, they begin to prepare for their own economic security in old age. They spend less time cultivating ties with their parents and shift to an almost exclusive concern with launching their own children into adult jobs and marriage.

In urban areas, old age does not precipitate such an exclusive concentration on the child with whom the parent lives. Even in the last years of life, household composition may change. New members may move in with the oldest generation, or the elderly parents may move out to join the child with more room or better access to medical care. As a result, the urban elderly maintain strong ties with all their children throughout old age, and it is common for siblings to split the financial obligations for elderly parents.[9]

Since household tasks that are the focus of parent-child exchanges are traditionally defined as women's work, mothers become closer to their children than fathers, and elderly women continue to report higher levels of solidarity than elderly men.[10] Yet in times of crisis, fathers are not at a clear disadvantage, being able to depend on their adult children as often as mothers.

Interdependence, not dependency, remains the primary characteristic of close parent-child relations.[11] In rural areas, where the shared family home is a primary unit of production as well as the single most valuable piece of private property, the interdependence of parents and child is obvious in the daily division of household labor. Each generation focuses on tasks that maximize the profit for the entire household, and neither can live as well independently as jointly.

In urban areas, it is not as readily apparent how the two generations define and maintain high levels of interdependence. Each working member is employed as an individual without regard to the earning power of others, and parents and children do not invest jointly in their homes. Nor do members pool all of their salaries into one budget. Even when parents live with children, it is common for urban children to contribute only 50 or 60 percent of their wages to cover the joint living expenses and to keep the remainder for their own savings or personal expenses. A look at how one urban family shares responsibilities illustrates the high levels of interdependence that prevail within the economic and social constraints of contemporary city life:[12]

> Ma Xinwang and his wife, Ouyang Xiu, live in three tiny rooms on the northern side of an old courtyard house in Beijing. Neither has an outstanding past or unusual prospects for the future. Ma is over seventy, a recent retiree who worked for the railroad before 1949 and later became a guard in the warehouse of a medium-sized state enterprise. Ouyang Xiu, just over sixty, has been a housewife her entire life.
>
> Ma Xinwang stands nearly six feet tall. He is big boned and has strikingly broad shoulders. He bears his age easily. Despite a mild case of rheumatism, he

Ideal Elders of the 1970s

A still from the feature film *Pine Ridge* shows Communist Party member and poor peasant Chang Wan-shan reining in runaway horses. 1974.

Lin Jen-kuei, a Red Army veteran, exhorts young people to continue the revolutionary struggle. 1976.

A Party agronomist in eastern China discusses the improved peanut harvest with an old peasant. 1973.

People's Liberation Army medical workers treat a peasant. 1976.

Elderly join young members of a rural work team. Shandong, 1976.

Rural Reality After Mao

Hebei harvest work, 1979. *Paul Pickowicz.*

A Hubei farmer carries a pig to market, 1982.
Robert Morowchick.

Hubei Province, 1981.
Lawrence Bates.

A Hubei rural laundry, 1981. *Lawrence Bates.*

Urban Reality After Mao

Beijing, 1983. *Gail Coulson.*

Qinghai, 1982. *Cynthia Sung.*

Beijing, 1981.
Mark Sheldon.

A stonecutter at Xian mosque, 1982.
Robert Morowchick.

An urban laundry, 1982.
*United Global Methodist
Ministries.*

A game of checkers
at an old age home.
Gene Stockwell.

Xian City, 1982. *Gail Coulson.*

Suzhow, 1982. *Mark Sheldon.*

City housework,
Nanjing, 1983.
Gail Coulson.

Wuhan City, 1982. *Robert Morowchick.*   Shanghai, 1982. *Gail Coulson.*

Xian City, 1982. *Gail Coulson.*

can still thread his bike through the heavy Beijing traffic and moves quickly and with agility when necessary. In 1975 he was selected as a model worker and rewarded with a metal teacup emblazoned with a commendation. In 1978, nearly a decade after he met the minimum requirements for retirement, he was awarded his pension and permanently withdrew from the labor force.

Good health and a fine work record only partially explain Ma's delayed retirement. The major reason for the postponement was financial. His son and daughter entered the work force in the late 1960s. By 1975 they both were married and had children. Their jobs and those of their spouses are in the state sector, and in terms of national averages they are rather privileged. Nevertheless, before 1977 neither had received a promotion, and they have a hard time making ends meet. In addition, neither the son nor the daughter has been assigned an apartment near their place of work. As a result, the couples live separately in factory dormitories for single workers, sending their children to live with their grandparents. Ma and Ouyang have full-time responsibility for the son's two boys and the daughter's girl.

In general, Ouyang takes care of the housework and Ma watches the children. Every day, he spends six to eight hours wheeling them to the park, joining them in building towers and forts with bits of discarded lumber, and disciplining the two boys. When Ouyang feels poorly, Ma steams bread for lunch and then takes an afternoon rest with the children. On summer nights when the inner, windowless room is too stifling for sleep, he takes the children for a stroll. During the day Ouyang's main responsibilities are shopping, cooking, and washing. Usually these tasks occupy her for the entire morning and part of the evening.

When the grandchildren are sick, Ouyang takes them to the neighborhood clinic. If the symptoms last more than a day or two, one of their parents comes and fetches them home. But generally the parents come only on their day off, and since the free days of brother, sister, son-in-law, and daughter-in-law only coincide during the three-day New Year holiday, the grandparents are always responsible for at least one grandchild.

One afternoon a neighbor of Ouyang's stops by to show off her new grandson. With her is the baby's mother, who has brought him from the factory daycare center to stay with his grandmother. The neighbor goes out of her way to describe to her daughter-in-law Ouyang's many burdens. The daughter-in-law expresses astonishment that one person should be responsible for three toddlers. Ouyang smiles and admires the infant. As her neighbor continues with the litany of Ouyang's onerous labors, Ouyang neither protests nor concurs. She remains, as always, rather subdued.

From Ouyang's perspective, life has not been particularly hard. In contrast to many women in her generation, and certainly in contrast to the women she knew in her natal village, she and her family have done well and will do better. They buy what they need. Her husband has a pension and is in good health. Both her children are married and have state jobs. Ouyang even has time to herself. When her housework is finished and her husband takes the grandchildren, she can go to a movie. She knows and enjoys leisure as her contemporaries in the countryside do not. She is free to sit on her stoop and visit with neighbors, her hands at rest because she need not busy herself continually with knitting, embroidery, or handwork.

Ouyang Xiu and Ma Xinwang maintain an egalitarian relationship with their children. Even though the son is openly protective and solicitous of his parents, the general impression is that neither generation wants to be financially dependent or force its opinions on the other. One Sunday the son-in-law brought back the granddaughter at the end of his day off, and before leaving he laid down a large bunch of fresh vegetables that are not regularly available in the city market. As soon as Ouyang saw them, she protested at his generosity and chased after him to the bus stop, thrusting a dollar into his pocket.

Another evening, as Ma was watching the grandchildren, an old colleague stopped by. The man had come straight from the shop and still wore his work clothes. The two men spent an hour in intense conversation, squatting on two wooden stools they had pulled out under the street light. The next day Ma left early on his bicycle and returned just before lunch. That evening he told his son that there were problems at the warehouse of his old workplace and that his workmate had suggested he return to his old job. Ouyang Xui said nothing, but the son dismissed the idea immediately. He argued that his father needed to rest and that in any case Ouyang Xiu needed help with the grandchildren. Xinwang drew in sharply on his pipe and replied that the children could go to a day care center. The son replied that there were no openings and repeated that his father should stay at home, take care of his health, and help his wife. No action was taken. But the next year the eldest grandson did enter the nursery school at his father's workplace. Ma, however, has not returned to work.

Ideally Ma's son would like his parents to live with him. The present arrangement is unsatisfactory. He also feels that his parents would consider living with his sister and her family if she could get a new apartment with two rooms. Neither Ouyang nor Ma, however, has ever expressed any eagerness to move. Furthermore, the even-handed way in which they treat their two children and the frequent and regular contact with the daughter and her husband suggest that they have no definite preference for a joint household with the son and that a move to join either child is not imminent.

Multiple Supports for Interdependence

In both rural and urban families, the migration restrictions that encourage joint living also intensify family relationships even when the two generations live separately. Unable to move far from their parents' village or town, children usually establish themselves in a community where their family is already well-known. With each passing year, parents and children accumulate an ever longer history of shared experiences. Their everyday lives converge, mutual obligations multiply, and the young find it increasingly difficult to envisage a life without their elderly parents nearby.

In addition to these external constraints which foster higher levels of voluntary interdependence, two pieces of legislation explicitly prevent children from abandoning their parents. The Marriage Law of the PRC, in both its 1950 and 1981 versions, requires children to support their elderly parents.[13] In general, however, children do not support parents from fear of judicial reprisals, and neither the Hong Kong nor the PRC interviewees reported any cases of elderly parents having to go to court to obtain a financial settlement.[14]

The guidelines governing the distribution of benefits for the indigent also hold children responsible by granting long-term government financial aid only to those elderly who are unable to work and are deprived of any "responsible kin."[15] In rural areas responsible kin are defined as sons, according to the traditional patrilineal preference, and those elderly who have surviving daughters but no sons can be considered to be childless. In urban areas, sons and daughters are equally responsible, and only those elderly without any progeny qualify for government assistance.

Externally imposed restrictions are not the only supports of parent-child solidarity. Personal commitments also create strong bonds of loyalty. Elderly men and women repeatedly make clear that infrequent contact with adult children has only negative connotations. Separation is equated with rejection, independence with selfishness, and having minimal relations with one's children is tantamount to failure in life's work.

Fundamental to these values is the assumption that through the gift of life and early nurturing, parents become eligible for a lifelong claim on their children's resources. Children provide for elderly parents, and parents turn to adult children without guilt, because both generations believe that the creation of the children's physical existence and the care given them in childhood require children to reciprocate in their parents' old age. The values instilled by this family-centered ideal of reciprocity encourage strong solidarity between elderly parents and their children in two ways. First, because obligations incurred in childhood are expected to continue throughout life, neither young nor old envision an extended period of complete independence from one another. Dependency, as experienced in childhood or old age, is viewed as a normal phase of every life. Thus the elderly need not view dependency as an attack on their self-esteem, and the young and middle-aged cannot plan for extended disengagement from the old.

Second, because lifelong reciprocity is an integral part of the common definitions of the "good parent" and the "good child," each person does not need individually to negotiate a code of social obligations in old age. Nor is it necessary for the old to maintain constant physical contact with the young to receive help and attention. For example, if natural disaster or work obligations separate members of different generations for years or even decades, the sense of obligation and the willingness to accept dependency remain strong.

Overall, urban and rural children have a similar respect for the importance of reciprocal obligations. They do, however, use a different time frame and stress different criteria to justify their responsibilities to their elderly parents. Urbanites cite the sacrifices and hardships their parents made for them in childhood, and their sense of duty rests on intangible emotional supports generated by memories of the past. Often the events occurred thirty or forty years earlier, yet they are the first justification cited in the explanations of a middle-aged child's support for an elderly parent.

Rural residents, in contrast, are strikingly unsentimental and oriented toward the present. Children define their obligations to elderly parents in terms of specific financial arrangements between the generations, frequently focusing on the conditions for the division and inheritance of family property. In these circumstances those who have received little material assistance from their parents as adults, or who have maintained no joint investments, have few obligations to support elderly parents. As one former rural resident succinctly put it, "The one that feeds them [the elderly parents] is the one that gets it [the house and family property]."

Despite these differences in tone and emphasis, both urban and rural residents agree on one basic limitation on the degree of responsibility. Regardless of age, they all believe that claims by the elderly for help from their adult children take second place to the immediate needs of the grandchildren. It is not that children are unwilling to sacrifice for their parents or that the parents feel insecure about their children's support. Instead, both generations want to give priority to grandchildren because they represent the future of the family, in whom all generations prefer to invest.

Dependency and Reciprocity

Overall, interdependence is the dominant characteristic of the ties between elderly parents and adult children. But families vary in their degree of solidarity, and not all parents experience the same levels of support. One reason for this variation is the difference in the quality of parents' earlier efforts to meet the needs of their children. Those elderly whose children remember their parents as generous and supportive enjoy the highest levels of support. This phenomenon appears in both rural and urban families, but as in other dimensions of family life, rural residents are more concerned with exact calculations, and they often focus their attention on specific transactions or breaches of contract.

The more objective calculation of debits and credits among rural families is a result of the importance of child labor in rural areas and the higher cost of rural weddings. Rural children begin to contribute to the family income by age eleven or twelve. By their late teens, they earn close to a full adult wage. Consequently rural parents view their children as an investment, not an expense, and both parents and children can easily calculate the relative contributions of each family member to the total household income.

The only major drain that a rural child places on the family finances occurs at the time of marriage. Most rural marriages are arranged matches which require large expenditures, especially by the parents of the groom.[16] Although marriage by purchase has been technically illegal since 1950, the groom's family in rural areas routinely gives substantial gifts of food, clothing, and cash to the bride's parents in the weeks before the wedding. The groom and his parents are also expected to provide to the bride new furniture and such special gifts as a bicycle, wristwatch, or sewing machine. In addition, they must give a bridal feast to introduce the bride and her family to her husband's relatives. On the average, the total cost of a wedding, excluding the price of new housing, exceeds 700 yuan, a sum nearly five times the yearly collective income of a young man in his twenties.[17] Since few rural men of marriageable age can meet such large expenses on their own, the typical arrangement is for parents and son to save jointly over a period of several years and for the parental investment in a son's wedding to obligate the son and his wife to support his parents in old age.

The marriage of rural daughters imposes substantially lighter financial burdens on parents, and subsequent ties between adult women and their families are therefore less affected by the size of the parents' contribution. Dowries, unlike the gifts and cash payment to the bride's parents, have largely disappeared. Thus, when the expenditures of the groom's family exceed the costs incurred by the bride's family for a wedding dinner, new clothes, and gifts to her new in-laws, the parents of a bride make a profit, which they usually put toward the marriage expenses of a son. Among the poorest families, two sets of parents may agree to exchange a daughter for a daughter-in-law, marrying "out" a girl without demanding money in exchange for receiving a daughter-in-law on similar terms. For most parents, however, even the marriage of a daughter involves considerable expense, and the profits from a daughter's wedding rarely cover all the expenses of the wedding of a son. Nevertheless, the arrangements for a daughter's wedding never represent the same type of investment for economic security in old age as does the marriage of a son, and therefore the demand for parent-daughter reciprocity does not focus as narrowly on parental investment in marriage as it does for sons.

In urban families, by contrast, the dependency of children extends over several decades, and daughters are at least as likely to incur obligations to repay parental investment as are sons. Until urban children are at least sixteen, they have little opportunity to make any cash contribution to the household. Furthermore, because urban parents pay cash for their children's food and clothing, they can easily calculate the cost of each child as a percentage of the family's monthly budget.[18]

Urban parents also contribute to their children's wedding expenditures, and in many cases the payments can amount to several hundred yuan.[19] However, in contrast to the uniformly heavy outlays by rural parents for their son's weddings, urban wedding costs are highly variable. Urban children nevertheless still consider their marriages to be a family decision, and even sophisticated party members will reconsider their choice of a prospective mate if a parent raises serious objections.

Even after marriage, many sons and daughters continue to depend on their parents for financial support. For example, in the households of Ma Xinwang, Zhang Aiguo, and Chen Youli, parents regularly give financial help to married children. Unlike the rural case, this type of parental aid is rarely drawn from joint household incomes but comes instead as a gift from the parents to the child. Thus, through their long-term dependency, urban children incur heavy obligations to reciprocate when later in life the direction of dependency shifts and it is the parents who must rely on their children.

Another salient urban-rural difference is the willingness of urban parents to aid all their adult children and, in particular, to accept prolonged financial responsibility for adult daughters. Whereas village parents treat a widowed or deserted daughter as the responsibility of her husband's family or as a ward of the community, urban parents do not lose their obligations to daughters after they marry. An urban woman in trouble can almost always return to her parents confident that they will support her for the rest of their lives. A look at a man with daughters in both the country and the city highlights the differences between rural and urban expectations of adult daughters:[20]

> Chen Jinzhong is forty-seven years old, a father of eleven and a grandfather of five. He has had two wives. He married his first wife when he was sixteen. They had five boys and four girls. The eldest four children have now married. Two sons and one daughter relied on their father and a matchmaker to find them spouses. The eldest girl, by contrast, acted independently from her parents, marrying a classmate from the village school. Both she and her husband had graduated from junior high school, and they have since been groomed to be local cadres.
>
> Chen's second wife is a Guangzhou office worker by whom he has a girl and a boy. He met her in 1958 while working on a large construction project. At first he told her he was unmarried. Later she learned about his family in the countryside. Already pregnant with her second child, she continued the relationship.
>
> Chen's disparaging description of his country daughters, the eldest of whom has had more education than her brothers, makes clear that he holds the

daughters in low esteem and has very little interest in their long-term futures. He only grudgingly acknowledges that they are hard workers, a virtue he attributes to his iron discipline at home, and repeatedly laments the substantial outlays he made at the time of their weddings. He shows no interest in discussing their employment prospects and reserves all his praise for his eldest grandson.

When he speaks about his city daughter, however, his attitudes are transformed. He pulls out a photo and points proudly at the girl. He explains that she was awarded a pencil set for outstanding performance in junior high school and that her teacher thought she could even make it to the university. He concludes: "She is very clever, very well behaved, and very obedient. She will be even more successful than her brother."

Chen's description of his daughters reflects a fundamental gap between urban and rural values. In this father's dreams there is one scenario for the village daughters and quite another for the city daughter. For the daughters in the village he can only foresee marriage "out" of the family, and he makes no plans to grant them a share in the family estate. In contrast, for the urban girl, he envisions the highest possible success. She will surpass her younger brother in her career and be a source of vicarious achievement for her father. Chen's ability to identify with the future of the urban daughter and not that of the rural ones reflects a critical difference in the attitudes of rural and urban parents toward their daughters. Once again it also illustrates how traditional values persist even after many of the original economic and social supports have disappeared.

Preference for Sons

In the preindustrial West, parents also observed the custom of patrilineal inheritance, and the elderly were often in closer daily contact with married sons than with married daughters. But as industrialization created a more impersonal workplace and as rural young people left the family farms to live and work among strangers unknown to their parents in the city, the economic supports for the traditional preference weakened, and the focus of parental loyalty became more flexible.[21] When fathers lost responsibility for the professional training of their sons and could no longer guarantee their employment, they lost control over their son's futures. Except among the wealthy, urban sons could establish themselves as their father's social and financial equal without parental support.

One consequence was that parental preference in old age for one child over another became a highly individual, emotional decision. In many instances, because elderly parents and daughters continued to have a strong interest in housework and child care which sons did not share as keenly, daughters became the preferred children among elderly parents. In addition, within the household, elderly mothers usually accepted their own daughters more easily than daughters-in-law. In turn, daughters preferred to be closer to their own mothers than to their mothers-in-law. As a result, in Europe and North America, increased industrialization and urbanization reduced the preference for sons among the old and noticeably strengthened the ties of parents with adult daughters.

In many ways the communist revolution created similar conditions for change in Chinese families. After the collectivization of agriculture and nationalization of commerce, elderly parents could no longer pass on any income-producing property to their male descendants. The CCP revolution also reduced parental control over a son's educational opportunities and job placement. Yet these changes have not dramatically changed the preference for sons in rural areas. For one reason, although collectivization prevents rural fathers from denying their sons employment, fathers still exercise considerable control through joint ownership of the family house.

Another reason for the continued preference for sons is that despite the establishment of CCP organizations at the grassroots level, villages are still closed to outsiders. Consequently young men in rural areas do not easily depart from the ideals of their fathers. Nor are their workplaces and homes distinctly separated. When adolescent males first enter the paid labor force, their incomes are paid to their father as the family head, and they are often supervised by their father's kinsmen and friends. Thus, young rural men usually succeed by accepting the values of traditional family loyalties.

In urban China, young men also find it difficult to break completely from their parents. They cannot always establish a separate household until after marriage, and in the periods of high unemployment that have prevailed since the mid-1960s, many men must rely on their parents' connections to secure jobs.[22] The replacement option of the 1978 retirement provisions, which permits parents to designate one child as a successor, is an extreme manifestation of this type of dependency among young urban males, but even through milder forms such as letters of introduction, parents have signficant leverage over their sons' futures.

Housing shortages and scarce employment opportunities make both rural and urban sons dependent on parents, but specific CCP policies toward urban women explain why urban parents draw closer than rural parents to daughters. After 1949, the CCP took several steps to improve the social position of women, and in general these changes came first and went farthest in urban areas. For example, in principle the CCP is committed to extending a basic education to both boys and girls in all communities. In practice, they were at first able to realize this promise only in urban areas.[23] Similarly, their promise to guarantee full employment and and equal pay to women has been best fulfilled in the cities.[24] In addition,

urban areas.[23] Similarly, their promise to guarantee full employment and
equal pay to women has been best fulfilled in the cities.[24] In addition, the
CCP enforces the provisions of the Marriage Law, which outlaws child
betrothal, dowries, and the bride price, more completely among urban
than rural families.

These changes in the economic and social status of women prolong
the adolescence of urban girls and enable them to marry later and on
more favorable terms than their rural peers. As a result, urban brides
who are older and more economically independent than rural brides are
able to stay close to their parents after marriage. During the time between entry into the labor force and marriage, both sons and daughters
live at home. For urban daughters, who still are more likely than sons to
live with their in-laws, this time before marriage cements the childhood
bonds of loyalty and greatly strengthens the strong emotional
attachments which will bind the two generations together even after the
daughter has left home permanently.

At no time since 1949 has the CCP overtly advocated separate family models for urban and rural elderly. Yet the communist revolution has
so significantly altered the nature of the parent-daughter bond in the
cities that two distinctive family forms have emerged. Just as differences
in the organization of work and the distribution of wages between urban
and rural China have encouraged different strategies for economic security in old age, so too the CCP's educational, employment, and marriage
policies for women in the cities have prompted urban families to evolve
patterns of contact that diverge significantly from the more traditional
arrangements prevailing in the countryside.[25]

5

FUNERALS AND FILIAL PIETY

FROM THE HAN to the Qing dynasties, Confucian orthodoxy presented the filial *(xiao)* son and daughter as the human ideal.[1] While the parents lived, filial children gave priority to the parents' needs for material comfort. After a parent's death, filial children spared no expense to provide as elaborate a funeral ceremony as possible. Within the Confucian tradition, the funeral of an elderly parent became a critical, public testimony to an individual's moral worth, and the intensity of the child's mourning reflected the depth of that person's commitment to Confucian ideals.

Since 1949, CCP leaders have intermittently attacked filial piety as anticommunist and have worked hard to popularize simple, secular funerals as the postliberation norm. Definitions of filial piety given by young urban residents indicate that for some individuals CCP efforts at ideological re-education have been successful:[2]

> Filial piety is a feudal theory that makes people into slaves. It means to listen unconditionally to the words of parents.

> Filial piety is used by landlords to make their children loyal to them. It is criticized because the government does not want people to think just about their families.

> Filial piety means that the young must give whatever they have to the old.

During the Anti-Lin Biao Anti-Confucius Campaign of 1973-1974, the CCP attacked filial piety with particular vehemence.[3] To be filial to one's parents was seen as the first step toward being submissive to all superiors; it was a key ideological underpinning for the oppression of the people. During the high tide of this campaign, anyone who openly instructed the young in the tenets of filial piety was equated with those who wished to sabotage the revolution. In practice, however, even during the height of the campaign rural and urban parents taught their children to respect the old, and only a minority enthusiastically supported the simple, secular funerals advocated by the CCP.

Belief in the efficacy of the Buddhist and Daoist rituals that surround ancestor worship and dictate many of the traditional burial rituals has encouraged resistance to CCP policy on funerals and ancestor worship. Old rituals have continued, and many people still equate elaborate funerals with proof of family loyalty and moral virtue. Death remains a mystery, and religious belief and familiar traditions give comfort and a sense of control.

Active resistance grounded in religious belief is only one reason that traditional funeral practices persist. Equivocal guidelines and irregular enforcement of funeral policies have also prevented rapid change. In the early years after Liberation, CCP leaders believed that improvements in the material standard of living, access to modern medicine, and the popularization of science would gradually eliminate the need for religion. Therefore they focused their energies on drives for economic development and redistribution of wealth, and gave less attention to the ideological re-education of religious believers. CCP leaders also opposed coercive measures for fear that such repression would provoke resistance to the CCP and thereby further retard real acceptance of communist ideals.[4] Mao's own attitude toward handling religious beliefs among the peasant majority is expressed in his guideline for party members responsible for cadre rehabilitation in 1965: "Idols are set up by the peasants. There will come a time when the peasants themselves will throw out these idols with their own hands, and it is not necessary for others to do it for them prematurely."[5]

In accord with these guidelines, local CCP cadres are generally instructed to rely on persuasion and to reserve punishment for those who proselytize or profit financially from the performance of religious ceremonies. In the case of funerals, this policy has meant the confiscation of temple properties, the destruction of religious artifacts, and the arrest of geomancers and Daoist or Buddhist priests who openly collect fees for religious services. Usually family members who participate are only lightly reprimanded. Policy implementation, however, has been inconsistent. In some years the CCP pushes harder to simplify funerals than in other years, and throughout the post-1949 era it has tolerated traditional rituals more readily in rural than in urban areas.

Shifts in Funeral Policy

In the early 1950s religious professionals were classified as "members of the exploiting classes."[6] The land and temples of lineage organizations were seized as state property, the public worship of ancestors was prohibited, and former priests and nuns were required to become ordinary laborers.[7] Yet these changes had little immediate effect on funeral practices. The cessation of the civil war provided a sudden sense of material well-being all over the nation. In this atmosphere of prosperity and peace, CCP propaganda for simple secular funerals often went unheard, and families spent their small savings on the most elaborate funerals that they could afford.

Cremation was rare and, particularly in the case of elderly parents, was viewed as a barbarous innovation. Geomancers continued to practice, and former priests and abbots attended funerals rather openly.[8] Family members still wore the traditional white mourning clothes in the funeral procession and hired professional musicians to escort the coffin through the streets to the grave. Before and after the burial, survivors gathered for family banquets, and after the funeral, lineal descendants observed forty-nine days of mourning. Because temples had been closed, no one could continue the practice of placing ancestor tablets on public display. But in the privacy of their homes, many people, particularly those over forty, kept memorial tablets on a family altar and offered appropriate sacrifices on the anniversary of a death and on the first and fifteenth of the month.

By 1949, many urban residents had already given up temple and home worship, and the hold of traditional beliefs was generally weaker in the cities than in the villages. The gulf between CCP ideal funerals and actual practices was less deep in urban than in rural areas.[9] Nevertheless, in the first five or six years after 1949, urban residents did not greatly reduce their expenditures for funerals. Instead, in several ways CCP policy actually encouraged an increase in the expense of the average urban funeral. For example, the Labor Insurance Regulations, as drafted in 1951 and amended in 1953, guaranteed urban workers in the most advanced, modern sector between 50 and 100 yuan for their own funerals and for those of their lineal dependents, namely parents, spouse, or children.[10] When families combined this insurance benefit with their own savings, urban workers were in an even better position than they had been before 1949 to fulfill traditional expectations for elaborate funerals. Urban residents thus spared no expense, particularly for funerals of elderly parents.

After 1955, CCP leaders became more strident in their criticism of lavish funerals and supernatural rituals.[11] Nevertheless, they still approved the financial support that allowed old customs to continue. The 1958 Regulations of the State Council on retirement of workers in the state sector repeated the earlier guarantees for funeral benefits.[12] Furthermore, should the relatives of an insured worker be unable to cover all funeral expenses, they then could borrow up to three months' salary from their workplace.[13] In 1956, the legislation establishing agricultural cooperatives extended some funeral benefits to rural areas. Henceforth, rural indigents without any family were guaranteed a decent burial at public expense.[14] In most cases this meant an earthen burial in a wooden coffin, several pallbearers, and a graveside ceremony with incense and candles. In the official press accounts of these funerals, costs averaged between 50 and 70 yuan.[15]

The onset of the Great Leap Forward in the summer of 1958 abruptly interrupted the policy of compromise and moderation.[16] In the desperate search to expand cultivated acreage, the CCP urged and in some cases forced peasants to level old graves and to establish public cemeteries on nonarable land. Temple worship had by this time disappeared, and sacrifices of incense and food at the grave were now outlawed. The CCP made its first concerted push to popularize cremation, and crematories were built in rural areas.[17]

The collapse of the Great Leap in 1960 signaled a return to the earlier, more lenient approach to funeral practices. Concerned with reestablishing confidence in the communist revolution and the efficacy of its leadership, the CCP again permitted local cadres to take a more accommodating attitude.[18] In urban areas they resumed distribution of funeral benefits to workers in the modern, industrial sector, and in rural areas they made no efforts to force cremation or deny a ground burial.[19]

In 1962 Mao launched the Socialist Education Movement to revitalize the revolution in the countryside. The primary target was corruption among local CCP cadres, but a secondary target was the traditional beliefs and practices that had returned in the wake of the Great Leap's collapse. As the movement gained momentum, the policy on funerals again became less lenient. This time the CCP went beyond verbal attacks on traditional ritual and made a sustained effort to alter people's beliefs in the supernatural.[20]

When the Socialist Education Movement merged into the early phases of the Cultural Revolution, the efforts to eliminate old practices intensified, producing significant changes in burial customs. In the cities, the relay stations that had previously held the encoffined dead for transshipment to rural areas were closed, and cremation became common among the urban old as well as the young.[21] In rural areas, public cemeteries replaced the scattered gravesites in suburban villages, and the number of rural crematories increased.[22] During the height of the attack on traditional customs in 1966, ancestor tablets that many rural families had maintained in their homes after 1949 were seized and destroyed by youthful Red Guards. During this period of radical upheaval, very few people dared to spend lavishly, and funerals became very simple. However, as soon as the Cultural Revolution turned away from attacks on traditional customs and the most radical phase had passed, funerals quickly re-emerged with many of their attendant rituals. The funeral of Wu Chenglong in 1970 is typical:[23]

In 1970 Wu Chenglong, the father of a brigade-level CCP party secretary, died at the age of eighty. At the time of his death, Wu was living with his wife and younger, unmarried son in a small hamlet. His funeral was elaborate by local standards. Wu had been sick for several months before his death, and in preparation for his funeral he had secretly consulted a geomancer, who chose an auspicious gravesite for both the old man and his wife on a hillside located just outside the village proper. There the graves would face a grassy slope in such a way as to guarantee that only the most benevolent powers would flow from the gravesite, thereby ensuring that Wu's children and grandchildren would accumulate more honor and wealth with each succeeding year.

Within hours of the death, the younger son left the village to register the event at the commune center. With the death certificate in hand, he received special ration tickets to let him purchase cotton cloth. At the burial the lineal descendants would wear white drapes, using the material later to make ordinary clothes. These expenditures were covered by the savings of the old man, his wife, and his younger son.

While her son was at the commune center, the widow washed the body and prepared it for burial. Local custom dictating the appropriate dress faithfully reflected the earthly inequalities between men and women. Men wore three rather than two sets of clothing; their shoes were embroidered in a distinctive fashion; and their jackets had additional pockets in order to carry more money into the afterlife.

Relatives came from surrounding villages to help prepare the meals for the village feast which was to last three days according to tradition. The elder son slaughtered a pig, more distant relatives brought chickens, and neighbors loaned the family cooking oil.

The burial was also guided by tradition. A middle-aged villager instructed the younger men how to carry the coffin from the village to the grave, so that they could alternate pallbearers and never let the coffin touch the ground. At the grave there was additional instruction on how to lower the coffin properly and cover it with earth. When the last spadeful was throw in, a shovel filled with candy was offered to those who had helped so that they would leave with only the sweetest thoughts for the deceased. This fulfilled the obligations between the dead and the living who had helped bring the body to its earthly resting place.

For the family members, however, the rituals continued. As the final part of the graveside ceremony, the elder son burned a paper strip upon which the name of the deceased was written. The sons and grandsons bowed to the ground, and then the family returned to a banquet meal at home.

In the weeks immediately following the burial, there were no additional public ceremonies. All the funeral rituals, however, were not complete. In the home of the widow and in that of her elder son, one member, usually the mother, would burn incense on the first and fifteenth of the month in honor of all deceased family members. If conditions still allowed, seven to ten years later, the family would have a second burial. They would hire a local expert to exhume the body, clean the bones, and rebury the remains in a small funerary urn. The urn would be placed on the hillside, half-buried in the earth to prevent dislodgement during heavy rainfall. Unlike residents of the more prosperous delta plains, villagers in this part of the province have never built elaborate tombs. Instead they leave the urns uncovered, and nature is permitted to follow her inevitable course. Even as the bones and urn decay, however, local residents believe that supernatural forces of the ancestor pass outward and continue to affect the destinies of the descendants.

In 1971, Wu Chenglong's younger son died. Although he had suffered from an advanced case of schistosomiasis, the family had made no advance preparations comparable to those for the father. They built a simple coffin of poor quality wood. The elder brother did not slaughter a pig, and the family held only one day of feasts. Unmarried and without any descendants, the brother did not merit kowtows or a geomancer. When the burial was complete, the widowed mother closed up her house and left the village to join the household of her elder son.

In urban areas by 1970 most of the old traditions that Wu Chenglong's family observed for him had disappeared. Cremation was almost universal, religious professionals no longer practiced, and graveside sacrifices had fallen into disuse. Yet even when burial rites are simplified, costs to the surviving family remain high. The fees for transportation to the crematory, the cremation, the rental of the memorial hall, and the storage of the ashes total approximately 50 yuan. Beyond these essential costs there are discretionary expenditures. Paper funeral wreaths that cost between 5 and 50 yuan are still permitted, and a family usually buys two or three and may have as many as twenty. If families are large, they may rent a truck or van to take them to the cemetery where the ashes are to be kept. Before and after the memorial service there usually are family dinners, or at least a small reception. When all these expenditures are added up, an urban family still finds it necessary to spend three or four months' salary on an elderly parent's funeral.[24]

Occasionally in smaller towns outside the major industrial and administrative districts, children still have lengthy corteges for their parents with marching bands and elaborate banquets. The children involved in the most lavish rituals have been high-ranking CCP officials.[25] But even ordinary urban dwellers will sometimes make extraordinary efforts to circumvent the general restriction so as to fulfill an elderly parent's last request for traditional burial:[26]

> In 1975, Wang Yen died in Huhehot, the major industrial city of Inner Mongolia. Widowed for ten years, Wang Yen had shared a home with her son, his wife, and two grandchildren. For several years prior to her death she had been chronically ill. Like many of her age, she was terrified of cremation and applied to return to her native village in South China where earthen burial was still permitted. Unfortunately, Wang Yen died before her request could be approved. But because she had made known her fears, her son and daugther appealed for special consideration.

Inner Mongolia is the home of many Muslim Chinese to whom creation is a sacrilege. Mindful of the need for these people's loyalty, the Chinese government has exempted Muslims from the general ban on earthen burial. Although not a Muslim, Wang Yen's daughter taught in a Muslim village in the suburbs of Huhehot, and through her connections there the family gained permission to bury their mother on the outskirts of the settlement.

The actual ceremony was simple. The children hired a truck to take them out to the burial site and paid the driver and his assistant to dig the grave and bury the coffin. After the funeral, the children and grandchildren wore small black arm bands for one month. The total cost of 300 yuan was divided between the siblings, with the better-paid brother contributing the larger share.

Although Wang Yen's fears are widespread among urban residents in their seventies and eighties, they are by no means universal. Instead, younger or better educated elderly already generally accept the communist ideal of cremation and a simple memorial service. Yet even when the ceremony is simple, funerals remain important family rituals that reaffirm the continuity between the generations:[27]

Li Danhua died in the winter of 1979 just before her seventieth birthday. She was a highly educated, nonparty administrator who had spent her entire adult life in service to her country. Her three children were also well educated and established in professional careers. At the time of her death, Li Danhua and her husband lived separately from their son and daughters, and unlike many couples of their generation, they had an extremely close, affectionate marriage. In the final months of her illness, her husband cared for her at their apartment, but when the pain became extremely acute, she was moved to a city hospital. A few days later she died.

Funeral arrangements were made by the husband and children in accord with the usual urban practices. Li Danhua was cremated within a day of the death, and her ashes were given to the family. They placed them with her photograph in a memorial hall at a public cemetery outside the city limits. The cemetery was located near the site of the original tombs of Li Danhua's own parents, who had died before 1949. Thus, even though the land was under cultivation, the family still could identify where the original markers had stood, and the survivors found meaning in observing this continuity between the several generations of the family.

After Li Danhua's death the son and his wife moved in with his father. They visit the cemetery regularly, and although the family makes no ritual sacrifices of fruit or incense at a family altar, a large memorial photograph of Li Danhua dominates one room in their home.

In the first years after Liberation, CCP funeral policy was ambiguous and permitted many irregularities at direct variance with stated CCP goals, particularly as it was applied to funerals of the elderly. Thus, at the same time that the new communist leaders vehemently favored simple, secular burials, they failed systematically to alter actual funeral practices and even went so far as to provide financial subsidies that neither the emperors nor the KMT had ever contemplated. The result of these inconsistencies has been strong popular support for a continuation of many traditional ideals and only gradual change in customary practice.

Underlying Personal Values

The motives of those people who resist CCP efforts to simplify funerals are often straightforward. When people believe in an afterlife where the dead have feelings and emotions identical to those of the living, they oppose cremation because they fear that cremation will cause a person they love excruciating pain. They continue to offer prayers and ritual sacrifices of incense and paper effigies at the gravesite to placate restive spirits, and they maintain the cult of the ancestor by worship within their homes.

In communities where funerals continue to be seen as an index of an individual's social respectability, many spend as lavishly as possible, as much from fear of public censure as from fear of supernatural retribution. In rural areas such social pressures are very strong, and adult children who do not exert themselves to hold a proper funeral are viewed as mean and selfish. To adhere voluntarily to the government ideal of a minimal, secular ritual is seen as a direct affront to the parent's memory, and such children find it hard to maintain face within their village community. An illustration of this type of social pressure comes from Guangdong:[28]

> Two middle-aged men living in a village split into two households after their father's death. Their mother lived with the elder son and shared fully in the household work until a few months before her death. When she died, the neighbors expected the son to buy a coffin and bury her with ceremony. Instead, he wrapped her in a reed mat and buried her quickly in the public cemetery. For several years afterward, the other villagers taunted the son as one "who first ate his mother's rice, and then ate her bones."

In urban areas fewer people are overtly concerned with the power of the supernatural, and there is less pressure to equate elaborate funeral rites with moral rectitude. Among the urban elderly, however, many are still religious and have continued the ritual worship demanded by the cult of the ancestor throughout the post-1949 era. In the early years after Liberation they worshiped quite openly, but since the CCP intensified ideological education and eliminated the production of such essential ceremonial objects as incense sticks, enterprising elderly believers have been forced to hide their religious activities from public view and to find substitute offerings. They dye red the smoking mosquito coils that are burned to repel insects and use them to venerate the dead at small family altars on the first and the fifteenth of each month. Some maintain vegetarian diets separate from other household members. Others keep a small shrine in an alcove of the house or hidden behind calendars or family photographs. And with very few exceptions, elderly parents tell their children that they are terrified by the idea of cremation and request a traditional burial in the earth with a few essential graveside ceremonies.

Although young and middle-aged urban residents do not appear to share their parents' beliefs and fears, they rarely express open contempt for relatives who continue with old rituals. Instead, they stress their own inability to share the beliefs and sympathize with the difficulty of the oldest generation in totally rejecting the practices that gave shape and purpose to their lives for so many years before 1949. A defense of his parents' beliefs by one man in his thirties is representative:[29]

"My father burns incense secretly every month. He remembers all the old customs and goes to a lot of trouble to buy the stuff on the black market. My mother is also superstitious about death. She doesn't like the idea of cremation and told me she hopes she can die in the countryside and have a ground burial. Even my father, who has survived so many terrible things in his life, is still afraid of cremation. They both have these strong beliefs. But myself, well, I just can't make myself believe them."

Most young urban residents express similar views on the generational differences in attitudes toward religion, but in virtually no instance do they use their own professions of atheism to deny their parents' requests. Instead, as in the case of Wang Yen's son and daughter, most urban residents, no matter how vehement in their support for CCP efforts to institute simple, secular funerals, provide their parents with the best funeral they can afford. Even when earthen burial is impossible, as is usually the case, children spend as lavishly as they are able, not from fear of angry ghosts or of public censure, but from a fundamental desire to be the filial son or daughter whom traditional Chinese culture has valued for centuries.

Filial Piety since Mao

When they died, Wu Chenglong was eighty years old and Wang Yen was in her seventies. They both were illiterate and had spent most of their lives in precommunist Chinese society where ancestor worship had government approval and funerals were a central rite generally presumed to shape the destiny of the deceased and their descendants. Throughout the post-1949 era the CCP has directed relatively little energy toward changing the beliefs of the elderly and has concentrated most of its ideological re-education on young adults and children. Particularly in religious matters the CCP holds a rather consistent view that with the passing of the oldest generation, the old rituals and superstitions will disappear and funerals will become totally secular ceremonies stripped of any connection to ancestor worship or traditional concepts of filial piety.

The funerals of Wu Chenglong's younger son and of Li Danhua suggest that with relatively little suppression or coercion, the gradualist policy of the CCP has achieved substantial success. Strong disclaimers of belief in the supernatural among the urban young also confirm such conclusions. But government publications appearing since 1976 suggest that old practices and traditional values may continue even after religious beliefs have weakened and those in their seventies and eighties have died. In a wide range of popular magazines filial piety has returned as a desirable trait for socialist heroes and heroines, characterizing outstanding young or middle-aged men and women who provide extraordinary care for an elderly parent or parent-in-law.[30] These individuals demonstrate their filial virtue by being attentive to the physical needs of the old, regardless of the hardships imposed on their own health or comfort. To be filial, therefore, has the connotations of being hard-working, responsible, and unselfish. There is no contradiction between being filial and being a good communist. One article even went so far as to claim that filial piety is "the highest virtue of the Chinese proletariat."[31]

Significantly, these official paeans to the virtues of filial piety totally ignore the issue of funeral practices. Thus they provide no information on the opinions of these official heroes and heroines toward cremation and burial ritual. The focus of the official accounts is exclusively on the care and support given when an elderly relative is alive. Several high-level CCP spokesmen, however, have dealt with the issue of funerals and ancestor worship in this same period, and their statements reveal a similar accommodation to old values.[32] Basically they agree with Mao's position on the counterproductive effect of coercion when applied to changing religious beliefs. Although they condemn ancestor worship and predict its eventual disappearance, they oppose the use of force against people as long as their involvement in religion does not produce political instability or reduce economic productivity.[33]

The official policy toward the Qing Ming festival also explicitly supports the ideals of filial piety in the context of funeral observances. Qing Ming, the festival of "The Clear and the Bright," is the annual spring pilgrimage to clean ancestral graves. In urban areas there has long been a secular element in its celebration, and even before 1949 Qing Ming had become as much an occassion for a family picnic as a sacred holiday. At its core, however, Qing Ming remains tied to the cult of the ancestor, and even in the most secularized celebrations of it remembrance of the dead and reaffirmation of family loyalties are central. Yet the CCP has taken a remarkably casual attitude toward the implications of continuing

Qing Ming observances. In the late 1960s CCP leaders briefly renamed Qing Ming the National Memorial Day.[34] They did not, however, change the timing of the holiday or seriously interfere with private family observances. By the mid-1970s even the original name was restored, and Qing Ming is once again an officially recognized holiday.[35]

Thus, despite the official goal of eliminating all vestiges of ancestor worship within the funeral ceremony, the actual implementation of government policy has permitted many traditional practices and beliefs to continue. It is not unusual for individuals during the day to participate in a collective Qing Ming service at their place of work in memory of a CCP hero, and then at night to hold a private family meal in remembrance of a deceased parent or grandparent. Even when the Qing Ming meal and the trip to the family graves are secular occasions on which the continuity of the family line is only recognized implicitly, government recognition of the Qing Ming holiday and official approval of family gatherings undermine the long-term CCP goal of eliminating family ceremonies built around the traditions of filial piety and ancestor worship.

Between 1962 and 1976 CCP leaders were not as tolerant of filial piety and the return of traditional funeral rites as they have been since the death of Mao. In fact, during these years funeral rituals were simplified and stripped of many of their supernatural dimensions. As a result, the identity between lavish expenditures and filial virtue was weakened. Yet even in families where neither generation believes in the supernatural, there is a compassion and commonality between generations that is ultimately the core of filial piety.

During an informal lecture in the summer of 1979, one Marxist philosopher of fifty defined the "true" meaning of filial piety as the willingness of the young to identify with the needs of the old and to recognize one's obligations to those who sacrificed for one when one was young.[36] This capacity to be filial distinguishes men from animals. It also, he explained, distinguishes the cultures of the East from those of the West. Far in advance of the Europeans, the Chinese had evolved a stable society where ethical behavior with filial piety at its core, was systematically promoted. In stressing the critical role of filial piety, this philosopher criticized the view that equates filial piety with blind obedience of the young to the old and emphasized a "purer" concept that stresses bonds of mutual respect and parent-child reciprocity. Using this definition, children who reject the ideals of filial behavior not only ignore their parents' legitimate claims but also deny their own inescapable connections with others. In this philosophical exposition, as in the funerals of the urban elderly, only pale vestiges of the old religious beliefs remain. But the moral imperative survives, and in this way, the ideals of filial piety continue to bind parents and children at death as they do in life.

6

INTERGENERATIONAL CONFLICT

THE CHINESE ELDERLY expect to have good relations with their adult children, and in general they do. But this predominant pattern of solidarity does not mean that elderly parents never experience conflict with their children, nor that only the minority of remarried widows and political outcasts experience estrangement. Everyday life in China is strenuous. Homes are overcrowded, and families struggle to live within their tight budgets. Under these conditions, patience wears thin, and parents and children quarrel. But more interesting than the mere incidence of conflicts are their forms and outcomes. Sons and their parents rarely quarrel in public, but when they do, the rupture is more serious for the old than for the young. Ties with daughters are generally weaker, but in times of acute distress, elderly sometimes turn to daughters more easily than to sons. Power within the family is usually most concentrated in rural families, yet total estrangement between the generations is more common in the villages than in the cities. The causes of family breakdown, the alternative sources of social control, and the distribution of power within families account for these somewhat anomalous findings and explain how post-1949 economic and social pressures shape the pattern of typical parent-child conflicts.

The official sources suggest that the Chinese elderly and their adult children fight almost exclusively over political ideology.[1] Politics causes the conflicts, and political education restores family harmony. In short, the same issues that divide teachers and students, workers and cadres, and competing factions in the CCP Central Committee also cause splits between elderly parents and their children.

Individuals tell a different story. In their personal experience, elderly parents and their children fight over private, not public, concerns. They squabble over finances, the care of the grandchildren, and personal betrayals. Although political campaigns do heighten tensions, and undermine family cohesion, ideological differences are not the fundamental

source of conflict, and political re-education rarely resolves real-life mis-
understandings.

For several reasons, the personal accounts of stress and conflicts
seem more credible than the official picture of harmony. The Chinese
press is a controlled, didactic medium, whose official purpose is to set examples. Stories of failure are not printed unless they can serve as negative
role models that caution readers against antisocialist thinking or behavior. As a result, the official media have a vested interest in minimizing the
incidence of conflict and ignoring cases where resolution of conflict fails.
Individuals operate under no such constraints. They describe a wider
range of problems, provide richer detail, and do not always experience a
happy ending.

Family Quarrels

Most conflict between elderly parents and their children begins within
the confines of the family home. Social pressures encourage parents and
children to keep their family problems private, and when the conflict involves an elderly parent, a special effort is made to hide the hostilities
from public view. Traditional values regarding poor relations between
the elderly and their children as proof of moral failure on the part of
either generation persist, and even the most modern and sophisticated
urbanites cannot afford to jeopardize their social prestige by overtly un-
filial behavior.

Not all quarrels, however, can be contained within the home, especially when there is so little private space, and family conflicts do spill
out into public view. In both rural and urban families, quarrels between
an elderly mother and her son's wife are the most likely to come to the attention of others. The continued preference for living with sons and the
sons' inability to find separate housing explains the dominance of the
mother-in-law/daughter-in-law feuds. Even in the cities, many new
brides begin their married life as newcomers in the established home of
their mothers-in-law. In rural areas, where the conflicts seem to be most
acute and violent, the bride not only enters as a newcomer to the household but also as a stranger to the community and even to her husband.
Thus rural daughters-in-law are in a particularly stressful position, and
initially power rests in the hands of the older woman.

In the lean months after the spending spree for the son's wedding,
the mother-in-law is especially watchful of any waste, and the possibili-
ties for conflict over household mismanagement are endless. The new
bride, unfamiliar with family routines, may use too much cooking oil,
sleep later than her mother-in-law, or return from the fields too late to do
her proper share of the evening chores. Rural family members have a
seemingly endless supply of stories of household spats, and they expect

frequent conflict as a matter of course in the first year or two after a son's marriage. Most, in fact, presume that completely harmonious families are exceptions worthy of comment.

In urban families, a new bride enters her husband's home under more favorable circumstances. Many have known their in-laws for several years prior to the marriage and are thus well aware of the idiosyncrasies of the household. Equally important, urban brides tend to be three or four years older than their rural counterparts and therefore are more socially and economically independent.[2] They have also benefited from the abolition of the payment of bride price, which in rural families encourages the groom's parents to take a proprietary view of the young woman. Since urban daughters-in-law are not evaluated in terms of their "purchase price," they enter their new home on a more equal footing with the other members. Nevertheless, urban daughters-in-law are not immune from the frictions generated by joint living. Coresidence requires greater cooperation than occasional visits, and often the arrival of the bride forces established family members to reorganize the existing apartment and crowd even closer together.

Adjusting to shared living presents the first challenge, the arrival of a grandchild the second. In almost all families, mothers return to work within six to eight weeks after the baby's birth, and primary care for the infant falls to the grandmother. The young mother returns from her job worried that the child is not gaining weight or has too many colds or fevers. The baby cries at night and disturbs everyone's sleep. If it is a girl, the father and grandparents may be deeply disappointed and find fault with both mother and child.[3] Thus child care precipitates some of the worst conflicts.

Over the long term both grandparents, but particularly the grandmother, who expects to outlive her husband by several years, want good relations with their son and his wife. In most families the elderly mother's awareness of her eventual dependency persuades her to avoid conflict and resolve the arguments that arise. This is especially true in urban families where the daughters-in-law have steady employment outside the home and where the mothers-in-law are totally dependent on the financial support of husband and children. But even in rural families where mothers-in-law contribute as much to the family budget as do the daughters-in-law, the older women seek harmony in view of their eventual need for family support. In the families of Li Hoizhong and Li Laoer, for example, the elderly mothers soon found accommodation more practical than domination, resistance, or argument.

But there are also examples of elderly women who disregard the advantages of compromise. These families, by the severity of their conflict, attract more attention than most. Despite their more extreme manifestations, they embody common problems. Two such families graphically illustrate the substance and context of typical family quarrels. The two cases, one from a village and the other from a city, also show how differences in the economic and political resources of urban and rural women decisively shape the outcomes of private family relationships:[4]

Song Meihua is a widow of sixty-five who lives with her only son Wu Deming, his wife, and three small grandchildren in a mountain hamlet in central Guangdong. The standard of living here is lower than in the Guangzhou Delta. There is still no electricity, and only one rough cart track connects the fields on the lower slopes to the main truck route to the commune center. The villagers are therefore rather isolated, and acceptance of new socialist ideals has come slowly.

Wu Deming is a slight man with only average ability as a field worker. The family's income, however, is better than average. Song Meihua is an expert with pigs, and the family's fruit trees are the best in the village. Thus when Wu Deming married in 1969, his family was able to spend almost 1000 yuan for the wedding preparations.

Wu's father and mother had both been married twice. Each had several daughters, but Wu is their only son. In addition, neither of Wu's paternal uncles have had a son survive to adulthood. Therefore, if Wu Deming does not have male progeny, the family line will die out. To avert this tragedy, Wu's parents, his uncles, and even his half-sisters pooled their savings to find the finest daughter-in-law possible. The old house was completely refurbished, the wedding feast was elaborate, and the bride was the most desirable the matchmaker could find. She was strong and capable, though not especially pretty, and came from a more prosperous village in the valley. Her parents demanded a bride price of 300 yuan and 25 kilos of dried fruit. The terms of this marriage set the stage for the protracted conflict to follow.

By arranging such a fine match for their son, Wu's parents, particularly his mother, believed that they had earned the obedience, respect, and gratitude of the new bride and their son, and in the first few months after the wedding things went rather smoothly. The new bride made a good impression on her in-laws. Rumor has it that when she entered the house for the first time, she immediately gave the traditional kowtow to Song Meihua and thereafter sought to please her in every way.

Relations began to deteriorate after the birth of the first grandchild when burdens increased for Song Meihua. After the death of Wu's father and the birth of his second child in 1972, the conflict between the two women intensified. The daughter-in-law was no longer the same tireless worker, her housework became sloppy, and she developed a reputation as a big eater. Song Meihua criticized her continually and urged her son to beat his wife to make her more obedient. In these fights, Wu Deming openly sided with his wife, which further strengthened her loyalty and affection toward him but also increased the fury of his mother and ultimately heightened the pressures on his wife. After an especially harsh argument, Wu's wife would take her two children and return to her parents. After a week or two, she would come home. She had no plan to leave her husband; she merely wanted to escape her mother-in-law's wrath and abuse.

In 1973, Wu's wife had a third child. She is now exhausted by her many burdens, and she can longer escape her mother-in-law by taking three children to visit her parents. Wu feels powerless to subdue his mother, and Song Meihua will not declare a truce. Wu has grown sullen and spends as few hours as possible with his family.

Luo Erniang is a widow of sixty who lives in Guangzhou with her son Feng Dao, his wife Hu Shihping, and two granddaughters. Both Hu and Feng work in a state-owned drydock, and by Chinese standards they have a comfortable life. Their joint income exceeds 100 yuan per month. Their apartment is large, containing two rooms measuring ten feet by twelve, a balcony, a separate kitchen, and a private toilet.

Hu Shihping and Feng Dao have a modern marriage. They met in 1961 through a mutual friend at their workplace. They courted for two years while waiting for an apartment. When Feng was promoted to supervisor of his workshop, they were assigned the apartment they still occupy. Within a few months after her marriage, Hu was pregnant. Even before the baby's birth Luo had moved in from the countryside, taking the front room as her bedroom. Later the two granddaughters joined her in the bedroom, and the apartment became crowded with furniture and family belongings.

Despite all their material advantages, Feng and Hu are very unhappy. Luo and Hu have a terrible relationship and quarrel incessantly. Luo's husband had died in 1940, and as a young widow in her sister-in-law's house, Luo had enjoyed a status barely higher than a maid. After her husband's death she was able to keep Feng Dao with her but was forced to marry her fourteen-year-old daughter to distant relatives in a village she had never seen. At family meals she was served last, and her only new clothes came grudgingly as presents from her brother-in-law. During those years, she invested all her hopes in her son's future. When Feng did well, she was eager to share his success and enjoy the security and status she had been denied by her husband's early death.

Under any conditions Luo and Hu might have had conflicts, but in this case the problem was accentuated by Hu's failure to have a son. After the birth of her first granddaughter, Luo remained optimistic, reasoning that it was best to have a girl who could help her mother with the boys that would follow. But when the second child was also a girl, born in the spring of 1966, Luo became frantic.

This family crisis could not have come at a worse time. By the fall of 1966 the political struggles of the Cultural Revolution had reached the shop floors. Hu had never hidden the fact that her grandfather had been a rural landlord, because she had grown up in the city where her father had been a petty clerk. But during the Cultural Revolution her heritage became a potential liability that could tarnish Feng Dao's political reputation and make Hu a target for ideological re-education.

In 1972 the drydock intensified its family planning campaign and urged all families to adopt the goal of the two-child family. Hu, already anxious about jeopardizing her husband's career, was one of the first to pledge herself to honor the ideal. Nevertheless Luo Erniang continued to harp incessantly on her need to see a grandson to carry on the family line before she died. She brewed fertility tonics and went back to her village to consult with old friends.

After learning of Hu's public commitment to have no additional children, Luo began to criticize Hu openly in front of her son. The arguing was incessant. Feng did not take his mother's side, but he gradually spent less and less time at home, eating most of his meals in the cafeteria. Hu was also stubborn. She would come home from work, take a bowl of rice, help herself to the condiments Luo had prepared, and go eat her supper on the doorsill of a neighbor.

In 1974 Hu applied to work permanently on the night shift and thereby avoid her mother-in-law totally. The reassignment would also mean little contact with her husband and children, but at that point she felt it was the only solution to the ceaseless arguments. Eventually, she reasoned, the old lady would have to accept the government's decision on family size, and until then, she would avoid drawing attention to herself and her family by reducing the conflict with Luo.

The families of Song Meihua and Luo Erniang are unusual only in the duration of their conflicts. One explanation for the atypical length of these conflicts is that both mothers-in-law have resources not readily available to other elderly women. In the case of Song Meihua the special resource is strong ties with her married daughters. In addition to Wu Deming, Song Meihua has three daughters. The two eldest, who contributed to Wu's wedding, are factory workers in the county seat; the youngest is married to a professional soldier stationed in Guangzhou. Unlike most rural women who let the ties with their married daughters atrophy, Song Meihua actively cultivates relations with her girls by frequent visits and exchange of presents. They in turn give her financial support and have invited her to move into their homes. Because of the continuing, strong relationship with her urban daughters, Song Meihua is able to push for domination of her daughter-in-law with total disregard for her own dependency needs in advanced old age.

Unusual circumstances also explain the uncompromising behavior of Luo Erniang, but in this case the older woman's power comes not from her own special strength but from her daughter-in-law's unusual weakness. Like most women of her generation, Luo Erniang never worked in the state sector. Therefore she has never earned a wage comparable to Hu Shihping's and will never qualify for a pension. As soon as she gives up her part-time babysitting job, she will become entirely dependent on her son and his wife for financial support. Furthermore, unlike most elderly urban women, Luo Erniang joined the household of her daughter-in-law and therefore lacks the usual advantage of being the established housewife. Despite her objectively subordinate position, Luo nevertheless refused to compromise because Hu's class background made her socially insecure.

Between 1966 and 1978, the children and grandchildren of former landlords, merchants, and other "bad elements" lived under a cloud of perpetual suspicion which made them loathe to create any public disturbances that would draw attention to them or their families. Thus, although Hu Shihping was never actually attacked for her bad class background, she lived in fear of an investigation. Feng Dao's mother did not overtly use her own spotless political pedigree of "former poor peasant" to chastise or control Hu Shihping, but she sensed Hu's vulnerability and therefore refused to take a quiet subordinate position.

Irreconcilable Differences

The overwhelming majority of Chinese elderly remain in close contact with at least one child throughout their lives. Even in families where relations are as tense as those in the families of Song and Luo, children do not threaten to discontinue financial support or take steps to divide the household permanently. Over the long run, both generations accept their lot and keep their conflicts out of public view. But among a minority, the two generations fail to reach a workable accord.[5] These parents and children eventually sever all meaningful contacts with each other, and each generation is left to fend for itself.

In average families friction over ordinary household decisions fuels family quarrels, and the main protagonists are the women, who take responsibility for the management of the household. In families with irreconcilable differences, however, the cause of the breakdown and the main protagonists differ. Parental misdeeds outside the home, particularly violations of social customs or political crimes, precipitate and justify the rupture, and sons, not daughters-in-law, are the critical protagonists. Yet while these families' problems are atypical, the causes and contexts of their breakdown have several familiar elements. Most elderly parents have sons, and almost everyone is capable of political or social transgressions. Thus deviant families highlight areas of vulnerability where even families with outwardly high levels of solidarity are also at risk.

In contemporary China, sons have far greater responsibilities for their parents' well-being than do daughters. Similarly, men have more influence outside the home. Consequently, a man's success or failure at the workplace or in political activities is more important to him and to the status of his family than is the case for a woman. When the superiority of male influence and obligations is realized in a society that practices the custom of patrilineal inheritance, the result for elderly parents and their sons is often a polarized choice between total interdependence and complete separation. The tie is too powerful and men's public life is too important for parents and sons to have only ambiguously defined obligations.

The consequences of this pattern of gender inequality for family conflict are most clearly seen among rural families where the son has inherited a bad class label from his father or grandfather.[6] In the Cultural Revolution, children and grandchildren who had inherited the class label of former landlord or former rich peasant could not attend senior high school or take the entrance exam for the universities. Often the entire family was prohibited from joining the collective health insurance plan. In political campaigns they were frequent targets to be dragged out as undercover agents of the KMT or antisocialist elements. This systematic discrimination severely strains intergenerational loyalties, and among rural families former landlords or rich peasants are far more likely to break permanently with their adult sons than are elderly parents from poor or middle peasant backgrounds.[7]

In urban areas elderly parents with bad class backgrounds also suffer higher levels of family breakdown than those without political stigma.[8] But in the cities, the inability to find alternative housing and the greater willingness to live with married daughters reduces the incidence of total isolation from all children. In rural areas, families that suffer prolonged distress can divide their home or move one generation out into an unused woodshed. The standard of living, especially for elderly parents, will dramatically decline, but unless they are severely handicapped, elderly people will not starve or freeze to death if they separate permanently from a child. In the cities, however, houses are too small to subdivide, and municipal real estate bureaus are unwilling to relocate a family "merely" because parents and children fight. In order to survive in the cash economy of the city, an elderly parent must have a job, a pension, or support from children. When an elderly urban parent has no pension and can no longer work, city governments hold adult children strictly accountable. If they refuse to provide support voluntarily, the state is empowered to find the errant child's place of employment, authorize a monthly deduction of ten or fifteen yuan, and require the payroll office to send the money directly to the elderly parent.

Housing restrictions and the threat of government intervention force urban children to stay with their parents under conditions of stress that would cause rural households to split apart. The relative equality between urban sons and daughters also reduces the number of isolated elderly by giving urban parents a wider choice than rural parents about the child with whom they will live. Rural parents of all ages continue to rely almost exclusively on sons for essential financial support, but urban parents turn to daughters almost as easily as to sons. For urban elderly of bad class background who are deserted by sons, these strong ties with adult daughters provide an escape route from total isolation. Because urban parents do not routinely polarize their affections in favor of sons, they have more options than rural parents in times of need, and this greater flexibility of the urban family substantially decreases the incidence of total abandonment and desertion among elderly political outcasts.

In families where the children, but not the parents, have become politically suspect, there is not so strong a destabilizing effect on family loyalties as when the elderly parent is the deviant member. Because elderly parents are well aware of their ultimate need for their children's financial support, parents are more hesitant than children to desert an established household. Furthermore, parents in these families often feel a responsibility for their children's misdeeds that children who merely inherit a bad class label do not. As a result, the elderly parents whose children have made political errors avoid bringing further shame on themselves and their family by additional unconventional behavior. In cases like Luo Erniang's where the daughter-in-law is the one with a questionable political background, the younger person does suffer a loss of power within the house, but for that reduction of influence to precipitate total breakdown would require financial resources that Luo lacks or a level of political pressure against Hu Shihping that has not materialized. Usually elderly parents protect themselves against this problem of tainted class background among their in-laws by counseling children against marrying anyone with a political background worse than their own.[9] In Hu Shihping's case, however, her husband's family did not exercise this leverage because, at the time of their marriage, Feng Dao's father was dead and his mother was a rural widow who had lived separately from her son for many years.

A second group of elderly parents who experience noticeably greater risk of permanent estrangement from children are those who violate the traditional taboo against remarriage of widows. Unlike elderly political outcasts, however, these elderly are found almost exclusively in rural areas.[10] Thus while urban children may deeply resent the replacement of their dead mother or father with a stepparent, they do not act in as extreme a fashion as their rural counterparts. Greater acceptance of remarriage in urban areas accounts for this urban-rural difference. In the cities, the local community does not reinforce a child's anger with overt support for the ideal of the chaste widow but instead encourages the children to support both elderly parents. As a result, in urban families the remarried elderly are less likely than their rural counterparts to be abandoned and totally cut off from children and kin.

Power and Conflict

Most elderly parents and their children can readily identify one individual as the head of the household *(jia zhang)*. But the duties and power of the head of household differ greatly between rural and urban families. Usually the head of household in rural families is the resident adult who earns the highest income. In most rural families this is a married man, in good health, between the ages of thirty-five and sixty. In two-generation families and in families where a father in his fifties is in poor health, the family head may be a young man in his twenties or early thirties. Examples of rural heads of household over the age of sixty are rare, found primarily in families where the elderly father, through membership in a political organization, commands influence outside of the village which supersedes the status and power of even the best-paid young farm worker. Elderly rural women are heads of household only when they live independently from husband and married son. Yet even then they are usually preparing to transfer authority to their eldest unmarried son and therefore rarely exercise the autocratic powers of a male rural head of household. In rural families, the heads of household have final authority over all family resources. They are the family spokesmen in all important community meetings, and the wages of all family members are totaled up in their name. In all family disputes, their word carries the greatest weight, and younger members rarely contradict them directly in either public or private debates.

In urban families the title of head of household has a different meaning. Here it designates the member who keeps the household budget and handles daily expenses. Thus in the family of Li Fulan, all agree that Li is their head of household, and each month all but the new daughter-in-law hand over their entire salaries to her, receiving pocket money as they need it. Yet in using the title head of household, Li Fulan and her family explicitly state that their definition does not confer the same degree of power that rural heads of household exercise, and they use the title in a rather light-hearted fashion.

The relative youth of the effective family heads in the countryside and the general lack of power vested in urban heads of household might suggest dramatic shifts from the pre-1949 custom as well as a clear preference by the CCP for the interests of the young over the old. But family structure during the three decades prior to Liberation does not substantiate such conclusions. In rural families during those years elderly patriarchs and matriarchs were rare phenomena.[11] In general, the size of income and the ability to organize the delegation of work between family members determined the distribution of power between parents and children. Since family income usually varied in direct proportion to changes in the health and strength of working adult members, control of family assets fell to the most vigorous, best-paid worker. Because most men in their fifties were less effective laborers than men in their thirties, fathers in the pre-1949 decades typically handed over authority when the supremacy of the son as the major breadwinner became self-evident. In the minority of cases where family wealth derived from land ownership, control of capital, or entrepreneurial talent, the oldest generations delayed the transfer of power and maintained control over their children until death.

Collectivization eliminated these pre-1949 sources of parental control, and in the 1970s the pattern that had previously prevailed among ordinary farm laborers and poor peasant families came to predominate among rural families of all economic classes. However, among rural parents who have access to resources outside the village by virtue of political or occupational connections, there is an interesting parallel with the upper-class elderly of pre-1949 China. In these families, sons in their forties continue to be subordinate to their fathers, and the entire family may be dominated by an elderly autocrat who decides upon the job assignments, housing allocations, and marriage partners of the next generation.

In urban China, elderly parents who are politically more powerful than their children or professionally better connected also exercise an exceptional degree of control over their adult children.[12] Although the source of their power is distinct from that which once enabled wealthy merchants or landowners to dominate, the phenomenon of men and women well into their forties still dependent on elderly autocrats represents a significant continuity between pre- and post-1949 China. In both instances, the concentration of power in the hands of the elderly parent testifies to frozen and inadequate channels of upward mobility and to the continuing importance of family connections as a means to allocate scarce opportunities among the young.

In rural areas where the head of household still exercises considerable power over all other family members, the transfer of the title from father to son greatly affects the subsequent position of the elderly in the household and in the community. Once the title of family head passes to the younger man, the father views himself as a subordinate member, and his status is, at best, that of senior adviser. Surprisingly, despite this major loss of power, no formal rite of passage initiates the event or eases the transition.[13] Each father and son negotiate their own transfer of authority, and it is potentially a period of great tension and conflict. In reality, however, resignation of the headship does not seem especially difficult, and it often turns out to be an easy transfer that legitimizes an earlier de facto shift of responsibility from old to young.

Disruptive splits are most likely to occur when the father is less than twenty-five years older than the son and neither generation exhibits obvious superiority in the workplace. However, even in the early 1970s such families were in the minority. Pre-1949 disruptions in rural family life, high rates of infant mortality, and the tendency for the poorest rural men to delay marriage had produced a generation of rural families where fathers were thirty-five or even forty years older than their eldest son. Thus, as in the case of Li Hoizhong, by the time of the son's marriage, fathers were already incapable of financial dominance, and the transfer of power to the next generation went rather smoothly. However, as the children born to young men who married in the 1950s come of marriage age, vigorous fathers and sons will compete for economic control of the household, and struggles for headship may emerge among many rural families.

In the cities, the financial superiority of one generation over another has a less direct effect on the distribution of authority within the household. Thus, even when parents' incomes exceed those of their children, as in the case of Zhang Aiguo and Chen Youli, parents do not single-handedly dominate family debates. Furthermore, withdrawal from the workplace decreases the power of the old in relation to the young. When the urban elderly leave the work force permanently, their families suddenly become their universe. They have few legitimate reasons to leave the house, and the separation from their workplace deprives them of the social status they earned as employees of a large, public enterprise.

Some elderly break away from the confines of the household through involvement in community organizations. In the early 1960s the largest industrial enterprises and some municipal governments established clubs and service groups to provide pensioners with appropriate leisure activities and an official means to do volunteer work in their neighborhoods.[14] During the Cultural Revolution most of these organizations were disbanded, but they reemerged after the rapid increase in the number of retirees in 1978. Calisthenic groups and chess clubs are two of the most common recreational activities. Jobs as babysitters, telephone messengers, and housekeepers for invalids are typical forms of social service.[15] In general, however, only a minority spend more than a few hours each day away from their families.[16] Significantly, the morning calisthenic groups, which draw the largest numbers and include men and women from a wide variety of social backgrounds, begin at dawn before the housework of the day starts and are disbanded by seven-thirty or eight o'clock in order to permit elderly participants to complete the family shopping or deliver a young grandchild to nursery school.[17]

Even among elderly activists heavy responsibilities at home take priority over public duties. This primacy of private over public obligations is especially obvious among elderly women. For example, in

Changzhou city near Shanghai a former textile worker and long-time CCP member is vice-head of a residents' committee which between 1972 and 1978 started sixteen different service and production groups.[18] The vice-head herself is paid twenty yuan per month beyond her pension for her work as administrator, and she appears to spend almost all of her waking hours on the committee's various projects. Yet her work does not take her far from home. The committee office is in the vestibule of her house, and her own family's courtyard doubles as a committee meeting place.

In Beijing, a retired nurse of sixty-seven heads a small health station. She too is a long-time CCP member. But in contrast to the former textile worker, the retired nurse is highly educated for a woman of her generation and was a middle-level adminstrator for twenty years prior to her retirement. She is confident, articulate, and forceful. Yet housework in her son's home severely limits the degree to which she can participate in public life. At home she is responsible for the daily shopping, the noon meal, and the full-time care of her three-year-old grandson. By her own report, these family obligations take the majority of her waking hours.

Most elderly have even fewer community responsibilities than these two CCP members. Their political activity is limited to weekly or bi-weekly study sessions and they have few social obligations. As a result, even in the cities the family home is the undisputed center of everyday life, and participation in politics or community work rarely substitutes for the power lost by an individual's withdrawal from the full-time labor force. Like the rural elderly who cede the role of head of household to the next generation when their income falls below that of their children, the urban elderly relinquish power within their families when they lose the status provided by a job outside the home. Although a large pension equal to the wages of another family member reduces the degree of power lost, retirement still signals a retreat to a less active position. Initiative for new family ventures passes to the younger generation, and elderly parents take up a subordinate position in the household of a child.

Today, as before Liberation, the culmination of a successful life is a harmonious family. Economic necessity, vestiges of traditional morality, and explicit government policies converge to reinforce high levels of interdependence, and only a deviant minority fear abandonment or must be satisfied with superficial, intermittent contact with their children. Yet despite the firm desire for strong family ties and the many external supports for intergenerational solidarity, good relationships are by no means guaranteed. One generation may be unwilling or unable to contribute as fully as another to maintain an acceptable level of interdependence. One individual may become a political liability or social outcast, and this stigma may threaten to damage the social status of the entire family. A new member who has no memory of the past contributions of older family members may fail to accept the duties and obligations of family reciprocity. In theory, these sources of stress could weaken the loyalties of the old as easily as those of the young. But in practice, severe ruptures are most threatening to elderly parents, who therefore carry the major responsibility for maintaining harmony between the generations.

7

THE CHILDLESS ELDERLY

IN TRADITIONAL CHINA where ancestor worship was widely practiced, to die without a surviving child was a tragedy. Without any survivors, no one would offer sacrifices on feast days, and so for the poor, life in the afterworld would be as meager as it had been on earth. For the childless rich, death also promised anguish because without descendants to send offerings to departed ancestors, these previously secure individuals would be eternally denied the comforts they had come to enjoy on earth. So grim were these prospects that the childless of all economic positions worked energetically to establish ties of fictive kinship through adoption and sororal or fraternal associations.[1] Using these surrogate family relations, the childless elderly partially compensated for their lack of progeny and thereby participated in the central rite of ancestor worship.

At least as frightening were the earthly realities confronted in the years immediately preceding death. While most elderly prepared for death surrounded by their family, the childless were alone. Since the childless were often those who had been too poor to marry and maintain a family in the prime of life, many of them lived in dread of an old age where they would be forced to become beggars or vagrants.

Within the traditional society there were charities which were obligated to support those bereft of kin. But in the decade of ceaseless fighting before 1949, very few of the benevolent associations or family organizations were prosperous enough to honor their commitments to destitute members. The Nationalist government and various religious groups offered sporadic aid, but here the elderly had to compete with orphans, war widows, and others who were considered better "investments" for scarce charity funds than the old.[2] For the childless elderly, life after death held no comfort, and life before death was precarious, painful, and often desperate.

When the People's Republic was established in 1949, the demands on the new government for improved social services were staggering. The majority of the population was under twenty-one, illiterate, and vulnerable to the most common infectious diseases. Yet balancing their enormous demand for education, steady employment, and minimal health care was their equally great potential for becoming productive workers, deeply loyal to the new national leadership. In comparison to the needs of these several hundred million young people in the prime of life, the claims of a few million childless elderly, whose most productive years were forever lost to themselves and to the new regime, did not seem pressing.[3]

One reaction could have been for the CCP to ignore this needy minority. The total population of destitute elderly was small, and the party's successes with children and youth could easily have overshadowed this relatively minor area of neglect. The new leaders could have argued that in times of scarcity, the first priority was elimination of the underlying conditions that created the problems and that direct care of those who had suffered under the previous regime was only a secondary concern. In fact, however, the CCP leadership chose a dual strategy that would simultaneously eliminate the underlying causes of childlessness and reduce the suffering of those too old to raise a new family. By outlawing concubinage and polygamy, prohibiting expensive bride prices, and reducing infant and child mortality, the CCP hoped to provide all citizens under the age of forty with the opportunity to marry and raise at least one child to maturity. In this way the agony of the childless elderly, as a social problem, could be eliminated within one generation. At the same time the government addressed the poverty of the childless elderly whom they had "inherited" from the earlier regimes. Their effort on behalf of these destitute individuals has affected the lives of several million elderly men and women and fundamentally altered the experience of growing old in China.

The Rural Childless

In the first six years of CCP rule, the government did not single out the childless elderly in rural areas for any special attention. Instead the new national leaders planned to meet the needs of this small minority through the general program of land reform and rural development that was designed to improve the situation of all rural poor.[4] Often this solution, which relied on the redistribution of land, tools, and livestock, was inappropriate for the childless elderly because they lacked the strength and the material resources to maintain their homes and farm their new land productively. In cases of desperate need, the provincial or county grain reserves carried the most destitute through the winter and spring, but in the first years after Liberation the rural childless were generally required to manage as best as they could on their own.[5]

The collectivization of agriculture in 1956 significantly improved this situation. The law establishing the new cooperatives required each small collective to support all members who could not work and who had absolutely no kin to take responsibility for their needs.[6] Initially each production team within a cooperative was responsible for supplying necessary food, fuel, and clothing, but whenever possible they were also to guarantee school fees for orphans and a decent burial for those who died without next of kin. Because the original legislation stipulated five items — food, fuel, clothing, school fees, and burial — families or individuals who received this type of aid were known as five-guarantee households (wu bao hu). Later as economic conditions improved, many communities also provided housing and medical care, and by 1970 most of the childless elderly could expect to receive six of these seven "guarantees."

In contrast to the Western habit of housing frail or destitute elderly separately from other age groups, the Chinese have generally shown little interest in building age-segregated housing. The guarantee of housing for the rural destitute has generally meant allocation of a private house amidst those of other villagers. During land reform, all rural residents were given some form of housing as their personal property. Provisions were frequently minimal, but as a group, the childless elderly were adequately housed by local standards and benefited just as well as the homeless of other ages.[7]

During the peak years of the Great Leap Forward this policy of keeping the childless elderly in their homes temporarily shifted to a policy of universal institutionalization. Shortly after June 1958, the government announced that elderly five-guarantee households should no longer live scattered throughout the villages in their own homes but instead should be grouped together in collectively owned old-age homes.[8] A desire to reduce the cost of existing welfare programs and to increase the resources for capital construction projects was the primary motive behind this drastic change in housing policy. The CCP planners hoped that when all the childless elderly were grouped together, the healthiest would care for the sick and all members would contribute to operating costs by growing their own food and producing handicrafts or raising livestock for sale to local marketing cooperatives.[9]

Over 100,000 old-age homes with over 2,000,000 residents were reportedly established between June and November 1958.[10] The number of residents in each home ranged widely, but generally the homes accommodated less than fifty. Facilities were simple, such as a converted wing of an unused storeroom or a portion of an old ancestral temple. In only a few instances were new structures built specifically to be old-age homes.[11]

This abrupt departure from the previous emphasis on home care lasted only a short time. Within one year problems surfaced in the management and financing of the old-age homes. Nursing care was difficult to organize, and the homes often placed heavy financial burdens on already strained local budgets. In some mountain communes where small villages were scattered over large areas, or in suburban communes where per capita income equaled urban standards, the old-age homes continued to be economically feasible and remained an essential part of the welfare system. In general, however, the quickly established homes of 1958 were disbanded, and by 1960 most childless elderly had returned permanently to their own houses in the villages.[12]

County welfare officials interviewed in 1979 about the sudden discontinuation of the rural old-age homes after the Great Leap Forward echoed complaints heard from refugees in Hong Kong. The PRC officials stated that the 1958 policy was premature. Personnel were insufficient, and the plans were too hastily implemented. They stressed the excessive costs of establishing separate old-age homes and for the present, as in the past, recommended institutionalizing only a small minority of five-guarantee households.[13]

In five rural communities visited in 1979 where old-age homes had once flourished, the homes had survived and prospered in three cases; in the two others they had been abandoned in favor of a return to the alternative of home care. The experience of the surviving old-age homes illustrates the key considerations that determine whether or not five-guarantee households enter an old-age home. The largest and oldest of the three surviving old-age homes is in Nan Yuan Commune in the suburbs of Beijing. Established in an abandoned courtyard as a temporary home for ten completely destitute elderly in 1958, the Nan Yuan home has grown into a sizable complex with thirty-six bedrooms, a dining hall, a medical station, gardens, and auxiliary buildings for a staff of sixteen. By 1979 there were sixty-six permanent residents—forty-nine men and seventeen women. Three years earlier there had been ninety residents, and one hundred could be accommodated. New residents are admitted at the request of their brigade leaders. Elderly people with criminal records are excluded, but those who come from "former exploiting" classes are theoretically eligible. Local cadres noted, however, that because elderly landlords and rich peasants are the least likely to reach old age without any surviving kin to care for them, no "former exploiters" have ever applied to enter.

Since the late 1970s the average income at Nan Yuan has nearly matched that of city workers.[14] Not only do the commune members resemble city residents in their material conditions and expectations, but they also lack the strong identity with their community that characterizes most rural residents. Nan Yuan Commune was formed by an administrative fiat that imposed a new collective identity on a group of scattered suburban settlements. Because the different segments of the commune are subdivided by a network of public highways that connect Beijing to outlying rural areas, Nan Yuan lacks the territorial integrity common to most other communes. In addition, many of the childless elderly there are former itinerant peddlers, contract laborers, or seasonal agricultural workers who have no strong networks of extended kin in the community. Thus, because Nan Yuan is an exceptionally prosperous commune with an unusually high number of elderly "sojourners" and a weak collective history, an ambitious program of institutionalization has been both feasible and necessary.

The second of the three surviving old-age homes is in Tian Family Brigade in Tian Family Commune seventy kilometers from the capital of Hebei Province. Although the home was founded in 1970, it represents a return to many of the ideals of 1958. The home consists of six small rooms grouped around a courtyard with a common latrine and a large kitchen. In 1979 there were eight residents—three elderly couples and two single men. All were too frail to do any work, and five were so disabled that they spent most of their time indoors. A middle-aged woman cared for them during the day, and a man in his sixties prepared their meals. Because all eight residents were five-guarantee households, brigade welfare funds covered the costs of their food, supplies, and services.[15]

Like Nan Yuan Commune, Tian Family Brigade has several characteristics that favor group care. The first and most important is an extremely high number of needy and isolated elderly.[16] Although the brigade is named after the Tian family, there are at least fourteen different surname groups. Many brigade members are first-generation residents who settled in the area either as farm laborers in 1949 or as former CCP guerrilla fighters who were demobilized after 1950. Thus, by the late 1960s and early 1970s Tian Family Brigade experienced a sudden upsurge in demand for five-guarantee aid as the childless men and women who had matured in the turmoil of the 1930s and 1940s entered advanced old age.

As long as the childless elderly remain relatively healthy and mobile, even as many as twenty individuals do not pose an excessively heavy burden on brigade resources. But when they fall ill and are bedridden, the brigade leadership has to mobilize many members to work full-time providing nursing care. This type of drain on brigade labor power was the primary incentive for establishing the Tian Family Brigade home.

Affluence and special organizational resources explain why this particular community is actually able to establish and maintain an old-age home for its large population of needy elderly. In Tian Family Brigade, a full-time worker earns twice the national average for agricultural workers, and the community can therefore provide higher than average levels of social services.[17] Unlike most brigades, Tian Family Brigade maintains a full-time kindergarten, a well-equipped health station, and a junior high school. Even more striking is its enormous auditorium, built entirely through brigade surpluses and seating two thousand people. But affluence and high levels of need do not totally account for these excellent community facilities. Tian Family Brigade also has an unusually talented group of leaders, and much of its success in establishing a local old-age home is attributable to this essential and scarce community resource.

The third example of a surviving old-age home is located in a small county seat high in the Taihang Mountains in Hebei Province. Unlike the first two homes, where admission is available to all five-guarantee households in need, this county institution accepts only the childless dependents of revolutionary martyrs and disabled servicemen. Although its seventeen residents in 1979 — thirteen men and four women — had just moved into a particularly spacious building complete with dining room, library, and first aid station, the home's origins were humble. It first opened in 1958 as a small hostel. In 1964 a young demobilized soldier from Jiangsu Province was sent to cook, clean, and care for the several residents. Single-handedly he met all their needs, mending their clothes, bathing the bedridden, and nursing those in ill health. As their numbers increased and as the county welfare budget grew, two women were sent to help him in 1972. Between 1958 and 1979, forty-seven people drawn from eighteen of the county's forty-two communes lived there. The county government covers 80 percent of the expenses. The production teams in which the residents had previously lived make up the remainder by supplying the cash equivalent of fifteen kilos of grain each month.

To be admitted into a county home, the elderly in theory first apply to the leadership of their brigade. In practice, the village leaders often take the initiative prior to a request from the elderly and offer them the opportunity of moving to the county seat. After the brigade leaders have approved a move and the elderly person consents, the application is sent to the commune, which in turn passes it onto the the Bureau of Civil Affairs at county level. After the bureau takes action, a request is made to the director of the home, and as soon as the director certifies that there is space and the county government guarantees to cover all expenses, the eldely person can move.

When communes run old-age homes, there is similar pressure from village level cadres eager to pass on the financial burdens of five-guarantee households to higher administrative levels. When five-guarantee

households live in their village, their team or brigade members bear all
the costs, including household or nursing aid when necessary. When the
destitute elderly move to a commune home, however, the burden light-
ens. The team must provide only a minimum grain ration and in addition
gains first claim to the house and all household possessions that the five-
guarantee household leaves behind in the village. Consequently, while
the lowest-level cadres have clear incentives for maximizing the number
of people who enter the commune home, the commune leaders seek to
restrict entrance to the most needy cases in order to reduce financial
drain on commune welfare funds.

The sources of income and the levels of expenditure in these three
old-age homes differ significantly, yet the circumstances forcing the elderly residents to accept relocation are strikingly the same. Uniformly
the elderly who move to old-age homes are the physically weakest and
most socially isolated. In most instances, the homes are a choice of last
resort, and even officials agree that the initial adjustment is often difficult
for many residents. They have trouble sleeping, become boisterous, an-
noy fellow residents, and refuse to eat properly. In part, the difficulties
are the consequences of the dramatic and sudden discontinuity in their
established way of life. Most of these people have not left their homes for
many years, and for those who have to move to the unfamiliar and distant county seat, the move is extremely unsettling. The transition to an
institutionalized life in a totally unfamiliar surrounding would be
disturbing for anyone, but for these frail elderly it is especially difficult.

In virtually all instances the move is also permanent. Moving to an
old-age home is thus directly associated with death. To a generation
raised to believe that death at home is essential for a peaceful existence in
the afterlife, the uprooting becomes especially difficult, and only the
most desperate agree to leave their homes.

The final reason that old-age homes have not proliferated since 1958
is a long-term decline in need. Since 1949, political and economic conditions have favored stable family life, and improved public health has
greatly reduced the incidence of the most common infectious diseases
among the young and middle-aged. As a result, most elderly people who
had children living during the first five years after Liberation have been
able to see at least one child marry and continue the family line. Because
the childless elderly "inherited" from pre-1949 society have not been
"replaced" in equal numbers from members of the next generation, the
percentage of elderly needing the five guarantees has declined even as the
population of rural elderly has steadily increased.[18]

Within twenty years of its first formation, implementation of the
five guarantees has become routine procedure throughout rural China,
and benefits have increased as the general standard of living has im-

proved.[19] By the 1970s most communities provided a basic grain ration of fifteen kilos plus a monthly cash payment of between two and five yuan.[20] Although these payments meet only the most basic needs, they do guarantee survival for those who have no other source of support. Because the benefits remain near subsistence level, however, many childless elderly supplement the aid either by growing cash crops or by creating special personal relationships with younger villagers. Throughout the post-1949 era, the most commonly cited means by which the childless elderly have increased their economic security are special relationships with younger villagers. This supplementary assistance does not jeopardize the monthly welfare payment. On the contrary, since the mid-1950s the government has explicitly encouraged these individual solutions and even urged the elderly to seek additional financial aid on their own.[21]

Because this strategy requires a great deal of initiative and depends on a variety of individual characteristics, there is no single prescription for success. Nevertheless the life situations of the childless elderly clearly show that childless women are far more likely to rely on special friendships to supplement their welfare stipend than are men.[22] Two childless elderly from one small Guangdong village illustrate the general context in which aid is sought and the significant difference in the coping strategies of rural men and women:[23]

Great Uncle Li is a feeble man of seventy who lives in the same village as Li Hoizhong and Li Laoer. As a young man, Great Uncle Li worked alongside his father and elder brother on the family's small landholdings. Later, at a time not precisely known to other villagers, the family fell upon hard times, lost their land, suffered several deaths, and drifted apart. By 1949 only Great Uncle Li survived, a solitary bachelor working as a day laborer. In 1952 the ancestral temple of the Li clan was partitioned into public storage rooms. Great Uncle Li served as the watchman and slept amidst the large grain barrels and harvesting equipment. After the collectivization of land in 1956, he worked at light tasks in the collectively owned fields. But by 1965 his eyesight had completely failed, and he was designated a five-guarantee household.

Unmarried and affiliated with a family line that had produced no descendants, Great Uncle Li had no close relatives. As a Li in Li village, he could consider all those who shared his surname as cousins of some sort, but such ties were extremely weak. At New Years no one could remember him sharing in the family reunions that brought together long-separated family members. At holidays, as on ordinary days, good weather found him resting in a sheltered spot under the eaves of the old temple, and rainy days kept him in his room.

In 1974 Li village had four other childless elderly dependents receiving the five guarantees. One of the most feeble was a widow of seventy who had also lost her eyesight. She lived alone in a tiny mud-walled house that had belonged to her husband's family prior to land reform. No one knew her full name, and she was usually addressed by the pejorative nickname of the "useless old woman" *(wu yong po)*. Although she did not use this phrase in describing herself, she readily answered when so called.

But while this old woman was useless to the collective work force, she was by no means idle. She raised several laying hens and carried on a rather brisk trade, bartering her eggs for salt, vegetables, and cooking oil to supplement her regular grain rations. Her house stood immediately before the best well in the village, and whenever anyone passed to fill a bucket, she asked them to draw an extra pail or two for her. She was a furious housekeeper, sweeping her house several times a day and scrubbing and airing her meager set of bedding for hours at a time. Before holidays or during the busy harvest weeks she took in wash for her neighbors. In return they shared with her a portion of their evening meal. Usually, however, she cooked and ate by herself. Her blindness made it hard to build a proper fire or control the heat in her stove, and she was often forced to settle for lukewarm gruel and burnt vegetables.

During the worst turmoil of the Cultural Revolution the Useless Old Woman sat on the sidelines. She was not a featured speaker during the mass meetings, and she never rose before the crowd to accuse village leaders of treachery or deceit. Yet indirectly she got pulled into the upheavals of village politics.

In 1964 a group of city youngsters, just barely out of junior high school, were dispatched to settle in Li village. Upon arrival, these "educated youth" were introduced to the Useless Old Woman so that later they would be able to distinguish which of the impoverished elderly were the official dependents of the village worthy of aid and succor and which were the unreconstructed former landlords and "bad elements" whom the young newcomers were expected to shun. Most of these youngsters came from families in Guangzhou, but a few were Indonesian Chinese without any relatives in the PRC who had originally come to China in the early 1960s to get advanced education. At first the Chinese government had supported them, educating them in special boarding schools and subsidizing their daily living expenses. By 1964 this policy had begun to change, and many of the Indonesian students were asked to make it on their own. Poon Yuk was one of the Indonesian emigrants to Li village.

Poon, a garrulous, funny, and self-sufficient teenager, arrived in the village eager to be a success. He became an outspoken but controversial leader among the urban youth, and during the Cultural Revolution he was severely criticized. His opponents in the village succeeded in getting him branded a counterrevolutionary, and for several months he was locked up in the village detention center with several of the former village leaders. Every day the "jailer" brought a thin rice porridge to the prisoners. The families of the others supplemented these meals with food from their homes. However, Poon's city peers spurned him and refused to visit him.

The only friend who did not desert him was the Useless Old Woman. Poon had always been one of her favorites. He loved to joke with her when he went to the well, and he gave her medicinal brews that he had learned in Indonesia. After Poon was incarcerated, the old woman continued the friendship. Every morning she crept out before sunrise to take him some bits of salted vegetables and a hard-boiled egg. Although everyone in the village knew that she fed Poon Yuk, she still could not directly flout the village justice system, so it was necessary for her to carry out her mission in the half-light of dawn.

After several months Poon Yuk was released. Later the verdicts were reversed, and most of the former prisoners returned to their positions of leadership within the village. Poon Yuk, however, had grown cynical and desperate about his future in the village. In 1972 he went back to Guangzhou, and within six months he legally emigrated to Hong Kong. But even in Hong Kong, Poon did not forget the Useless Old Woman. At least through 1974 he regularly sent her cash remittances large enough for her to buy a good supply of cooking oil as well as black market grain for her chickens.

Rural women such as the Useless Old Woman consistently earn less than men. As a result, throughout their lives, childless women occupy an economically inferior position to that of childless men, and they anticipate their vulnerability in old age long before their male peers. Often while still in their forties, they seek to ingratiate themselves with younger and stronger villagers by offering to help care for their children, do their wash, mend their clothes, or prepare meals while the youger person devotes maximum energies to productive tasks with high economic return. The childless women perform these tasks in the hope that their contribution to the younger person's welfare will subsequently justify a claim for help in advanced old age. The childless women extend their offers of help deliberately, and the young do not accept them casually. Both young and old adhere to a village morality that demands reciprocity, and thus childless women whose offers of help are accepted can be relatively certain that they made a good investment toward their long-term financial security.

Childless rural men experience more favorable economic conditions. In the prime of their lives, they are able to support themselves easily and see no necessity to cultivate economic ties with unrelated younger villagers. As a result, when old and frail, the men can not fall back on a reservoir of good feelings or a past history of repeated exchanges of aid. Because childless women perceive the economic hardships of a childless old age at an earlier stage in life than do childless men, they begin to plan for supplemental arrangements in middle age, and in the stable rural communities of post-1949 China these strategies prove successful.

However, male-female differences among the childless elderly are not attributable entirely to women's early financial insecurity. The "success" of women like the Useless Old Woman is also the consequence of gender differences in childhood socialization and village sexual mores that favor women's adjustment to the role of dependent.

Before 1949, parents prepared their daughters for an arranged marriage to an unknown man in a distant village by training girls to take subordinate, support roles within the household. In contrast, they raised their sons to become heads of household either within or near the natal home. Thus, although both daughters and sons were prepared for "blind marriages," sons were not socialized to establish their future livelihoods as dependents in a community of strangers. Consequently, childless old men today are not as adept in establishing or sustaining ties of fictive kinship and dependency with younger villagers.

But childhood socialization is only one "cultural advantage." Elderly women also succeed in maintaining surrogate family relations better than their male counterparts do, because an alliance between an old woman and a young man is deemed more socially acceptable than one between an old man and a young woman. In the eyes of the village a relationship between an old woman and a young man parallels that between a mother and her son. In contrast, relations between an old man and a younger woman have sexual implications that make the relationship slightly illicit. Since most ties between an older and younger man would almost always involve a relationship with the younger man's wife, the prevailing sexual mores create a barrier to close relationships between destitute old men and younger villagers. Because these attitudes have dominated throughout the post-1949 era, childless females are generally more successful than males in developing the surrogate family ties that provide extra financial and emotional supports in advanced old age.

The Urban Childless

In the first years after 1949, the CCP did not address the needs of the childless elderly in the cities differently from the needs of the poor in general. As in rural areas, CCP leaders presumed that programs that helped any segment of the urban destitute would automatically improve the livelihood of the childless elderly. Between 1949 and 1950, municipal welfare associations loosely allied with the All-China Welfare Institute provided food and shelter on a temporary basis.[24] In the absence of a national welfare policy or funding organization, the success of these early efforts depended on the experience and commitment of the local city officials and on the size of competing financial demands. By 1952, however, most cities had a predictable routine for providing monthly cash grants through the municipal offices of the Ministry of Internal Affairs (Nei Wu Bu). As the hierarchy of political organizations matured in economic and administrative spheres, all facets of urban welfare work became similarly bureaucratized.

For those in the full-time labor force, the work unit took total responsibility for the welfare of the workers and their dependents.[25] Only those without any ties to a workplace remained the responsibility of the city. Within a few years after 1949 most of the urban population —

either directly through their employers or indirectly through their spouses, parents, or children — had become associated with a work unit, so that municipal welfare work came to be synonymous with aid to the childless elderly without regular employment.

By 1970 many of those without families were retired workers who had qualified for a monthly pension. Thus only those unable to collect retirement benefits and too weak to continue in paid employment depended on city welfare stipends. Increasingly this group of recipients has come to be the elderly in their late seventies and eighties who lost contact with their families prior to 1949. The local Street or Neighborhood Committees *(Jie Dao Wei Yun Hui)* take major responsibility for the welfare work for the elderly, certifying final decisions on eligibility and allocating funds.[26] But in practice, the elderly first confront welfare personnel at the lower administrative level of the Residents' Committee *(Zhu Min Wei Yun Hui)*. Procedures here are informal. Often cadres in charge are housewives or pensioners working as volunteers, and a favorable review of an application frequently depends on a favorable report from nearby neighbors.[27]

The actual size of the monthly payment varies from one city to the next and according to the special needs of the individual, but certain general guidelines prevail nationwide. Usually housing and medical services are provided free of charge. In addition, each person receives a monthly cash grant of between eight and fifteen yuan to cover the cost of food. To those who need help with household chores or require nursing care, the Residents' Committee assigns a neighbor or retired worker in the vicinity. At other times, help is given spontaneously.[28] These informal arrangements are at least as common as the formal assignments, and such situations can continue for many years. As in rural areas, informal arrangements are essential to the well-being of the childless, and neither local cadres nor the elderly recipients are eager to introduce any significant changes in existing guidelines.

Despite the similar emphasis on self-sufficiency and community volunteers for rural and urban programs, the childless elderly living in cities are far more likely to move to an old-age home than are those living in the villages, and since 1950 old-age homes have been an integral part of the urban welfare system. Within this overall acceptance of old-age homes, however, there are noticeable patterns of variation over time and in different regions of the country.

In the first five years after Liberation, policy toward housing the childless elderly varied according to the particular circumstances of each city. In Shanghai and Guangzhou where beggars were deemed a major threat to public security and public health, the earliest policies toward the childless elderly were frequently identical to those toward vagrants.

All elderly who inhabited the streets or had uncertain residences were gathered together, and efforts were made to verify the economic and political position of the family members still living in the person's natal village. Whenever possible, these people were given temporary shelter and then sent back to the countryside to reside with distant kin.[29] Less frequently they were sent to settle in state farms.[30] Those whose families could not be located and who were too weak to join the labor force were housed in municipal old-age homes. In this way the number of the institutionalized was kept small, and expansion of existing homes was not given priority. For example, by 1952 when Guangzhou had 1.4 million inhabitants, there were only two old-age homes — one small residence for twenty Moslem widows, and one large dormitory accommodating approximately two hundred and fifty residents.[31]

According to news reports from Shanghai and Guangzhou, the overall policy in the first years after 1949 was to house only those elderly who posed an immediate threat to public safety. Those not brought to the attention of the government workers were permitted to continue with their existing and often makeshift arrangements.[32]

In those early years the highest levels of institutionalization occurred in the industrialized cities of the Northeast, where large numbers of single men had emigrated in search of work between 1910 and 1930. Here the childless elderly were less likely to be vagrants and more likely to be single men who had worked for many years in the mines, the forests, and the city transport and sanitation services. There were few efforts to resettle these elderly in the countryside. Instead, the city or provincial unions moved immediately to house them permanently in old-age homes. The homes with the highest standard of living, as indicated by the size of their monthly food allowance, were those established and maintained by the labor unions. Financial support came from union welfare funds, and in some cases the residents themselves covered all monthly expenses from their pensions.[33] In the nonunion institutions funds came from meager city welfare funds. The standards here were lower, and there was greater emphasis on the need for residents to grow their own vegetables or manufacture marketable handicrafts.[34] Nevertheless, even in the large northern cities the number of old-age homes remained small, and no efforts were made to recruit the childless elderly who were still self-sufficient.[35]

In the smaller cities the migration to urban areas did not disrupt family life as drastically as it did in major industrial areas. Therefore, in the smaller urban areas the absolute number of childless elderly was small. Moreover, many elderly still had recourse to some residual kin networks in the surrounding countryside.[36]

In 1956 this initial policy of minimum institutionalization was revised so that the number of homes was expanded and existing facilities were improved.[37] For example, in July 1956 Beijing opened a third municipal home, and within one month it accommodated over nine hundred new residents.[38] Between July 1956 and July 1957 this pattern of expansion was repeated in other large cities.[39] Welfare standards were upgraded for all needy groups, and for the childless elderly this often meant increased opportunities to enter an old-age home.

The next shift in policy occurred during the Great Leap Forward. Although the changes instituted were not nearly as radical as those experienced in the rural areas at this time, the shift produced noticeable, short-term changes in household arrangements. Under the impetus of the drive for self-sufficiency and for higher levels of employment and productivity, some cities opened small, locally run homes called "Courtyards of Happiness" *(Min Ban Xi Fu Yuan)*.[40] These were small residences established in formerly unused public spaces. Quickly converted into housing, they provided both a collective home and a workplace for the childless elderly who had previously lived scattered throughout the community. At the same time that these small local homes were established, residents in the existing municipal institutions were asked to increase the time they spent in productive labor.[41] Unlike the rural program for the childless elderly, however, the changes in the urban areas did not necessitate relocating millions of elderly; even during the greatest push of the Great Leap Forward, the nationwide figure for the urban elderly in old-age homes remained at the relatively low level of 65,000 residents.[42]

In the years that immediately followed the Great Leap Forward, references to the locally run homes disappeared, and reports from the 1960s emphasized improvements to a select number of large, well-established institutions.[43] Since the late 1960s preference has continued to be given to home care. Institutionalization is reserved as a last resort, and the number of municipal old-age homes remains small.[44]

Two elderly men's efforts to maintain their independence explains why some childless elderly are more successful than others in using their personal resources to avoid institutionalization:[45]

Lao Yeh was born in the Dong Tai area of Jiangsu Province at the beginning of the twentieth century. Orphaned at four, he was supported by his older brother until old enough to be hired out as a full-time laborer. After only a few years of working for a local landlord, Lao Yeh left Dong Tai to seek his fortune in Shanghai, where he worked as a rickshaw coolie. Within three years his health was broken. Unmarried and cut off from kin in the countryside, he survived for the next twenty-five years as a scavenger in the city streets. After 1949, he first worked briefly for the sanitation department and later was assigned a job as a doorman at a small kindergarten. In 1966 just prior to the Cultural Revolution, he stopped work and relied entirely on a monthly stipend of fifteen yuan supplied by the Neighborhood Committee.

Four years later cadres from the local Residents' Committee approached Lao Yeh and suggested that he move to one of the city's old-age homes. There he would receive two meals a day, free medical treatment, and two or three yuan each month for incidental expenses. Two women from the committee took Lao Yeh to visit the home, where he stayed less than a day. The home did not compare favorably with his existing situtation, and he made no further efforts to move. According to Yang Meihua, Lao Yeh's neighbor and long-time confidante, life in the home was too regimented, and he greatly preferred life in his old neighborhood.

For over twenty years Lao Yeh had lived in an old residential area of central Shanghai. The houses were wooden tenements packed together with little or no space between the buildings and only narrow alleys to serve as roadways. As families grew and new in-laws and grandchildren joined existing households, the apartments were further subdivided so that frequently four or five families shared one floor. Yang Meihua lived in three rooms above a small noodle shop. Lao Yeh rented an attic room in a larger house on the corner. The two had been friends since the early 1950s when Yang had been a young housewife and Lao Yeh an elderly bachelor.

Yang Meihua and her husband had met in 1948 through a matchmaker hired by his mother. She was a teenager who had never left her native place; he was already a worldly man from Shanghai who had been on his own since the age of twelve. They stayed together for ten years. They had five children in quick succession, and then he left her for another woman. He sent her money irregularly and occasionally returned home, but most of the responsibility for the family fell to Yang Meihua. She became a full-time worker in the weaving room of a large textile mill.

It was in those hardest years, when her children were too young to work and she had no relatives to share her burdens, that she and Lao Yeh became close friends. He had already transferred to his job as watchman. When Yang Meihua worked the night shift, he stayed with the children. When someone was sick, he brewed the medicines or took the children to school. Gradually, the two households cemented ties of fictive kinship. He became her foster father, and her children call him grand-dad.

After Meihua's two eldest children entered the labor force, Yang Meihua began to assume the protective role. She did Lao Yeh's wash, cooked for him, and prepared tonics to clear his lungs. When he was sick and she was on a night shift, she sent her youngest daughter to prepare his supper. Even when the cadres from the Residents' Committee returned to urge him to visit a second home with better facilities and a nicer location, Lao Yeh refused to make even a preliminary visit, preferring to stay near Yang Meihua and her children.

Wu Laoliu is a blind musician living in the municipal old-age home of Shijiachuang, the capital of Hebei Province. Wu began to lose his sight as a young child, and in his teens he started to work in teahouses as an itinerant blind musician. He and his mother were the only survivors of a large family of eight which was devastated in the late 1930s by a particularly severe cycle of drought and floods. His mother took in washing, but Wu was the primary financial support of the family.

After 1949, Wu joined a city orchestra and lived with his mother in a room that they rented near the municipal bureau of culture. After her death, he moved to the dormitory of his work unit. It was a comfortable and secure life. He ate in the cafeteria, went to work with his colleagues, and received special instruction in braille. In 1960 he was the Shijiachuang representative for the National Conference of the Blind and Deaf in Beijing.

At the dormitory and through a study group for blind CCP members, Wu made friends. Some were his age, but many were older. Most of these men have since died. In this community Wu represents the last generation in a long tradition of blind musicians. Since 1949, few city children have been blinded by infectious disease, and therefore Wu Laoliu has no "successors" to repeat his professional and personal career.

In his early sixties, Wu Laoliu began to suffer severe circulation problems in his legs. He could no longer manage the stairs in the dormitory, and daily trips to and from work became impossible. He qualified for a pension of forty-six yuan per month. Although this is a large income for a single person, he could not maintain a separate household and was forced by necessity to move to the city old-age home in 1979.

Shijiachuang is a city of one million inhabitants, yet in 1979 only ninety-eight elderly lived in the single municipal old-age home. In the 1950s when the home was first established as a center for the destitute and disabled of all ages, there were two hundred residents sheltered in a scattered collection of mud-walled dwellings. By the early 1970s the orphans had found jobs, the oldest had died, and the total number of residents fell below one hundred. Nevertheless the city upgraded the facility, tearing down the oldest buildings and adding a new courtyard with large bedrooms, meeting rooms, and an enormous kitchen. Some of the residents still worked in the fields or the piggery belonging to the home, but most were too weak to do physical labor and spent their days entirely in their rooms. Direct state subsidies cover most of the expenses, and the home has a prosperous appearance.

In contrast to conditions in the 1950s and 1960s, the Shijiachuang home in 1979 was exceptionally comfortable and attractive. Yet few new residents entered. The only other new resident beside Wu Laoliu was an 85-year-old former Catholic nun who had outlived all the other sisters from her original convent and had nowhere else to move.

The living conditions and housing choices of Lao Yeh and Wu Laoliu emphasize the key role of personal relationships in determining the very practical decision of where to live. Since Liberation, old-age homes have greatly improved. Their housing arrangements are above rather than below average, and they have trained staff to provide adequate food and medical care at no cost to the individual. Yet in the eyes of the urban elderly, old-age homes continue to be seen as charnel houses. As in the early years after 1949, only the poorest or most disabled move into an old-age home. But as the case of Wu Laoliu suggests, destitution is not entirely a question of finances. As in rural China, the key to security in old age still lies in the quality of personal relations, in particular in the existence of strong friendships built on long-term bonds of reciprocity.

In summary, in both rural and urban areas, the success of the post-1949 welfare policies for the childless elderly is predicated on the ability of elderly individuals to create bonds of fictive kinship or to sustain ties of mutual obligation with kin other than children. Through special relationships with younger neighbors, colleagues, and nieces or nephews, the childless elderly obtain essential material and emotional support. In this way they avoid institutionalization, and the overall financial burden on the government is substantially reduced.

In the three decades before 1949 there were inadequate public provisions for the destitute elderly without families, so they scrambled desperately to find some way to escape starvation and a pauper's grave. Then too, ties to surrogate kin and friendships with younger or more prosperous people were common coping strategies, and throughout their lives childless adults worked vigorously to cement these personal relationships. But despite this similarity in the coping strategies of childless elderly before and after 1949, the differences between the two eras are substantial.

Since 1949, public rather than private solutions have dominated. Under the CCP, public programs provide the essential supports for daily living. Although welfare payments guarantee only subsistence-level aid, in comparison to the chaos and uncertainty that confronted childless elderly before 1949, the post-1949 order and routine represent decisive gains.

Under the CCP, even during periods of extensive political upheaval, public welfare programs have continued to meet the basic needs of the childless elderly. In contemporary China, fears of starvation and an unmarked grave no longer terrorize this unfortunate minority of the population. Although surrogate kin and ties to extended family remain vital to the well-being of the childless elderly, the communist revolution guarantees survival to those whom the previous regime cruelly cast aside.

8

OLD AGE UNDER COMMUNISM

BY THE LATE 1970s, Chinese elderly had reaped many benefits from the victory of the CCP. The collective economy guaranteed basic survival to those elderly who could no longer support themselves, and major improvements in public health created life expectancies that approached those of the developed world.[1] These economic and demographic gains positively affected the elderly throughout the nation and produced a level of material security that in the decades prior to 1949 had been available only to the rich or the exceptionally lucky.

The improved security and longevity, however, were not primarily the result of policies designed to help the old. Instead, thirty years of communism had greatly benefited the old because CCP policies had stabilized family life and in doing so created the material and social conditions that permitted adult children to support and care for their elderly parents. Basic support was guaranteed not by greatly expanded public welfare measures, but by expectations of intergenerational reciprocity and lifelong experiences of economic interdependence.

Nor were the gains of the revolution evenly distributed among all regions of China, or all generations of the elderly. After three decades of CCP rule, the greatest financial benefit explicitly targeted for the old — lifetime pensions replacing 80 percent of a worker's last wage — remained exclusively an urban privilege. And until the late 1970s, these pensions went overwhelmingly to men in their sixties who had joined enterprises and offices as young employees in the 1950s. Most urban women over fifty and men over seventy survived through the same strategies elderly adopted in the countryside: either they worked as long as their health permitted or they became the dependents of their adult children.

A second, more surprising, generational inequality was that between younger and older urbanites. After three decades of CCP rule, it appeared that in the most completely "socialized" urban sector, the communist revolution had in some ways brought greater benefits to the old than to the young. In the first years after their victory, the CCP had felt confident that it could offer the urban proletariat the full benefits of socialism: lifetime employment, an eight-hour workday, cheap food, public housing, free education, and medical care. By the early 1960s, however, the deep-seated poverty of the Chinese economy forced the leadership to reduce the scope of their original welfare promises through selective cutbacks implemented according to the principle of seniority. After 1963 urban high school graduates found it difficult to get good jobs in state enterprises, and many were forced to enter the collective sector, take temporary jobs, or move to the countryside. In this way, the incoming cohort of young urban workers was denied the job security and welfare benefits that had been routinely offered to school leavers in the 1950s.

Although all urban employees endured a wage freeze between 1963 and 1977,[2] those who already had achieved lifetime employment, free medical care, or subsidized housing kept their benefits, while those who followed them — often their own children — had to make do with the leftovers. In rural areas, where the state played a less decisive role in allocating benefits to individuals, cohort inequalities were of little consequence. There, physical strength was the final arbiter, and as workers aged, their incomes gradually decreased and within most families power slowly shifted to the younger, stronger members. But in the most modern state enterprises and among the more "advanced" proletariat, the imperatives of brute strength, or even of higher education, were muted. It was here that the communist revolution, in its reliance on bureaucratic entitlements and perquisites of seniority, created a distinctive pattern of age-sensitive inequality that compounded the longstanding cleavages of gender, region, and class.

The poverty that forced compromises with the original communist blueprint also decisively shaped the relationship between the party-state and Chinese families. Ideally under communism society, not families, would assume responsibility for the needy or disabled, and differences in family resources would not determine a person's material well-being, health, or occupational success. Each citizen would owe primary allegiance to the state and the party, and core identities would be public and fraternal, not private and familistic. However, as was clear from the discussion of housing and welfare arrangements in Chapters Three and Six, the CCP had from the first years of its rule rejected a frontal attack on family loyalties and family functions. Officials realized that the cost of jettisoning family support networks was too high, and drafted welfare policies that explicitly required families to fulfill their precommunist functions as primary providers and distributors of scarce goods and services.

Even in the areas of politics where insistence on the principle of individual autonomy and subordination of the family to society would not have imposed direct financial obligations on the state, the CCP did not break free of the past ideologically. On the contrary, it intensified the importance of family pedigree, creating a system of class labels based on a family's precommunist social and occupational standing that served as a major source of political capital (or liability) from the land reform of the 1950s through the Cultural Revolution. In both rural and urban political struggles, family history played a decisive role, and even loyal communist activists were not permitted to renounce family obligations or to create a political identity completely independent of the one they inherited at birth.[3]

By the late 1980s, economic and social reform had altered many of the Maoist institutions that once defined the responsibilities of family members toward one another. Collective agriculture was replaced by the functional equivalent of family farms.[4] Newly legalized private businesses and factories created jobs in which the young could advance their careers without depending on their parents or the state. Restrictions on residential mobility were eased, and by 1987 millions of rural residents had moved to work in cities and small towns.[5]

Also threatening the pre-existing relationship between the party-state and the family was Deng Hsiao-ping's renunciation of class struggle and stigmatizing class labels as primary tools of policy implementation. For the first time since 1950, people were free to ignore family pedigree, and, theoretically at least, young people could focus on advancing private interests with a single-minded concern that would have brought heavy censure only a few years earlier.

Were these changes by policy makers and individual families so substantial that the security of the old was significantly reduced? Without the same external pressures pushing young and old toward high levels of interdependence, were the elderly more vulnerable than they had been in the late 1970s? Were the opportunities for the young to strike out on their own so abundant that cohort inequality disappeared as a significant social cleavage? Would the elderly of the 1980s find a new basis for a secure old age, or had reforms so undermined the Maoist support structure that growing old had become more painful and unpredictable? To answer these questions, we must re-examine in some detail those arenas where the changes were of greatest consequence, i.e., the worlds of work and family. But first I would like to make a brief detour to introduce some basic demographic considerations that both document the diversity within the elderly population and place the concept of cohort inequality in broader historical perspective.

Demographic Considerations in the 1980s

In 1953 the age distribution of the Chinese population conformed to the pyramid configuration typical of countries with high fertility and falling

TABLE 1

Size and Age Distribution of Chinese Population,
1953–1987

Age	1953	1964	1982	1987
0–4	15.6%	14.4%	9.3%	9.3%
5–9	11.4	13.6	10.9	9.0
10–14	10.1	12.4	13.0	10.3
15–19	9.2	8.9	12.4	11.9
20–24	8.4	7.3	7.3	11.3
25–29	7.5	7.3	9.1	6.9
30–34	6.8	6.7	7.2	8.4
35–39	6.2	5.9	5.3	6.6
40–44	5.5	5.1	4.8	4.9
45–49	4.9	4.4	4.7	4.4
50–54	4.2	3.8	4.0	4.3
55–59	3.5	3.2	3.3	3.7
60–64	2.6	2.5	2.7	2.9
65–69	1.9	1.7	2.1	2.2
70+	2.1	1.9	1.7	3.2
Population (in millions)	582	694	1.003	1.067

SOURCES: For 1953, 1964, and 1982, Banister, *China's Changing Population*, pp. 25, 27, and 34. For 1987, *ZGTJNJ 1988*, p. 105–7.

infant mortality (see Table 1). The absolutely largest birth cohorts were the youngest, and as one moved up the age pyramid, each older birth cohort was smaller than the last. A decade later, as a result of fluctuating fertility and mortality rates, the overall shape of the population had become more irregular.[6] During the three famine years that followed the collapse of the Great Leap Forward in 1959, mortality soared, especially among the old and the very young. Fertility plunged, and entering cohorts were approximately half the size of those that had immediately preceded them. Then, in 1962 as economic conditions improved, the trend reversed itself. Birthrates soared, infant mortality dropped, and new cohorts were almost three times as large as those of the famine years.[7]

By the 1970s remarkable declines in fertility created a second indentation in the pyramid, and the newest birth cohorts were again smaller than older ones. Between 1970 and 1980 the total fertility rate (TFR) for women of childbearing age fell from 5.8 children per woman to 2.2,[8] and even as the number of women entering their childbearing years dramatically increased, annual total births remained below those of the early 1960s. As a result, the distribution of the population by July 1987 was quite "lumpy," bulging outward to indicate a large population between the ages of ten and twenty-five, but tapering inward to reflect the smaller birth cohorts after 1972.

By the late 1980s, the relative size of the elderly population had noticeably increased. In 1953 there had been 27 million people aged sixty-five and older, representing 4 percent of the total population; by 1987 there were more than 58 million people over sixty-five, 5.4 percent of the population.[9] In 35 years the elderly population had grown at a faster rate than the total population, and among the elderly over seventy, the rate of increase was twice that of the total population.[10] Nevertheless, as Table 1 shows, the elderly were still a small minority within a generally young population. It was also true, however, that by 1987 the Chinese population, while still predominantly young, had passed through what is known as the demographic transition and was about to enter a period in which those over age sixty-five would double in absolute numbers and triple as a percentage of the population by the year 2020.[11]

At first glance it might appear that the sheer size of the elderly population in a poor, agrarian nation would create a heavy burden on society and on families with dependent elderly. Dependency ratios actually declined, however, during the first four decades after 1949, and the demographic shifts generally made it easier, not harder, for society and families to provide for the old. In 1953 there were 94 dependents for 100 workers; by 1964 the ratio had dropped to 78:100, by 1982 to 62:100, and by 1987 to 52:100.[12] Moreover, because of the high fertility in the 1960s and early 1970s, the percentage of elderly among the dependent group did not sharply increase.[13] The overall impact of these demographic trends was therefore an increase in the number of working-age people and a steady decline in the number of dependents each worker had to support.[14]

As with other dimensions of Chinese society, however, macro-demographic trends were not uniform throughout the nation. Until the mid-1960s the elderly had been concentrated in rural areas, and cities had noticeably younger populations.[15] This seemingly anomalous finding is actually quite easily explained by looking at fertility, mortality, and migration patterns during the last years of the Republican era and the first years of the PRC. In the 1940s and 1950s, fertility was equally high among urban and rural women but migration was highly skewed; massive numbers of young people left the villages, but few young people left Chinese cities. The result was young cities, and relatively old villages.[16] After 1962, rural and urban areas developed divergent demographic patterns that reduced the overrepresentation of the old in the countryside. Birthrates plummeted in the cities, but not in the villages.[17] Rural residents were barred from permanently moving to the cities to work, and millions of urbanites were resettled in rural areas. By the late 1980s the cumulative impact of mortality, migration, and fertility differentials had reversed the situation of the 1950s, and there was a somewhat higher concentration of elderly in the cities than in villages and small towns (see Table 2).

TABLE 2

Size and Distribution of Elderly Population, 1987

| Age | Percentage of Total Population | | |
	Cities	Towns	Villages
50–54	5.1%	4.3%	4.0%
55–59	4.2	3.6	3.5
60–64	3.1	2.8	2.9
65–69	2.3	2.1	2.2
70–74	1.5	1.5	1.6
75–79	0.9	0.9	0.9
80+	0.6	0.6	0.6
Total Population (in millions)	193	200	674

SOURCE: *Zhong Guo 1987 Nian 1% Ren Kou Chou Yang Diao Cha Zi Liao,* pp. 136–40.

China in the 1980s had the largest population of people over age sixty-five of any country in the world. Yet as a percentage of the population, they had barely surpassed their moderate levels of the 1950s. As a result, the needs of the old did not loom disproportionately large, and it was still possible for the government to argue that this relatively small, physically frail group had special needs that both families and society could afford to meet. Thus even though the preferential treatment of certain cohorts of older workers was primarily created and maintained by the bureaucratic privilege of seniority, the relatively constant share of the old in the total population obscured the impact of massive increases in their absolute numbers, and thereby helped maintain a public commitment to treat the elderly as a favored group throughout the 1970s and 1980s.

New Patterns of Work and Retirement

Collectivization and the ideology of socialism directly increased the financial security of the old. In rural areas between 1955 and 1980, each production team was required to provide a basic grain ration to all members. In addition, most elderly could find some form of remunerative job within the village economy. Old men like Li Hoizhong who were able to do little more than scavenge in the lanes, or stand guard at the orchard, earned work points that entitled them to a share of the team's year-end profits. Rural women like Chen Pingfang earned cash by selling vegetables and pork. And all rural elderly were made more secure by the household registration system, which tethered Chinese men to the villages of their birth and thereby guaranteed that at least one adult son would be close by when elderly parents could no longer support themselves.

In a different but parallel fashion, the CCP's transformation of the urban workplace also increased the financial security and earning power of the old. After 1955, employment for most state and collective employees was guaranteed until retirement age.[18] National wage scales reduced income inequality between occupations and increased the rewards for manual labor. Seniority determined earnings and benefits, and even during periods of economic stagnation, the relative advantages of the established older workers remained untouched (see Table 3). Under these conditions older urbanites were protected from direct competition with entering cohorts of workers, and better educated or more productive newcomers found it impossible to surpass or even match the wage levels of those ten or twenty years their senior.

The communist revolution had promised the proletariat financial security in old age,[19] and for those who entered the urban labor force after 1949 the promise was realized. With as little as ten years' work experience retirees drew a basic pension that replaced 60 percent of their last wage and also allowed them to receive free medical care and subsidized housing. With twenty years' work, a retiree's pension replaced 80 percent of his or her last wage, and for model workers and those with only one child, pensions were 100 percent of wages.

Between 1978 and 1988, Chinese leaders directly attacked many of the institutional and ideological foundations of these Maoist supports for the urban and rural elderly. They praised individual initiative and private risk-taking, and they deliberately reduced the reach and power of collective organizations and the central plan. The most fundamental departures from past practices were in the countryside. The communes, which had been the core institutions throughout the Mao era, were dismantled between 1980 and 1983.[20] There was a functional return to family farming, and with the legalization of private trade, rural residents quickly redeployed household members to maximize the return on family members' labor power.

Following these fundamental institutional reforms came a major shift in migration policy. In 1984, the State Council passed new regulations allowing rural residents virtually unlimited access to jobs in 60,000 small cities and market towns.[21] In practice, the new rules invited massive migration to large and medium-sized cities, and by 1988, 50 million former rural residents — predominantly young men — were working in urban areas.[22]

In response to these fundamental policy shifts, one would expect to see a decline in the financial security of the rural elderly. A return to family farming removed the safety net of the collective, and eliminated the elderly's privileged access to high-income jobs in the private sector. Weaker *hu kou* constraints might permit the young to abandon the old, and to

TABLE 3

1982 Industrial Monthly Wages by Age and Type of Job
(in yuan)

Job type	under 25	26–30	31–35	36–40	41–45	46–50	51–55
blue collar	66.2	74.2	77.6	85.3	90.0	96.9	105.0
white collar	57.9	64.2	72.3	77.4	83.1	95.0	101.0

SOURCE: Jiang Ze-hao and Chen Bao-guang,"Distribution of Salary," *She Hui Ke Ji Xue Kan*, No. 4 (1984), p. 67.

begin new careers totally independent of parents and older male relatives. Were these in fact the immediate consequences?

Based on Chinese surveys in rural areas, it appears that in the first decade of decollectivization, the elderly on the whole did not suffer. Instead, the new opportunities to develop commercial sidelines and produce crops for local markets raised the labor value of all family members, and the old continued to play a central role in the household economy. Some of these surveys, however, also documented declining levels of self-sufficiency among rural elderly. One 1986 survey of rural counties outside Beijing reported that 78 percent of those over sixty could not support themselves but relied on their children for basic needs.[23] A 1987 study of rural Hubei reported that 57 percent of those over sixty relied on others, and 43.7 percent reported that they had no control over the spending of family income.[24] A 1989 survey in rural Liaoning reported the same trend among 87.5 percent of respondents.[25] Thus to the extent that we can generalize from early Chinese evaluations of the reforms, it appears that the most general consequence of decollectivization for rural elderly was a decline in self-sufficiency but no obvious or pervasive loss of security. Where incomes rose, elderly with strong family ties benefited by virtue of the redistributive functions of the family and traditional mores of intergenerational reciprocity. Where incomes fell or stagnated, they shared the family's poverty and reduced their demands in order to conserve scarce family resources.

Chinese sources also make it clear, however, that the shift to family farming and the dismantling of collective welfare supports created the potential for widespread insecurity in the future. During the Mao years, even when they were not immediately in need the collective economy had stood behind all elderly. Workpoints were registered for each elderly team member who came regularly to work, and if they had been good workers in the past their history was recognized and the local community felt obliged to support them. Under the household responsibility system, the village-level collective leadership no longer controlled the resources with which to protect the elderly against rejection by kin or the premature death of a child. In addition, in the late 1980s young family members were freer than at any time since the early 1950s to leave their parents and find work away from their village, and village leaders were less willing and less able to mobilize the local community to guarantee the security of old neighbors. To the extent that elderly rural parents were well cared for and respected by financially secure children, the collapse of the collective had no immediate or systematic negative impact on their financial security. But the potential for abuse and abandonment was noticeably higher than it had been ten years earlier. Moreover, when one turns from looking at the majority, who had good relations with adult children, and examines the impact of the reforms on the fledgling social security programs or the Five Guarantees, one sees that the negative potential has already begun to be realized.

After 1980, the destruction of the communes and the return to families as the basic unit of production and saving precipitated major cutbacks in all collective welfare programs at the village level.[26] Village health cooperatives closed, barefoot doctors became fee-for-service private practitioners, and the custom of allowing families in difficulty (*kuan nan hu*) to draw grain rations against future earnings disappeared. These cutbacks hurt both the young and the old, but for the childless elderly the collapse of the collectives had especially harsh consequences. In the Mao era, destitute elderly (*wu bao hu*) in almost every village could expect the team to guarantee subsistence and a decent burial; after 1980, the Five Guarantees fell on hard times. Between 1983 and 1986, the percentage of elderly who qualified for aid under the Five Guarantees but did not receive it rose from 4 to 26 percent,[27] and by 1988 some Chinese observers announced that the system had virtually collapsed.[28]

In addition, the retreat from collective welfare undermined any systematic effort to create a rural social security system to parallel the pensions given through the Labor Insurance Regulations. During the late 1970s, many rural areas had begun to discuss different ways to develop some type of rural social security system, and during my visits to model brigades in Hebei and Jiangsu in 1979, I had seen successful brigade-level systems in operation. Particularly after implementation of the one-child campaign, there was an even clearer impetus to reduce parental need for many sons. By the mid-1980s, however, examples of functioning rural social security systems had virtually disappeared from the national press, and the only concrete proposal I discovered explicitly emphasized individual rather than collective solutions. In this proposal, rural parents with one child or two daughters were urged to join a contributory insurance plan that required a down payment of 500 *yuan* and a monthly fee of ten *yuan*, and provided a final pension of only 30 *yuan* a month, payable after

TABLE 4

The Changing Composition of National Workforce
1953–1987

Year	Rural	Urban State	Urban Collective	Urban Private	No. of Workers (in millions)
1953	88%	7%	0.09%	3.80%	207.2
1957	86	10	3	0.40	237.7
1965	82	13	4	0.30	286.7
1970	82	14	4	0.20	344.3
1975	78	18	5	0.05	381.6
1978	76	18	5	0.02	401.5
1985	74	18	7	0.80	498.7
1987	74	18	6	0.90	527.8

SOURCE: *ZGTJNJ 1988*, p. 153

twenty years' participation.[29] Given the large cash investment required of participants, as well as their regular cash contribution of 120 *yuan* a year, this program was feasible only in affluent suburban areas. Furthermore, even in these villages, the final outcome would still provide an inferior, less secure old age than the one provided by one or more sons. Small wonder, then, that the press did not report widespread imitation in other regions of China.

In the cities, the structural transformation after 1980 was more modest. Despite enthusiastic promises to break "the iron rice bowl" and reduce the reach of the command economy, ten years after Mao's death 70 percent of the work force remained in the state sector (see Tables 4 and 5). Wages were still primarily determined by fixed wage scales, promotions continued to be on the basis of seniority in the wage grade, and workers could resign only with the permission of their supervisor and the unit's personnel office.[30] There was no institutional change in the cities comparable to the return of family farming, and no administrative deregulation as dramatic as the legalization of migration to cities. Nevertheless, some changes in the pay structure and the commitment to lifetime employment displayed the potential to challenge the previously favored position of the elderly.

After 1978 wages were less completely determined by hourly rates because bonus pay and piece work increased the chance for individuals to earn income in excess of that set by their basic wage grade (see Table 6). New hiring rules replaced lifetime employment with time-specific contracts, and general economic policy encouraged employment outside the state sector.[31] Taken together, the shift toward a more individualized reward structure and greater reliance on labor contracts theoretically undermined the advantages of seniority and permitted economic competition between individuals of different ages.[32] Under these conditions, the ad-

TABLE 5
Composition of Urban Workforce by Sector
(in millions)

Year	State (contract)	Collective	Private
1953	18.2	.3	8.98
1955	19.0	2.5	6.40
1957	24.5	6.5	1.04
1965	37.3	12.2	1.71
1976	68.6	18.1	.19
1978	74.5	20.4	.15
1979	76.9	22.7	.32
1980	80.1	24.2	.81
1981	83.7	25.6	1.13
1982	86.3	26.5	1.47
1983	87.7	27.4	2.31
1984	86.3	32.1	3.39
1985	89.9 (3.3)	33.2	4.50
1986	93.3 (5.9)	34.2	4.83
1987	96.5 (7.2)	34.8	5.69
1988	99.5 (9.9)	35.2	6.33

SOURCES: For 1957–87 *ZGTJNJ 1988*, p. 153; for 1988 *RMRB*, March 1, 1989, p. 2; and *Chinese Statistics Monthly*, No. 8 (Nov. 1989), p. 7; for contract workers, in 1985 *Xin Bao* (HK) March 13, 1987, p. 13, in 1986 *BR*, No. 9 (March 2, 1987), p. 26; in 1987 *Zhong Guo Fu Nu Bao*, June 13, 1988, p. 1; in 1988, *RMRB*, March 1, 1989, p. 2.

vantages of older workers could disappear and the possibility loomed of a retreat from the commitment to universal pensions that would parallel the collapse of collective welfare in the countryside.

Despite the clear potential for the post-Mao reforms to undermine the security of the urban old and erode the benefits of seniority, there was little evidence that precommunist levels of insecurity would return. On the contrary, the most obvious short-term consequences of post-Mao reform in the cities was a rapid expansion of pension benefits and a reduction in

TABLE 6
Different Sources of Monthly Wages in State Enterprises, 1978–1986

Type of wages	1978	1980	1982	1984	1986
time rate	85.0%	70.0%	64.0%	58.5%	59.0%
piece rate	0.8	3.0	7.6	9.5	9.0
bonus	2.3	9.0	11.0	14.0	13.0
subsidies	6.5	14.0	14.0	14.5	15.2
overtime	2.0	1.6	1.5	1.5	2.0

SOURCE: *Zhong Guo Tong Ji Zhai Yao 1987*, p. 101.

some of the most glaring inequalities among the elderly population. In the 1970s reliance on rules of entitlement had created large age-specific disparities, whereby those who had been too old to hold a post-1949 job that provided a pension, or those who had retired in the 1960s when wages and benefits were low, occupied a distinctly inferior position to the newly retired. Thus in contrast to the rural areas, in the cities the communist revolution had created an economically bifurcated elderly population, with only a minority as full beneficiaries of the best that the revolution could provide. But after 1979, these cohort inequalities within the older population diminished, and overall the promises of socialism were more fully realized among the urban old than in any decade since 1949.

During the 1980s, most urban elderly became financially independent of their children, and among those under age seventy, pensions became the norm for women as well as men, and for those retiring from jobs in the collective sector as well as for those who had worked for a state enterprise.[33] There was also less regional inequality. In 1978, pensioners had been concentrated in a few large coastal cites and the three provinces of the northeast; a decade later, pensioners were a common phenomenon in large cities throughout the country.[34]

The extraordinary speed with which the number of pensioners grew in the 1980s clearly demonstrates that initially the post-Mao reforms had positive consequences for urban elderly (see Table 7). Between 1978 and 1987, the number of pensioners grew sixfold, and the percentage of urban elderly receiving pensions approached the percentage of the total population who were urban employees (zhih yuan).[35] Equally noteworthy was the ability of the Chinese government to maintain benefit levels at about 90 percent of the average wage even while the ratio of workers to retirees precipitously dropped, from 33:1 in 1978 to 7:1 in 1987.[36]

However, despite extending basic pension benefits to the majority of urban elderly and simultaneously keeping benefits high, government policies did not eliminate the problem of inequality among the old, nor did they eliminate heavy dependency on children among the oldest and frailest. Instead, both problems persisted, albeit in slightly different forms. A comparison between the position of one group of privileged cadres and that of ordinary elderly documents these emerging disparities.

Li xiu, a shortened form of li zhi xiu yang, literally means a cadre who has "withdrawn from work for recuperation." The term seems to have first appeared in the mid-1950s as a special pension program aimed at disabled officers of the PLA.[37] In 1979 cadres from the Ministry of Civil Affairs told me that li xiu status was granted to only a few high-level CCP leaders who had made great contributions before 1949, and during that trip I did not meet a single li xiu pensioner.[38] According to documentary and interview materials gathered by Hong Yong Lee, the State Council had origi-

TABLE 7

Number of Elderly Receiving Pensions
(in millions)

	All pensioners	From state sector	li xiu	Cost to state (in billion yuan)
1978	3.14	(2.84)		1.7
1979	5.96	(4.73)		3.2
1980	8.16	(6.38)		5.0
1981	9.50	(7.40)		6.2
1982	11.13	(8.65)	(0.007)	7.3
1983	12.92	(10.15)	(0.470)	8.7
1984	14.78	(10.62)	(0.830)	10.6
1985	16.37	(11.65)	(1.080)	14.9
1986	18.05	(13.03)	(1.370)	19.4
1987	19.68	(14.24)	(1.520)	23.8

SOURCES: For number of pensioners *ZGTJNJ 1988*, p. 203; for number of *li xiu* cadres, through Dec. 1982, *Xin Hua News*, Feb. 6, 1983, translated in *Survey of World Broadcasts*, Feb. 12, 1983, Part 3, Fe B11/14; through July 1983, *BR* Sept. 12, 1983, p. 6; through April 1984, *RMRB*, Sept. 11, 1984, p. 4; through July 1985, *RMRB* (overseas edition), July 2, 1985, p. 1; through Dec. 1986, *RMRB*, Oct. 11, 1987, p. 1; through Dec. 1987, *Zhong Guo Lao Dong Ke Xue*, No. 10 (1988), p. 43.

nally planned to expand eligibility for *li xiu* status to a wider range of party veterans in 1965 to encourage retirement of its oldest cadres, but the Cultural Revolution killed the idea.[39] Only after 1978, when the top CCP leadership adopted mandatory retirement as part of a major effort to rejuvenate the top ranks of the party and the army, did the *li xiu* benefit emerge as a central component of Chinese retirement programs.[40]

State Council regulations in 1980 established the ground rules for expansion and implementation of the *li xiu* program.[41] Henceforth all those who had served the revolution during the Japanese War or the Civil War at the level of a county vice-head or its equivalent would receive preferential treatment in retirement. Pensions would equal last wage, there would be special cash payments for resettlement, special trips for the retiree and family, and continued access to internal party documents. Between 1982 and 1986 eligibility requirements were further relaxed and benefits improved, and by the late 1980s, virtually all those who could prove they had done "revolutionary cadre work" before October 1, 1949, qualified for *li xiu* status.[42]

The immediate goal of this liberalization of *li xiu* pensions was to implement the policy of mandatory retirement among the upper ranks of the CCP and PLA by easing the transition to civilian life. As is evident in Table 7, the upgrading of benefits had the desired effect. The number of *li xiu* pensioners grew rapidly after 1982, and by the end of 1987 60–70 percent of those eligible had retired.[43] On average their yearly pension was 400 *yuan* higher than that of ordinary retirees, and among those coming from the military the disparity averaged 1,000 *yuan*.[44] Nevertheless, there still remained a significant minority of almost one million for whom even these generous perquisites could not compensate for the loss of full-time employment.[45] In short, among the elite even the most privileged retirement status was inferior to lifetime employment.

The majority of urban elderly, however, had no choice but to accept retirement. After 1978, retirement for the first time became mandatory for women at fifty and men at sixty, and there were no provisions to increase benefits retroactively for those who had retired earlier under less generous circumstances as there were for *li xiu* cadres. Nor was any provision made to index pensions to increases in the cost of living. These disparities between ordinary and cadre retirees created a significant new class of privileged elderly among the urban population, and in years of high inflation such as those between 1984 and 1989,[46] the push to make retirement mandatory created new hardships among the urban old. As in the 1970s, the ones who were most disadvantaged were the oldest, who had retired in the 1950s and 1960s or had never qualified for a pension.[47] But by the end of the 1980s, even younger retirees were beginning to feel increasingly anxious about their long-term financial security. A significant minority took new jobs;[48] but for most, the response was increased awareness of their need for adult children as essential to long-term security and well-being.

Although inflation increased the sense of insecurity among urban pensioners, in the workforce cohort inequalities persisted and many young urbanites continued to be disadvantaged. During the 1980s, nearly 75 million young adults entered the urban workforce, and unemployment, which had plagued city school leavers since the early 1960s, was more than halved.[49] Average wages more than doubled between 1978 and 1987,[50] and in some cases differences began to narrow between older and younger workers as the result of increases for the lowest-paid workers.[51] Overall, however, these improvements did not suffice to eradicate the cohort inequities that had characterized the 1970s; nor did they establish the structural foundations for subsequent fundamental change. Higher rates of employment among young adults were largely achieved through the creation of jobs in the collective and private sectors (see Table 8), and although in a few widely publicized cases young entrepreneurs working outside the state system reaped huge profits, in general these jobs offered lower wages and fewer benefits than state employment.[52]

Media reports of rapid promotion of the young ahead of their seniors similarly represented the exceptions, not the norm. In the 1980s as in the 1970s, wage increases and promotions usually went not to individuals, but to entire wage grades.[53] Even bonuses could be given collectively to a shop, a division, or an entire enterprise, and except for workers who were

TABLE 8

Destination of New Entrants to Urban Labor Force

	1978	1979	1980	1981	1982	1983	1984	1985	1986	1987
Number										
(in millions)	5.44	9.02	9.0	8.2	6.65	6.28	7.21	8.13	7.93	7.99
State (%)	72.0	63.0	63.5	63.5	61.5	59.0	57.5	61.3	67.6	62.4%
Collective (%)	28.0	35.0	31.0	32.5	33.0	27.0	27.0	25.0	28.0	26.7%
Private (%)			5.5	4.0	6.5	13.0	15.0	13.6	4.0	10.6%

SOURCES: 1978–85, *Zhong Guo Lao Dong Gong Ce Tong Ji Zi Liao 1949–85*, p. 110; for 1986, *Statistical Yearbook of China 1986*, p. 104; for 1987, *ZGTJNJ 1988*. p. 175.

paid for piecework, bonuses typically were distributed on the basis of one's wage grade rather than individual performance.[54] Moreover, although bonuses grew at a faster rate than wages, they amounted to a relatively small share of total urban income.[55] In the 1980s as in the 1970s, young urban workers continued to work within a bureaucratic system dominated by rules of seniority that the reforms had done little to change.[56] Age differentials like those so graphically illustrated in Table 3 still characterized the urban opportunity structure, and in many enterprises a bias against the young remained a distinctive characteristic of the urban workplace.

Household Arrangements of the Old and the Young

When I examined housing arrangements of the old in the 1970s, both documentary and interview evidence indicated that about 85 percent of elderly parents lived with an adult child.[57] The primary supports for this trend were chronic housing shortages, which prevented the establishment of independent households at the time of marriage, and tight migration controls, which made it difficult for the young to leave their home village or home town upon completion of their education. In addition, multi-generation households offered both young and old certain economic advantages. They economized on such expenditures as fuel, electricity, and food and provided such domestic services as nursing care and baby-sitting, for which neither the state nor the market offered an equally low-cost substitute. However, despite similar rates of joint living in villages and towns, multi-generation living was viewed in a more positive light among rural families than among urbanites. In the countryside, a large household was an accomplishment, the successful result of a long-term strategy for family advancement. In the cities, by contrast, multi-generation households were seen by most as a necessary adjustment to housing shortages. Both generations would have preferred "intimacy at a distance," but the difficulty of securing separate apartments forced newly married children to maintain joint residence with their parents. Most of my urban respondents considered the arrangement inconvenient and, they hoped, temporary.

After 1980, economic and political reforms altered financial and administrative constraints on housing choices. In the countryside, newly prosperous rural families invested heavily in residential building,[58] and in the cities, the government and local enterprises poured money into urban housing construction on a scale not seen since the early 1950s.[59] The rate of growth was extraordinary. Between 1978 and 1987 per capita living space doubled,[60] average household size dropped,[61] and the number of households rose at a faster rate than the general population.[62] Did these macro-level changes reduce the predominance of multi-generation living among the old?

Initial documentary and survey data indicated that the housing boom of the 1980s had no major impact on the household arrangements of the old. A 1987 national census reported that 18.5 percent of *all* households included three or more generations, and that only 5.5 percent were composed of one person living alone.[63] In the same year a national survey focused exclusively on people sixty and older found that 82 percent of all elderly lived with at least one child, and throughout the country the most common arrangement was a five-person, three-generation household.[64] As in the 1970s, the rate of joint living was highest in rural areas. Only 1.9 percent of rural elderly lived alone, and 7.5 percent lived only with a spouse.[65] In urban areas, by contrast, 5.2 percent lived alone and 20.9 percent lived only with their spouse.[66]

This is not to conclude that the economic improvements of the 1980s and the greater opportunities for migration had no impact. From a range of sources, it appears that in rural areas, despite the clear overall preponderance of multi-generation living, there was a new tendency among the most affluent "young old" to create separate homes for their sons immediately after marriage.[67] These parents seemed to be responding to the sudden reduction in barriers to home construction, and to be pushing for an early division of the household in order to lay claim to land and put up new houses before policies changed or income fell. There was, however, a clear pattern of regional difference. For example, in some suburban areas the likelihood of elderly living jointly with their adult children noticeably declined during the 1980s, and in some areas multi-generation households were even more common in the cities than in the surrounding countryside.[68] In more remote areas, by contrast, where farmers grew rich by creating large family enterprises rather than dispersing members to work outside the village, it appeared that affluent households had become larger and more extended.[69]

Thus as China entered the 1990s, one saw clear evidence of parallels with Taiwan, where Myron Cohen observed that in labor-intense tobacco-growing areas households were large and complex, while in nearby rice-growing areas family division occurred early in the life cycle and households were smaller and less extended.[70] Or as L. S. Sung put it so well in a study of family division and inheritance practices that was contemporaneous with Cohen's: "[Taiwan] family patterns are more strongly affected by how families obtain their property than by whether they are rich or poor."[71]

In post-Mao China, even in areas where nuclear families have increased, Chinese surveys have explicitly noted that the preferred living arrangement for frail rural elderly continues to be a home shared with an adult child.[72] Thus what appears to have changed for rural families after 1979 is the timing of co-residence, not its desirability. Previously migration controls and housing shortages forced rural parents to house at least one adult son and his family. In the 1980s if parents could manage without a co-resident son, they encouraged him to work outside the village or to build a new home in the same village. Both generations assumed, however, that when the elderly parent was no longer self-sufficient, the two households would merge, with a son and daughter-in-law returning to live with the elderly parents while their own newly married son and his wife established a separate household in the house they left. Moreover, it should be emphasized that based on the 1987 national survey, nuclear households continued to be rare among rural elderly, and that by far the most typical pattern was a home shared with a married son, his wife, and their children.

In urban areas, as noted above, elderly were slightly less likely to live jointly with children.[73] However, overall housing shortages[74] and police controls over household registrations continued to favor multi-generation living for the majority of old people in the cities.[75] Moreover, even during the housing boom of the 1980s, apartments continued to be allocated primarily on the basis of seniority, and therefore middle-aged parents with several children, not newly married couples, were given priority for new housing.[76] As a result, the situation of Li Fulan, who had housed each married son in turn, appeared to be as common in 1987 as in 1979, and adult children often remained dependents in their parents' homes until well into their thirties.[77] In general, housing bureaus and real estate offices expected elderly parents to live with at least one child, urban children continued to look to their parents to solve their housing needs, and high levels of co-residence persisted even as per capita wealth increased.

Housing shortages and administrative constraints, however, were not the only barriers to one-generation households among the urban elderly. Long-term demographic trends also prevented rapid "nuclearization" of urban households. High birth rates in the 1950s and falling mortality rates in all decades after 1949 created denser networks of kin than had been available in earlier decades. For example, in the early 1950s, many brides and grooms had a widowed parent, a minority came from families with more than one surviving adult son, and it was most unusual for all four grandparents to survive to the birth of the first grandchild.[78] By the 1980s, survivorship rates had so drastically improved that a young couple who planned a marriage without both sets of parents was rare.[79] Most elderly parents had several surviving adult children, and most urban primary school students had two surviving grandparents.[80] Moreover, given the improved life expectancies among adults as well as children, there was a high probability that once created, multi-generation homes would not soon be dissolved by an elderly parent's death.

Another demographic trend of the 1980s that sustained joint living in urban areas was the success of the campaign for the one-child family. Begun in 1979, the campaign had been so effective in large cities[81] that there was less pressure on multi-generation households to split after the birth of grandchildren than had been the case in the 1950s or even the 1970s. Among the families I visited in Shanghai (1987) and Wuhan (1988), the most typical families included a couple in their early sixties, a married son and daughter-in-law in their early thirties, and one preschool grandchild.[82] The standard living arrangement in these families was for the newly married pair to be given one room in the parents' two-room apartment. The young couple would decorate the space as their own, often keeping their television and refrigerator at their bedside.[83] After the birth of their child the baby slept with them, but within three years or less, the child began sleeping with the grandparents and the young couple again had a room to themselves. Thus even though my respondents in Shanghai and Wuhan often expressed a desire for the young couple to have their own place, those single-child couples who had their own room appeared to feel no urgency about moving, and in the eyes of others (for example, my research assistant) such young couples had already achieved an adequate degree of privacy and independence.[84] Moreover, when I asked either generation to predict arrangements for the next decade, when older parents would be in their seventies, virtually all agreed that the elderly would certainly not live alone. To both young and old, the prospect of a frail parent living alone was a forlorn and lonely (gu du) arrangement that seemed almost inhumane. And in cases where the mother or father had already been widowed, the current arrangement had taken on a rather permanent character, with neither generation exploring alternative arrangements.

Relations between Elderly and Their Adult Children

Materials collected on elderly and their families in the 1970s consistently documented high levels of interdependence across the life cycle. Young and old were bound together by a morality of lifetime reciprocity and by material constraints that penalized those without family supports. Loyalties to kin systematically prevailed over those to peers, and once a man and woman had become parents, it was unlikely that they would ever live for any extended time without a child or grandchild in their home.

Interview and documentary materials also made it clear, however, that rural and urban elderly evaluated these high levels of interdependence differently. Rural elderly viewed joint living as essential to economic survival, and even as a strategy for individual and family advancement. They also consistently favored patrilineal loyalties. By contrast the urban elderly viewed joint living as a coping strategy, and attachments to their adult children were more emotional than economic. Urban families also were characterized by bilateral loyalties, with elderly parents often as intensely involved with daughters as with sons.

One explanation for these fundamental differences between urban and rural family relations lay in the more restricted economic functions of urban families. Urban parents and their adult children emphasized emotional ties and disregarded the greater earning power of a son because the communist revolution had provided pensions and made individual members more economically self-sufficient. Urban families were neither basic units of production nor the providers of essential welfare services.

In addition, political and economic power in the cities did not flow through the traditional channels of patrilineal kin groups. Authority relations within factories might be "neo-traditional" and paternalistic,[85] but they were rarely based on actual blood ties. In a city factory or government office, it would be rare for a man to find everyone in his shop a first or second cousin, for his father to be his foreman and his uncle the head of the factory. In a village, such a total overlap between work place and family was the norm.[86] Strong ties between male kin provided access to village power, for which a daughter and her offspring provided no viable substitute. Little wonder, then, that rural parents looked so one-sidedly to sons for support and protection in old age.

Published discussions of family relations after the death of Mao indicate that the patterns described above persisted into the 1980s. Ties between elderly parents and their children remained strong.[87] Rural elderly continued to favor patrilateral loyalties, while urban elderly were more likely to observe conventions of bilateral kinship. However, when I compared the materials I gathered in Shanghai and Wuhan in the late 1980s with those from my 1979 interviews, I discovered that despite the social and economic incentives for strong parent-daughter ties after marriage, only 20 percent of the joint families in my sample contained a married daughter.[88] In fact, the percentage of parents living with a daughter and son-in-law had been higher among the 1979 urban respondents.[89] Nor was this apparent bias against daughters in the 1987 and 1988 interview materials easily explained by the supports for bilateral ties I cited in Chapter 3.

Urban brides of the 1980s still faced no barriers comparable to that of village exogamy; in fact the norm was for bride and groom to have parents living in the same town or city. Young urban men also had more opportunities than their rural counterparts to develop strong peer relations that could rival the ties between a son and his parents. And perhaps most important, urban parents exercised only moderate control over a son's or daughter's choice of spouse.[90] How, then, can we account for the pronounced tendency for young urban couples to join the home of the groom's parents? And what are the implications of this pattern for understanding the character of the ties between urban elderly and their adult children?[91]

By comparing how different cohorts within the families of my 1987 and 1988 interviewees have benefited from the economic and political reforms of the Deng era, the persistence — even resurgence — of the traditional patrilocal households becomes more understandable. Between 1978 and 1988, city residents experienced a dramatic improvement in their standard of living. Urban wages nearly tripled, rationing of most foodstuffs disappeared, and color televisions and refrigerators — items that had previously been scarce luxuries — became almost commonplace.[92] And what did this new affluence mean for family life? Most immediately it unleashed a consumer revolution that dramatically redefined the external markings of social status. After 1980, status came increasingly to be defined in terms of material possessions: the quality of home furnishings, possession of a digital watch or a steady supply of imported cigarettes. In most of the families I visited, older members were less obviously affected by these indicators of wealth and status, but in decisions revolving around preparations for a wedding — an area of particular importance for understanding intergenerational relations — middle-aged and newly retired parents were as vulnerable as the young. A big banquet, a large trousseau, and a complete bedroom set were the minimum purchases necessary for a socially acceptable wedding. Anything less not only made the family lose face, it also could cause the children to claim parental selfishness or neglect, and thus justify their distancing themselves from parents and filial obligations.[93]

During the 1970s government media featured ideal young couples who celebrated their marriages with a simple tea party and began married life with a trousseau consisting of a new winter jacket, two quilts, and a thermos bottle. In practice, urban weddings of the 1970s typically had involved a family feast, and brides expected several sets of new clothes, basic home furnishings, and when possible a new bicycle or wristwatch. For the groom and his family, average expenditures for these items totalled three to five months' income, and for the bride and her parents only somewhat less.[94] But a family's reputation did not absolutely demand an expensive wedding, and it was possible (and of course politically correct) to marry with not much more than a new set of bedding, a table, and two chairs. A young couple could, therefore, start married life without any financial obligations or debts to their parents.

The greater affluence as well as the influx of a whole new range of consumer goods and appliances virtually eliminated the option of a simple wedding. Average expenses doubled, and then tripled, during the first years after Mao's death, and by the mid-1980s an average urban wedding cost 5,000–6,000 *yuan*.[95] With a monthly salary of 100–120 *yuan*, few young workers or staff members could hope to accumulate savings of this size. Thus, in order to cover the cost of such new necessities as a restaurant banquet, television, refrigerator, washing machine, and electric fan, young couples turned to their families, and in doing so they entered their married lives more dependent on their parents than had been true for earlier generations.

The parents in my 1987 and 1988 surveys grew up during the Japanese war, and were the young adults who had created the industrial growth of the First Five Year Plan. Almost half had been born in villages or small towns and migrated to the city as teenagers or young adults. In the Wuhan sample many of the men had come to the city via army service. In Shanghai the primary route had been apprenticeships in shops and textile mills, or day jobs as rickshaw pullers. Later in life a very high number joined the CCP,[96] and by retirement they occupied the middle levels of factory or office leadership. Thus although by virtue of their current CCP membership and seniority on the job, they represented the upper reaches of the working class and the middle strata of white-collar workers, only a minority began their lives in such comfort and security.

Their children, the young adults in my sample, had led very different lives. They were almost all born in the cities where they now lived. Except for those sent to the countryside after junior high school, none had begun work before age eighteen. Parents had played a critical role in securing their current urban job, and in many cases parents and children had the same employer. In the Shanghai sample 47 percent of families had at least one child in the same unit as a parent; in the Wuhan sample it was 89 percent. Whereas by age thirty-five their parents were financially responsible for three or four small children, as well as for an aging parent, these adult children could barely support themselves, and many still received regular help from their mothers and fathers.

In light of the exponential growth in the cost of an acceptable wedding and the high levels of dependency on parents among this generation of young urbanites, it is not surprising that parents frequently expanded their home to include the spouse of a newly married child. The question, however, remains, why did they more frequently welcome a daughter-in-law than a son-in-law?

If I were to adopt my respondents' replies to this question, the answer would be simple: "Because a man would lose face if he moved into his wife's house. He would have no status or power." In short, what these urban residents emphasized was that Chinese culture is patriarchal, and discriminates against females. But this answer, while true and relevant, does not explain why affluence and greater consumerism has strengthened these traditional patrilineal preferences, or why these biases might be more decisive for shaping living arrangements of the elderly in the 1980s than in the 1970s. However, if we place the explosion of consumerism and the prolonged dependency of urban youth in the larger framework of the post-Mao political and economic reforms, a causal link emerges.

The Deng reforms championed decollectivization, privatization, and depoliticization. In essence, the 1980s witnessed a retreat of the party-state and the emergence of a nascent civil society. For men and women in their fifties and sixties, reduction of state control over private life allowed them to express and realize traditional family values that the more intrusive Maoist regime had effectively censored. Moreover, in the Deng years there was also a retreat from earlier efforts to reduce gender differences in wages and job opportunities. As a result young women were again openly discriminated against during initial job assignments and subsequent promotions.[97] Given these constraints on a daughter's career and earning potential, it became rational to value a son's financial contribution more highly than a daughter's.

Depoliticization of urban job assignments also permitted higher returns on education and professional training;[98] indirectly, this shift reduced the value of a daughter's help. In the 1970s the job assignment procedures for young urbanites usually ignored educational credentials.[99] In some years all secondary school graduates regardless of training would be sent to the countryside; in other years only those with an older sibling already working in a village or state farm could be assigned a city job. Sometimes families could keep a child at home on the grounds that the elderly parent needed care. Where the parent was relatively young and in good health, the family would try to argue that the new graduate was too physically frail to withstand the rigors of rural life. Parents worked energetically to protect the interests of whichever child — son or daughter — was scheduled for a job assignment that year. In this environment, parents with several teenagers could not predict which one would ultimately be the best source of support in the future, or even which one would be allowed to live in the same city as the parents. Therefore, many parents were as intensely involved with their daughters' futures as their sons', and exclusively patrilateral strategies were discarded. The capricious system of job allocation and the massive outmigration of secondary and university graduates to manual jobs in the countryside depressed career prospects of both sons and daughters. But because males had historically been the primary candidates for leadership positions and high salaries, the labor policies of the Cultural Revolution years created greater relative losses for males. In the 1980s, therefore, when job assignments more predictably rewarded credentials for males and discriminated against females, parents quite rationally expected more material gains by living jointly with a son than with a daughter.

The depoliticization of work increased patrilateral biases in a third way. During the years when political connections, or merely a good class label, were a primary determinant of security and social position, daughters were as valuable as sons. In fact, as we saw in Chapter 6, in families where a political stigma had created especially severe discrimination or tension, daughters could offer more reliable support because women's work was not as politicized and therefore the regime did not police matrilateral ties as closely as patrilateral ones. Under these circumstances, affinal ties had great importance, and it made sense for some families deliberately to develop a matrilocal household. In the more depoliticized atmosphere of the 1980s, political blemishes no longer so directly determined family wealth and status. Daughters lost their previous comparative advantage, and elderly parents and young adults would tell a curious foreigner, "It is shameful for a man to move to his wife's home."

As in the 1970s, material scarcities were the most immediate determinants of urban living arrangements. Housing shortages denied many newlyweds the neolocal home they desired. Shortages of social services and the diminishing purchasing power of fixed incomes encouraged aging parents to construct households that included those younger members who were most likely to provide long-term financial and emotional security. Daughters faced the same housing crisis as sons; in fact, because many units provided housing for male workers before female workers, the needs of daughters could be greater.[100] Daughters were also as reliable a source of care as a son and daughter-in-law. Thus while necessity and external constraints explain why high percentages of urban elderly lived with one or more married children, cultural preferences and discrimination against women explain the bias in favor of sons.

Intergenerational Conflict and the New Inheritance Law

Among the elderly men and women I interviewed in the 1970s, family harmony was highly valued, and failure to maintain good relations with at least one adult child was a source of personal grief and public shame.

Aware of their future need for supportive children, elderly parents usually curbed their anger toward a recalcitrant child or quarrelsome in-law, and in most cases it was the elderly parent—especially the financially dependent mother—who sought accommodation and reconciliation. Parents with a bad class background were more often abandoned than children who had made political mistakes, and remarried widows, not divorced daughters, were likely to precipitate premature family division. The exceptions to this pattern of deference to the young were: the CCP patriarch whose political connections were superior to those of his children; the unusual rural widow like Song Meihua, who had strong relations to city daughters; or the uncommon family like that of Feng Dao, where the class background of the young wife was markedly inferior to that of the unemployed mother-in-law. In most families elderly parents were ordinary workers or peasants without political power. They had few resources with which to control their children, and thus as their influence over adult children waned, they adjusted to a subordinate position within the family and strove to maintain their children's solicitude and respect.[101]

After 1985, however, the passage of the PRC's first Inheritance Law introduced the potential for different calculations by both parents and children.[102] By specifying the rights of those who previously had been most vulnerable—widowed daughters-in-law or elderly parents with poor relations with their sons—the Inheritance Law theoretically empowered the previously weakest members of the household and thereby potentially altered typical expressions of family conflict. According to the 1985 Law, surviving spouses were guaranteed half of all property that had accumulated during the marriage (Article 26) and sons (or their widowed wives) and daughters were to divide the remaining half into equal shares. (Article 9). In critical areas, however, the Law was ambiguous on how these principles would be realized. For example, Article 13 stated that shares of an estate inherited by heirs of equal rank "generally should" (*yi ban ying dang*) be equal. However, those who had lived with the deceased or had fulfilled principal obligations "might" (*ke yi*) get a larger share, while those who could have helped but did not, "should get nothing or get a smaller portion" (*ying dang bu fen huo zhe shao fen*).[103] In three confusingly overlapping sections, the law supported equality between males and females (Article 9) and identified daughters as primary statutory heirs (Article 10), but then explained in detail how parents could use wills to disinherit statutory heirs or leave property to the state, a collective, or a person other than a child (Article 16).

In any circumstance such a strong legal endorsement of parental prerogative would have marked a clear departure from the customary practices of the 1970s, where the primary object of value—usually the house in which the parents lived—was passed on to the co-resident son, often during the parent's life. But in the context of the return of family farming and legalization of private trade, the law appeared to create an especially clear break with past practice. Theoretically elderly parents, even if they were no longer major contributors to the family budget, could now control their children through threats of disinheritance. They also could play siblings off against one another, or use threats to leave all the property to the state as a means of controlling or punishing an overly independent child or in-law.

Based on summary statistical data and on a review of inheritance disputes described in Chinese legal journals[104] and the *Bulletin of the Supreme People's Court*, however, it appears that during the first few years after the passage of the Inheritance Law, elderly parents did not treat the law as license to exercise greater control over adult children. In 1986 and 1987, inheritance disputes represented less than 4 percent of all formally mediated disputes,[105] and in 1987 there were 20,000 fewer such disputes than in 1986.[106] Most telling, the number of wills notarized fell from 11,200 in 1986 to 10,968 in 1987.[107] To the extent that the law altered family behavior, it appeared primarily to heighten conflict between siblings in atypical families where parents had been married more than once, or where some of the heirs were adopted, foster, or step children. For the elderly, the new law had had no obvious immediate negative impact on parent-child ties, and there was no sudden upsurge in the overall level of intergenerational conflict.[108]

Nevertheless, analysis of those few families where disputes did become public was revealing because although these families had atypical relationships, the need to divide joint households or distribute parental possessions was a universal problem. The ambiguity of the 1985 Inheritance Law affected all citizens, and thus the cumulative record of court decisions, particularly as they emerged in consecutive issues of the *Bulletin of the Supreme People's Court*, spoke directly both to the position of the CCP toward family autonomy and to the potential of individuals using the courts to challenge the weight of family custom.

Between 1985 and 1988, the *Bulletin of the Supreme People's Court* published eleven cases or Supreme Court instructions (*pi fu*) that involved inheritance disputes. In some cases the Court specified the grounds for reversing or affirming a lower court decision; in other cases the decision of a lower court was simply reprinted. However, by virtue of being chosen for publication in the main bulletin of the highest court, these cases articulated the goals of the CCP leadership at that time and effectively created precedents against which lower courts would make future decisions.[109]

In general, a review of these eleven cases documents strong continuity with the practices of the 1970s. The court affirmed that children owed care to parents in return for care they had received in childhood and also that children should inherit in proportion to the care they had given their parents.[110] In short, the court articulated the same guiding principle for inheritance of a parent's property as one of my 1976 respondents: "The one that fed them [the parents] is the one that gets it [the house, the furniture, and personal belongings]." Thus despite explicit legal backing for statutory heirs to inherit on the basis of blood ties and for equal division between sons and daughters, the Supreme Court stood behind the traditional morality of "concrete" reciprocity. And given the overwhelming tendency for parents to live with sons and not daughters, such a position meant that patriarchal inheritance practices continued to be the norm.[111]

Between 1980 and 1985, journal articles discussing principles for division of family property frequently cited Article 18 of the 1980 Marriage Law to justify division of property in proportion of care.[112] What such logic indicated was that the CCP granted the greatest claim to those who had given the most care, and in practice this meant that co-residence determined distribution of parental wealth. Based on the published debates in the legal magazines and the Supreme Court *Bulletin*, it also appears that even after 1985, the party continued to favor these traditional mores, which one Chinese commentator so aptly summarized as a concept of equal inheritance where "equal rights do not necessitate equal shares" (*tong deng quan li bu deng yu shi ping jun fen pei*).[113] For China's elderly, the consequence of these assumptions about a just division of property was a continuity with the Maoist era even as the leadership rapidly dismantled core institutions of the collective economy and rhetorically championed the rights of the individual.

Conclusion

In China since 1949, policies toward the family have been inconsistent, and CCP power has not unilaterally dictated the behavior of family members. For example, throughout the post-1949 era the official media often attacked exclusive family loyalties on the grounds that they deflected the energies of citizens away from a commitment to public responsibilities. Yet in order to minimize expenditures on welfare, keep pension programs in line with current rates of productivity, and reduce the demand for new housing, many welfare policies were predicated on the continuation of the very same particularistic loyalties that the CCP ideologically opposed. Therefore, even after the government created material and legal parameters that constrained the range of probable family relationships, it simultaneously continued to need autonomous families to provide goods and services that were too expensive for the government to supply directly. As a result, throughout the post-1949 decades the majority of Chinese parents knew that to guarantee security and care in old age, they had no viable alternative but to rely on their children, and from childhood on, mothers and fathers prepared their children for a lifetime of mutal dependency and reciprocity.

In general the boundaries between public and private responsibilities were well defined, and although the state's power and coercive potential made it the ultimate arbiter, for most of the post-1949 era the division of authority between the state and the family was complementary rather than antagonistic. Yet for individual men and women moving between the public world of work and the private world of family, there were both tensions and contradictions. As Max Horkheimer has taught us,[114] families as the locus of primary care and early socialization inculcate the private attachments and morality of earlier generations. When the young person leaves home first for school, then for work, the morality of the family is frequently at odds with that of the workplace, and the individual must learn to live a double life or jettison one morality in favor of the other. The contradiction can be especially acute in societies where the government seeks to eliminate dissent and nonconformity. In the case of China, however, the CCP, except during its most collectivist and totalistic phases, rejected both the destruction of family functions and the obliteration of traditional family morality.

CCP tolerance of family loyalties has been especially pronounced in matters relating to the elderly. Unable to finance a national pension system, unable even to fund fully the care of the minority of needy elderly living in the cities, the state encouraged and legitimated loyalties rooted in a precommunist past. While seeking to eliminate values and ambitions that sabotaged the collective economy or loyalty to an authoritarian state, CCP cadres simultaneously legitimated traditional obligations of mutual support and long-term reciprocal care. Sons who refused to support elderly parents could be taken to court to have support payments deducted directly from their monthly salary. Ancestor rituals were maligned and temples dismantled, but the most progressive labor regulations granted the rare privilege of paid vacation days to those returning home from a parent's funeral. Even where elderly had no immediate family, the government stepped in reluctantly, advocating whenever possible that childless elderly rely on networks of fictive kin.

Despite the potential for these strong private commitments to create conflicting demands, the contradictions that Horkheimer identified between private values and contemporary public mores failed to emerge as a divisive social force in matters related to care and respect for the old. Rather, in the PRC, filial behavior served the state as well as the individual, and past and present definitions of family obligations effectively merged. Like their imperial predecessors, CCP leaders found Confucian familism to be a powerful force in service to the state and the social order. In the context of socialist ideology and the reality of persistent scarcities, traditional ideals supportive of intergenerational solidarity survived, and were reproduced in succeeding generations. Chinese elderly have benefited from a basic continuity between the pre- and post-1949 definitions of filial behavior, and the communist revolution has had consequences for family life that the original CCP architects neither expected nor planned.

The following abbreviations are used in the Notes. Complete publication data on sources other than newspapers and journals are given in the Select Bibliography, pp. 171–174.

BR	*Beijing Review*
CL	*Chinese Literature*
FBIS	Foreign Broadcast Information Service
GRRB	*Gong ren ri bao (Workers' Daily)*
GWYGB	*Guo wu yuan gong bao (Bulletin of the State Council)*
JPRS	Joint Publications Research Service
KTSH	*Kan tu shuo hua* (Look at the pictures and tell a story)
NCNA	New China News Agency
PR	*Peking Review*
RMRB	*Ren min ri bao (People's Daily)*
SCMP	Survey of the China Mainland Press
ZGTJNJ	*Zhong guo tong ji nian jian* (Chinese Statistical Yearbook)

NOTES

Introduction

1. Irving Rosow, *Socialization to Old Age* (Berkeley: University of California Press, 1974), pp. 3–7; Ernest W. Burgess, *Aging in Western Societies* (Chicago: University of Chicago Press, 1960), p. 17; Simone de Beauvoir, *The Coming of Age* (New York: Warner Communications Co., 1973), pp. 16–20, 130–131,409–411; Joseph Britton and Jean O. Britton, "The Middle Aged and Older Rural Person and His Family," in *Older Rural Americans*, ed. E. Grant Youmans (Lexington: University of Kentucky Press, 1967), p. 46; Arlie Russell Hochschild, *The Unexpected Community* (Englewood Cliffs: Prentice Hall, 1973), p. 20; Donald O. Cowgill and Lowell D. Holmes, *Aging and Modernization* (New York: Appleton-Century-Crofts, 1972), pp. 9–10. Subsequent comparisons of the position of the elderly in developed and developing nations document a curvilinear relationship between modernization and the status of the old. That is, during the period of rapid change from a preindustrial to an industrial society the relative position of the old declines, but when a society reaches the economic standards of an advanced industrial or postindustrial country such as the United States or England, the position of the old steadily improves. Erdman Palmore and Kenneth Marston, "Modernization and Status of the Aged: International Correlations," *Journal of Gerontology* 29. 2 (1974): 205–210.

2. Albert P. Blaustein, ed., *Fundamental Legal Documents of Communist China* (South Hackensack, N.J.: Rothman, 1962), pp. 334–354.

3. Prior to 1981, 80 percent of the population was frequently presumed to live in rural areas. More recent Chinese sources that define urban areas as those with populations exceeding 30,000 indicate that the rural population is almost 87 percent of the total. Sun Jingzhi, "Guang yu zhong guo ren kou fen bu wen ti" (Concerning the distribution of the Chinese population), *Ren Kou Yen Jiou* 2 (1982): 10–12; Review of *China's Population,* in *Beijing Review* (hereafter *BR*) 44 (Nov. 2, 1981): 30–31.

4. "Caring for Middle-Aged Intellectuals," *BR* 33 (Aug. 16, 1982), p. 5, gives age 56 as the onset of old age. The age spread for the active workforce is elsewhere given as 16–59 for men and 16–54 for women. Wong Weizhi, "Dui wo guo jie fang hou ren kou nian ling jie gou de chu bu fen xie" (A preliminary analysis of the age structure of China's population since Liberation), *Ren You Yen Jiou* 4 (1981): 7–11.

5. John S. Aird, "Population Growth in the People's Republic of China," in *Chinese Economy: Post-Mao,* U.S. Congress Joint Economic Committee (Washington: U.S. Government Printing Office, 1978), p. 469. Nathan Keyfitz, "Popula-

tion and Employment in China," Working paper of the International Institute for Applied Systems Analysis A-2361 (Laxenburg, Austria, February 1982), p. 15, gives higher 1980 estimates of 160 million, 86.5 million, and 57.8 million for those over 49, 59, and 64 years respectively.

6. John S. Aird, "Recent Demographic Data from China: Problems and Prospects," in *China Under the Four Modernizations: Part I*, U.S. Congress Joint Economic Committee (Washington: Government Printing Office, 1982), p. 182.

7. In 1975 citizens 65 years and older were 4 percent of the total Chinese population. Estimates for 2000 vary between 6 percent and 7.6 percent depending on higher or lower fertility rates in the intervening 25 years. The respective averages for all of Latin America are 3.8 percent and 4.4–4.8 percent, for Asia 3.4 percent and 4.8–5.4 percent, and for Africa 2.9 and 3.2–3.5 percent. Jacob Siegal, "Demographic Background for International Gerontological Studies," Paper prepared for XIth International Conference of Gerontology, Tokyo, Japan, Aug. 20–25, 1978.

8. The gender, age, and emigrant status in Hong Kong, of the 29 Hong Kong respondents are:

	Men		Women	
Age	Legal	Illegal	Legal	Illegal
under 30	1	5	1	1
30–54	5	5	5	2
over 54	3	0	1	0
Totals	9	10	7	3

The gender, age, and type of interview sponsorship of the 88 PRC respondents are:

	Men		Women	
Age	Official	Unofficial	Official	Unofficial
under 30	1	0	1	1
30–54	5	3	4	5
over 54	30	4	29	5
Totals	36	7	34	11

9. In the summer of 1979 under the auspices of the Chinese Academy of Social Sciences, I paid halfday visits to Nan Yuan Commune on the outskirts of Beijing; Ninth Street Brigade on the outskirts of the county seat of Shu Lu County, Hebei Province; Tian Family Brigade 10 kilometers outside of the same county seat; and Hua Xi Brigade in Jiangsu Province. During the same visit I paid three one-hour visits to Beijing Textile Mill No. 3, Beijing Small Electric Machine Factory, Beijing Instrument Factory, Wuxi Clay Figurine Factory, Changzhou Railcar and Locomotive Factory, Nanjing Light Machine Tool Factory, Nan Jing (Panda) Radio Factory, and Shijiachuang No. 1 Textile Mill. In Shijiachuang I visited the Hebei Province No. 1 Hospital, in Nanjing the Medical College Hospital, and in Beijing Hospital No. 1. The old-age and convalescent homes visited were the Nan Yuan Commune Old-Age Home; Tian Family Brigade Old-Age Home; Guang Rong Home for Dependents of Revolutionary Martyrs and Servicemen in Jing Xing County, Hebei Province; Convalescent Home for Tangshan

Earthquake Paraplegics in Pu County, Hebei Province; Shijiachuang City Old-Age Home; Retirement Village for Retired Party Cadres in Zheng Ding City, Hebei Province; and Jiangsu Province Workers Sanatorium on Lake Taihu, Wuxi City, Jiangsu Province.

1. Attitudes Toward the Elderly

1. Chang Yu-chen, "Going into Battle," *Chinese Literature* (hereafter *CL*) 9 (1976):63.

2. See e.g. "Hong guan jia" (A red official home), *Guang Ming Ri Bao*, Mar. 9, 1970, p.2; "Dang guan, bu xiang guan" (An official who does not behave as one), *Ren Min Ri Bao* (hereafter *RMRB*), May 16, 1970, p. 2; *Xin Hua* (Guangzhou), no. 6174, May 15, 1971; "The Iron Man of Taching," *Peking Review* (hereafter *PR*), 47 (1971):10–11; *Xin Hua* (Guangzhou), no. 6528, July 5, 1972; Sui Hung-tzu, "A Lumber Dispatcher," *CL* 2 (1973):63–69; "Kuang shan gong ren zai pi lin pi kong" (Miners in the Anti-Lin/Anti-Confucius Campaign), *RMRB*, Feb. 10, 1974, p.1; "Wang Daxue de gu shih" (The story of Wang Daxue), *Guang Ming Ri Bao*, Dec. 19, 1974, p. 3; Hao Jan, "A Sea of Happiness," *CL* 1 (1975): 20, 38; "Revolutionary Grandmother Still Young in Spirit," *PR* 34 (Aug. 22, 1975): 11; "Management Is Good," *People's Daily* June 9, 1976, trans. in *China Mainland Press—Survey of PRC Press* (hereafter *CMP*) 76-31 (1976): I62–64; "Carry Forward the Revolutionary Traditions," Kwangtung provincial radio, Sept. 9, 1976, trans. in *Foreign Broadcast Information Service—China* (hereafter *FBIS*), no. 76-178, p. 47; Zhang Chengzhu, "Za men de da lao wei" (Our Old Mr. Wei), *Ren Min Wen Xue* 9 (1976): 91–93; "Down with Everything," *PR* 13 (1977): 14; "Sketches," *CL* 4 (1977): 36–66; "Taching Impressions," *PR* 21 (1977):20–24; Xiao Yuxuan, "Xi wang" (Hope), *Ren Min Wen Xue* 6 (1977): 38–55; "Chang Chung-liang," *China Pictorial* 7 (1977): 44; "Jan Ta-Ku," *PR* 11 (1978): 38; Kang Ke-Ching, "Women Revolutionaries I Have Known," *China Reconstructs* 27. 5 (May 1978): 19–22.

3. "The Demon of Demolition," *CL* 11 (1971):23–48; "Guo Xiao Yang," *RMRB*, Nov. 28, 1973, p. 1; Yueh Wen, "The Cave Hospital," *CL* 7 (1977): 45; Hsu KuangYao, "Sun Flower," *CL* 9 (1977): 10–27; "True Story of Heroism," *PR* 2 (1978): 26.

4. "Bao Bao Xue shuo hua" (Bao Bao learns to talk) *Kan Tu Shuo Hua* (hereafter *KTSH*), no. 5 (1982); "Chun Fung," *KTSH*, no. 4 (1982); "Hao Mao Mao" (Good Mao Mao), *KTSH*, no. 1 (1982); "Gai Shuo Shen Me" (What should we say), *KTSH*, no. 7 (1981); "Yu Tian" (A rainy day), *KTSH*, no. 8 (1981); "Huan Li" (Good manners), *KTSH*, no. 9 (1981).

5. See e.g. two magazines for this age group, *Xiao Peng You* and *Er Tong Shih Dai*, and four books for school-age children: Ke Yen, *Wo de yeh yeh* (My Grandpa) (Tianjin: Ren Min Chu Ban She, n.d.); Shen Qiaosheng, *Chang Qing Song* (Shanghai: Ren Min Mei Shu Chu Ban She, 1979); Yang Mo, *Zai Yen Xiao de Da Di Shang* (Above the smoldering plain) (Tianjin: Ren Min Mei Shu Chu Ban She, 1978); Lu Ping, *Yin Hai Zhi Ge* (The song of the silver sea) (Shanghai: Ren Min Mei Shu Chu Ban She, 1978).

6. Chou Yuan, "Tong Ling Lao Die" (Grandpa Brass Bell), *Shao Nian Wen Yi* 7 (1980): 19–29.

7. See e.g. the old concubine in *Zheng Duo* (To seize through fierce struggle) (Shanghai: Ren Min Chu Ban She, 1975), p. 12; old landlord in *Xin lai de xiao shu zhu* (The newly arrived young mainstay) (Beijing: Ren Min Ti Yu Chu Ban, 1976); old speculator in Yao Zhing-li, *Hong se xiao shan dian* (The little red shop)

(Shanghai: Ren Min Mei Shu Chu Ban She, 1976); old doctor in *Li Mei* (Beijing: Ren Min Mei Shu Chu Ban She, 1976); old landlord's son in Yang Hsiao, *Making of a Peasant Doctor* (Peking Foreign Language Press, 1976); old peddler in *Xiang yang yuan de gu shih* (Stories from a sunshine courtyard) (Beijing: Ren Min Mei Shu Chu Ban She, 1976); former wife of capitalist in "Xi Yang xin gu shih" (New Stories of Xi Yang), *Lian Huan Hua Bao* 1.2 (1977): 46–53; old speculator in Lin Guiyang, "Er jin Feng Huan cun" (Second visit to Phoenix village), *Lian Huan Hua Bao* 7 (1977): 25–32; old landlord peddler in He Yi, *Liu Wenxue* (Shanghai: Xiao Nian Er Tong Chu Ban She, 1979).

8. Merle Goldman, "China's Anti-Confucian Campaign, 1973–1974," *China Quarterly* 63 (Sept. 1975): 435–462.

9. *RMRB*, Dec. 1, 1973, p. 1; Feb. 10, 1974, p. 1; *Guang Ming Ri Bao*, July 9, 1974, trans. in *Survey of the China Mainland Press* (hereafter *SCMP*) 74–31 (July 20–Aug. 2, 1974): 80–84; *New China News Agency* (hereafter *NCNA*), Sept. 21, 1974, trans. in *SCMP* 70–40 (Sept. 30–Oct. 4, 1974): 184–186; *NCNA*, Nov. 2, 1974, trans. in *SCMP* 74–47 (Nov. 18–22, 1974): 22–24.

10. Francis L. K. Hsu, "Chinese Kinship and Chinese Behavior," in *China in Crisis*, ed. P. T. Ho and Tang Tsou, vol. 1, bk. 2 (Chicago: University of Chicago Press, 1968), pp. 587–592; Marion Levy, "Notes on the Hsu Hypotheses," in *Kinship and Culture*, ed. Francis L. K. Hsu (Chicago: Aldine Publishing, 1971), pp. 33–41.

11. Between 1966 and 1976 approximately 20 million urban junior high and senior high students were sent to live in the countryside as part of a national policy to speed up rural development and reduce population pressure in urban areas. *BR* 47 (Nov. 23, 1979): 6–7; "Guo wu yuan zhi qing ling dao xiao zu" (The leading small group on educated youth in the state council) and "Tong Yi Ren Zhi, Zuo Hao Zhi Qing Nian Shang Shan Xia Xiang Gong Zuo" (Develop a unified perspective and do well the work of sending educated youth up to the mountains and down to the countryside), *Hong Qi* 8 (1979): 58–62; Thomas P. Bernstein, *Up to the Mountains and Down to the Villages* (New Haven: Yale University Press, 1977). Chen Ximing is a pseudonym for a man interviewed in Hong Kong in 1976 two months after he illegally left China. He was a former member of the Communist Youth League and local-level cadre who had been deeply involved in the political and economic life of China.

12. Among the elderly described by Hong Kong emigrants, 9 out of 17 rural childless elderly and 2 out of 14 urban childless elderly relied extensively on long-term relationships with nonkin.

13. *The Red Lantern* (Columbo: Afro-Asian Writers Bureau, 1967). See also "Vice Minister Shen Hung: Model Ranking Cadres," *BR* 30 (July 28, 1980): 24–27; "Not a Lonely Old Man," *BR* 51 (Dec. 21, 1979): 28; "A Unique Family," *BR* 35 (Sept. 14, 1979): 26–27; *Da Gong Bao* (Hong Kong), Mar. 20, 1974, p. 3; Huang Shan, "Spring Comes South," *CL* 5 (1972); "On the Home Front," *PR* 27 (July 7, 1978): 46; "On the Home Front," *PR* 16 (Apr. 21, 1978): 30–31.

14. Wu Ruiqing is a pseudonym for an old lady who lived in a village near one of the Hong Kong emigrants when he was a short-term resident and investigative reporter.

2. Work and Retirement

1. James R. Townsend, *The People's Republic of China: A Basic Handbook* (New York: China Council of the Asia Society, 1979), p. 63; Victor D. Lippit, *Land Reform and Economic Development in China* (White Plains: International

Arts and Sciences Press, 1974), Ch. 4; Nicholas Lardy, "China's Economic Readjustment," paper prepared for the China Council of the Asia Society (Washington, D.C.: China Council, 1980); "The Agricultural Development Program," *BR* 12 (Mar. 24, 1980): 14–20; A. Doak Barnett, *China and the World System* (New York: Overseas Development Council, 1979), p. 30; Thomas G. Rawski, *Industrialization, Technology, and Employment in the PRC*, (Washington, D.C.: World Bank, 1978), pp. 93–94.

2. Dennis L. Chinn, "Basic Commodity Distribution in the People's Republic of China," *China Quarterly* 84 (Dec. 1980): 744–754; Nicholas R. Lardy, "Regional Growth and Income Distribution in China," (New Haven: Yale University Economic Growth Center, 1980).

3. E.g. in 1977 and 1979 when rural average per capita income from all sources was 117 yuan and 123 yuan respectively, urban per capita income was approximately 300 and 350 yuan respectively. *Xin Hua*, (Beijing), June 16, 1980, trans. in *FBIS* 117 (June 16, 1980): L4–5; Zhou Min, "Further Economic Readjustment," *BR* 12 (Mar. 23, 1981): 23–25; W. Klatt, "Chinese Statistics Up-dated," *China Quarterly* 84 (Dec. 1980): 739.

4. E.g. in 1980 when the average wage for an urban job in the state sector was 800 yuan, the average return to a full-time male agricultural laborer was under 400 yuan. *BR* 8 (Feb. 23, 1981): 8–9; 20 (May 18, 1981): 20.

5. William L. Parish and Martin King Whyte, *Village and Family in Contemporary China* (Chicago: The University of Chicago Press, 1978), pp. 30–35; Frederick W. Crook, "The Commune System in the People's Republic of China, 1963–1974," in *China: A Reassessment of the Economy*, papers submitted to the Joint Economic Committee, Congress of the United States, July 10, 1975, pp. 394–402. After the return of Deng Xiaoping in 1978, Chinese leaders began a radical readjustment of the commune system. The move toward higher levels of collectivization that was shifting ownership from teams to brigades was halted and the direction of change was reversed to put even greater responsibility in the hands of subteam units such as small work groups and individual families. Jurgen Domes, "New Policies in the Communes: Notes on Rural Societal Structures in China, 1976–1981," *Journal of Asian Studies* 41. 2 (Feb. 1982): 253–267.

6. John Burns, "The Election of Production Team Cadres in Rural China, 1958–1974," *China Quarterly* 74 (June 1978): 273–296.

7. Through the 1970s between 75 and 80 percent of urban workers were state employees. *BR* 20 (May 19, 1980): 20–24; "Present Economic Policy," *China Reconstructs* 30. 1 (Jan. 1981): 4–8; "Communiqúe on Fulfillment of China's 1980 National Economic Plan," *BR* 20 (May 18, 1981): 20.

8. "Labour Insurance Regulations of the People's Republic of China," trans. in Blaustein, *Fundamental Legal Documents*, pp. 534–554.

9. E.g. the Labour Insurance Regulations only cover the minority of state employees who work in rural areas. Most rural residents rely entirely on the resources of their village and extended families. Deborah Davis-Friedmann, "Welfare Practices in Rural China," *World Development* 6 (May 1978): 609–619.

10. Marion J. Levy, *The Family Revolution in Modern China* (New York: Atheneum, 1968), pp. 253–256; Lin Yueh-hwa, *The Golden Wing* (London: K. Paul, Trench, and Trubner, 1947), p. 130.

11. Among the 164 elderly peasants described in the Hong Kong interviews, only 16 percent of the men (N=11) and 10.6 percent of the women (N=10) did no daily work. For those between 55 and 59 years of age, 94.5 percent of men (N=21) and 66 percent of the women (N=23) worked full time in the collective

work force. For those 60 and older, 42 percent of the men (N=20) continued in the collective work force, 23 percent (N=11) worked halftime in the collective and halftime at home, and 12 percent (N=6) worked full time at home. Among the women 60 and older, 18 percent (N=12) worked full time in the collective, 32 percent (N=23) worked halftime in the collective and halftime at home, and 50 percent (N=35) worked full time at home.

12. *RMRB*, June 2, Sept. 18, Dec. 9, Dec. 15, 1972; Nov. 28, 1973; Jan. 10, 23, 1974; *Zhong Hua Xin Wen*, Oct. 13, 1973; Lin Min, *Red Flag Canal* (Peking: Foreign Languages Press, 1974), pp. 43, 48; *People's Daily*, Nov. 24, 1974, trans. in *SCMP* 75–04, pp. 57–58; *Da Gong Bao* (Xiang gang), June 4, July 5, 1976; Ho Hsiao-lu, "A Detour to Dragon Village," *CL* 12 (1971): 19–28; Yeh Wen, "A New Commune Member," *CL* 12 (1971): 55–61; Hsia Jensheng, "The Bridge," *CL* 12 (1972): 10–14; Hsin Jung, "Red Heart Plums," *CL* 12 (1972): 53–60; Mo Ying-feng, "The Roadside Inn," *CL* 12 (1972): 39–45; Ma Chin, "Selling Pigs," *CL* 3 (1973): 93–98; Chang Lin, "Diligence and Thrift," *CL* 12 (1973): 88–89; Shih Min, "The Breathing of the Sea," *CL* 3 (1973): 55–62; Li Hao, "When Peaches Ripen," *CL* 10 (1973): 79–82; Wang Shu-Yuan, "Notes on Art," *CL* 1 (1974): 114; Hua Tong, "Ye-nan de Zhong Ze" (Yenan seed), in *Shih Xiao Shuo* (A collection of short stories) (Shanghai: Ren Min Chu Ban She, 1974), pp. 153–166; Chao Yen-yi, "A Snowstorm in March," *CL* 1 (1975): 86–93; Yao Hua, "Old Wang of the Storeroom," *CL* 8 (1976): 44.

13. The same pattern in a Fujian brigade during a period in 1976 when work in the collective was stressed. Marina Thorberg, "Chinese Employment Policy 1949–1978 with special Emphasis on Women in Rural Production," in U.S. Congress Joint Economic Committee, *Chinese Economy Post Mao* (Washington, D.C.: Government Printing Office, 1978), p. 595. See also Zhan Wu, "Liao ning sheng jian she fu de hui zhu yi xin nong cun de diao cha bao gao" (Investigative report on Liaoning Province's development of rich and prosperous socialist new villages), *Hong Qi* 6 (1980): 39–44.

14. This story came from an emigrant in Hong Kong one year after she had left the village where Li and Chen lived. She had lived in the village 10 years and had helped the daughter-in-law care for Li and Chen for the five years that their son was away in military service. She knew the family well and had no obvious reason to distort the situation. This case history was one of the richest in detail, but its general outlines were repeated in many other sources.

15. Chen Muhua, "Controlling Population Growth in a Planned Way," *BR* 46 (Nov. 16, 1979): 17–20; "Readers Condemn Unfeeling Sons," *China Reconstructs* 27. 7 (July 1979): 38–39; "News from Harbin," *RMRB*, July 7, 1979, p. 2; *Xin Hua* radio broadcast, July 9, 1979, trans. in *China Report: Political, Sociological and Military*, July 25, 1979, pp. 140–141; *Xin Hua* (Beijing), Feb. 27, 1980, trans. in *FBIS*, Feb. 28, 1980, R 4–5; "The Land and the People," *BR* 18 (May 5, 1980): 28. In 1978 pensions to nonworking rural elderly were not entirely without precedent. Several respondents reported that after 1968 and sometimes as early as 1964 their villages had distributed old-age grain subsidies *(wu lao liang)* to elderly who could not work. These payments varied in proportion to the size of the local harvest and were initiated and managed by teams, not brigades. They were available to both men and women and did not contain the same requirements for twenty years of continuous employment as did the pensions.

16. The Labor Insurance Regulations usually replace 70–75 percent of the last salary, and model workers or former revolutionary fighters can replace 90–100 percent. By contrast, rural disabled or destitute receive a subsistence grain ration

half the size of a full-time worker and a cash payment of 20-30 percent of the rural pension.

17. Chinn, "Basic Commodity Distribution," pp. 745–747; Domes, "New Policy in the Communes," pp. 257–259; Crook, "The Commune System," pp. 394–402.

18. The Dazhai system, named after a small brigade in North China that experimented with a purer form of communism in the late 1960s and early 1970s, eliminated private sector jobs and evaluated the work of all brigade members in terms of their political attitude, past suffering, current need, physical strength, and skill level. It was widely emulated between 1968 and 1970 but soon fell into disuse outside of Dazhai because it could not provide enough incentives for the strongest team and brigade members to push themselves as hard as was necessary to guarantee a good collective harvest. Jan Myrdal and Gun Kessle, *China: The Revolution Continued* (London: Chatto and Windus, 1971), pp. 83–105; Jack Chen, *A Year in Upper Felicity* (New York: MacMillan, 1973); *Qiong Bang zi jing shen fang guang wang* (The Qiong Bang spirit spreads out) (Beijing: Ren Min Chu Ban She, 1975), p. 76.

19. These ratios were calculated by comparing the number of work points assigned grade 2 or grade 3 workers to those assigned grade 1 workers of the same sex. In most time-rate systems, grade 1 men received ten points, grade 2 eight points, and grade 3 five or six. For women it was usually eight, six, and four. When piece rates or skill rates replaced or supplemented time rates, the elderly did not fare as well because they worked more slowly, lost more work days because of illness, and were assigned less valued tasks. Zhan Wu, "Liao Ning Sheng Jian She Fu Du De She Hui Zhu Yi Xin Con" (Liaoning Province sets up prosperous socialism), *Hong Qi* 6 (1980): 39–43; Lei Pui-leung, *Ren Min Gong She* (People's communes) (Hong Kong: Chinese University Press, 1981), ch. 5.

20. Parish and Whyte, *Village and Family*, pp. 56–57, 60, 66, 77, 347; Martin K. Whyte, "Inequality and Stratification in China," *China Quarterly* 53 (Dec. 1975): 688–689.

21. Between 1956 and 1981 the percentages earned from private sidelines, even as an average, varied enormously. When the CCP stresses collective efforts, as it did in the early 1970s, the average percentages fall to as low as 10 percent. But when the CCP relaxes restrictions on private endeavors, even averages can go as high as 50 percent. Thus, private sidelines on the average provided 40 percent of total per capita income (47 yuan: 117 yuan) in 1977 and 32 percent (40 yuan: 123 yuan) in 1979. Because the range of incomes was extremely wide, some families in fact, earned at least half their total income from sidelines. *BR* 39 (Sept. 28, 1981): 3; *Xin Hua* (Beijing), June 16, 1980, trans. in *FBIS* 117 (June 16, 1980): 4–5; Parish and Whyte, *Village and Family*, p. 61; Fox Butterfield, "China Is Trying New Incentives," *New York Times*, Apr. 26, 1979, p. A11; "Quarterly Chronicle," *China Quarterly* 74 (June 1978): 449.

22. There is no central directive or national regulation requiring each household to send two workers to the collective. Instead, the national government stresses the principle of giving priority to the collective, and each team decides what is equitable. Most teams require all able-bodied members between 16 and 50 to work full time for the collective and then, depending on family circumstances and the skills of the individual worker over age 50, they permit the elderly to retire, provided at least two other family members are in the labor force.

23. Because prices for pork are nearly identical across the country, throughout the 1970s these averages held nationwide. Liu Chunlie, "How a Farm Family

Gets Its Income," *China Reconstructs* 21. 11 (Nov. 1972): 40–41; Parish and Whyte, *Village and Family*, p. 119.

24. Fieldwork in Taiwan confirms the observations of my interviewees on the difficulty of pig raising. Myron Cohen, *House United, House Divided* (New York: Columbia University Press, 1976), pp. 220–221.

25. E.g. when Chen Pingfong worked full time for the collective and was unable to raise any pigs at home, she earned 80–130 yuan during the five years Li Saikwok was in the army. When she retired to work at home, she raised two or three meaters plus a sow whose piglets she sold. In 1975 her cash contribution to the family exceeded 200 yuan.

26. See also Myrdal and Kessle, *China*, pp. 135, 169.

27. Although from the first years of the PRC there was a split within the leadership over the speed with which Chinese agriculture would mechanize, both Maoists and Liuists hoped for a radical reduction in reliance on manual labor. Mark Selden, ed., *The People's Republic of China: A Documentary History* (New York: Monthly Review Press, 1979), pp. 185, 235, 341–350.

28. "Labour Insurance Regulations of the People's Republic of China," 1951 version, trans. in Blaustein, *Fundamental Legal Documents*, pp. 534–554.

29. Franz Schurmann, *Ideology and Organization in Communist China* (Berkeley: University of California Press, 1968), ch. 4 and p. 284; Liang Junru, "Bi shu gai ge da ji ti zhi yeh de li run fan pei zhi du" (we must change the distribution of net profits in large-scale collective enterprises), *Jing Ji Guan Li* 1 (1980): 21–23. After 1978 small urban collectives drew workers increasingly from among unemployed urban youth. But throughout the 1960s and most of the 1970s collective enterprises were dominated by the old and middle-aged. In 1980, 80 million urban workers were in state enterprises with annual average incomes of 803 yuan, and 24 million worked in collective enterprises with annual average incomes of 624 yuan. *BR* 20 (May 18, 1981): 20; Ling Junru, "Bi shu gai ge," *Jing Ji Guan Li* 1 (1980):21–23; "Communiqúe of Fulfillment of China's 1978 National Economic Plan," *BR* 27 (July 6, 1979): 40.

30. The severance pay system was used almost exclusively in the small cooperatives that were less directly controlled by municipal organizations than the large collectives. By 1979, in Beijing factories union officials said that the system had fallen into disuse.

31. The modified pension system was begun in 1964 and was generally in place and functioning in most large urban areas by spring 1966. State Council directives nos. 292 and 224 (1965), Ministry of Internal Affairs and Ministry of Labor joint directives nos. 4 and 25 (1965), Ministry of Second Light Industry and the All China Association of Handwork Cooperatives joint directive no. 11/59 (Apr. 1966), Planning Committee of Fujian Province Revolutionary Committee, *Lao dong gong zi wen jian xuan pien* (Collected documents on wages), Oct. 1973, pp. 438–439, 458–460, 637–646.

32. The main periods of revision were February 1958, June 1962, August 1964, January 1965, August 1965, and June 1978.

33. The 1958 revisions (article 2) reduced the work requirement for a minimum pension for men at age 60 from 25 years' work experience with five years in the enterprise concerned to 20 years' total work experience with five consecutive years in any enterprise. For women the reduction was from 20 years total with 5 years in the enterprise concerned to 15 years with 5 consecutive years. This draft (article 3) eliminated bonuses for those who worked beyond retirement but also tied the payments more precisely to the number of years of consecutive employ-

ment. Thus (article 4), those with less than 10 years received 50 percent of their last wage, less than 15 years received 60 percent, and with 15 years or more received 70 percent. "Provisional Regulations of the State Council Concerning the Retirement of Workers and Staff Members," trans. in Blaustein, *Fundamental Legal Documents*, pp. 555–562. The 1962, 1964, and 1965 regulations primarily aided workers in the collective sector. In general, the minimum requirement of continuous employment was longer (8 years rather than 5), and the minimum pension was lower (40 percent rather than 50), but even with these limitations the new regulations significantly increased the financial security of the elderly in the collective sector. Planning Committee of Fujian Province Revolutionary Committee, *Lao dong gong zi*, Oct. 1973, pp. 438–439, 458–460, 637–646. The 1978 revisions reduced the requirement for a minimum pension to 10 years employment, raised the general benefit for those with 20 years' employment from 70 to 75 percent of the last wage, guaranteed a minimum pension of 25 yuan, and expanded benefits for those who had joined the CCP before 1949. *She hui wen jiao xing zheng cai wu zhi du ze bien* (Selected regulations related to the financial administration of social and educational affairs) (Beijing: Cai Zhen Bu, 1979), pp. 426–436.

34. *Nan Fang Ri Bao*, May 10, 1952; *RMRB*, Jan. 11, 1953.

35. *Hei Long Jiang Ri Bao*, Jan. 14, 1957; *Zhe Jiang Ri Bao*, Feb. 19, 1957; *Bei Jing Ri Bao*, Mar. 27, 1957; *Da Cong Ri Bao* (Jinan), July 19, 1957.

36. *Xin Xiang Ri Bao*, Dec. 22, 1954; Lu Da Ri Bao, Dec. 26, 1956; *Xia Tou Ri Bao*, May 23, 1957; *Wen Hui Bao*, Nov. 11, 1955; *Jie Fang Ri Bao*, Apr. 30, 1956; *Zheng Zhou Ri Bao*, Nov. 6, 1956; *Da Gong Bao* (Hong Kong), Sept. 10, 1956.

37. *Gong Ren Ri Bao* (hereafter *GRRB*), Jan. 22, 1958.

38. *Ibid.*

39. *GRRB*, July 7, Aug. 24, Sept. 3, 1958; Jan. 22, 1959; *Lu Da Ri Bao*, Oct. 4, 1958; *Liao Ning Bao*, Nov. 9, 1958; *Zhong Guo Qing Nian*, no. 23, Dec. 12, 1958; *Bei Jing Wan Bao*, Mar. 2, 1959.

40. Blaustein, *Fundamental Legal Documents*, pp. 555–562.

41. In the one reference found of pensions granted during 1958–1960, they were even lower than those listed in 1951-1956. Guangzhou retirees on the average received 141 yuan per year, or slightly more than 10 yuan per month. *Da Gong Bao*, (Hong Kong), May 23, 1959.

42. The population of retirement age is estimated to be, in millions:

Year	Women 50 years and older	Men 60 years and older
1962	41.3	18.8
1963	45.3	19.4
1964	46.4	19.4
1965	47.7	20.6
1966	49.1	21.3

U.S. Department of Commerce, unpub. materials on population estimates of the PRC prepared by Foreign Demographic Analysis Division, April 1976.

43. *GRRB*, July 26, Nov. 8, 1962; Oct. 25, Nov. 23, 1963; Mar. 14, July 10, and 24, 1964; *Yang Cheng Wan Bao*, Jan. 19, 1963; Feb. 27, 1965; *Xin Men Wan Bao*, Feb. 23, 1964; *Xin Wen Bao* Mar. 3, 1964.

44. "Zuo hao tuo you gong zuo" (Do child care work well), *RMRB*, Aug. 18, 1979, p. 1.

45. Ross Terrill, *Flowers on an Iron Tree* (Boston: Little Brown, 1975), pp. 144, 156; *Wen Hui Bao*, May 12, 1973, p. 4; John K. Galbraith, *A China Passage* (New York: Signet, 1973), p. 55.

46. Judith Treas, "Socialist Organization and Economic Development in China," *The Gerontologist* 19.1 (Feb. 1979): 34–43; "Excerpts from a Speech by Ulanhu," *BR* 7 (Feb. 16, 1979): 28.

47. The revisions, drafted in June 1978, went into limited operation in August 1978, and began a national trial period in January 1979. When I interviewed municipal union officials and enterprise cadres in charge of pension work in 1979, the revisions were read to me, but I was not permitted to see or copy them because they were considered to be only in draft form for internal circulation. In point of fact the draft was identical in every city and implementation was uniform in all twenty state enterprises visited.

48. The reduction from 20 to 10 years as the minimum work history for the minimum pension was first implemented in pension reforms adopted in 1962-1965. But because of the time lag between the drafting of reforms and the return to routine retirement in the 1970s, the 1978 regulations had greater impact. Also because the salaries of those with 10–14 years' experience were higher in 1978 than in 1962, the partial pension was significantly larger. Earlier revisions were made at least four times: June 1962; Aug. 5, 1964; Aug. 4, 1965; and December 1965. Planning Committee of Fujian Province Revolutionary Committee, *Lao Dong Gong Zi*, pp. 438–439, and 543–560.

49. Raising the minimum standard from the previous minimum of 10 yuan to 25 yuan for ordinary pensioners and 36 yuan for CCP members significantly reduced the burden on enterprises to give monthly supplements or emergency aid to help retirees. In Nanjing, a union representative from a textile factory reported that in 1978, prior to implementation of the new regulations, 55 percent (N=98) of the retirees needed such supplements.

50. In two families interviewed, one in the Changzhou Railroad Factory and one in the No. 2 Textile Mill in Changzhou, children had replaced parents in 1964 and 1965. This practice was a formal, published benefit. Planning Committee of Fujian Revolutionary Committee, *Lao Dong Gong Zi*, p. 646.

51. The only limitations were that the children be between the ages of 16 and 30 and not already have a permanent work assignment in the state sector. Thus all children sent to settle in the countryside, even those on state farms, and all those working in small cooperative street factories were eligible.

52. Changzhou Railroad Factory: 75 percent (N=530); Nanjing Light Machinery: 67 percent (N=12); Nanjing Radio: 78 percent (N=200); Nanjing Textile Mill: 80 percent (N=550); Nanjing Electric Power Plant: 95 percent (N=98); Shih Jia Chuang No. 1 Textile Mill: 100 percent (N=42); Beijing Small Electric Motor: 65 percent (N=25); and Beijing Fine Instruments: 100 percent (N=60).

53. Chen Youli is a woman I interviewed under the official sponsorship of the Chinese Academy of Social Sciences in summer 1979.

54. Among the 84 elderly parents interviewed in summer 1979 in 5 Chinese cities, 91 percent of the women and 100 percent of the men aged 50–59 had incomes equal to or in excess of their oldest working child, as did 50 percent of the women and 100 percent of the men aged 60–69, and 30 percent of the women and 73 percent of the men aged 70 or older. Among 29 elderly parents known to refugees interviewed in Hong Kong in 1976, 75 percent of the women and 100 percent of the men aged 59–59 had incomes equal to or in excess of their oldest working child, as did 0 percent of the women and 87 percent of the men aged 60–69, 0 per-

cent of the women and 60 percent of the men aged 70 or older. See also Terrill, *Flowers on an Iron Tree,* p. 97; Ruth Sidel, *Families of Fengsheng* (Middlesex, Eng.: Penguin, 1974), pp. 16, 99–100.

55. In PRC data 68 percent (8 out of 12) and in Hong Kong data 27 percent (5 out of 18) of elderly workers had children with 10 or more years' employment whose incomes were equal to or less than theirs.

56. Chen Ting-chung, "An Analysis of Wage Adjustment Implemented by the Chinese Communist Regime," *Studies in Chinese Communism* 7. 12 (Dec. 10, 1973): 1–10; Harrison Salisbury, *New York Times,* Nov. 5, 1977, p. 5; Frederick C. Teiwes, "Before and After the Cultural Revolution," *China Quarterly* 58 (Apr./May 1974): 337–338; Vice Premier Yu Chiu-li, speech at Fourth Session of the Standing Committee of the Fourth National People's Congress, *PR* 45 (Nov. 4, 1977): 6.

57. Teiwes, "Before and After the Cultural Revolution," pp. 337–338.

58. The major adjustments occurred in 1977 and 1979, affecting over 40 percent of the work force each time. In 1978 minor adjustments were given to 2–3 percent of the workers. *PR* 45 (Nov. 4, 1977): 6; 49 (Dec. 2, 1977): 3; *BR* 45 (Nov. 9, 1979): 4.

59. "Economic Readjustment Off to a Good Start," *BR* 20 (May 19, 1980): 17–19; Wei Min, "1979: More Than Seven Million Employed," *BR* 6 (Feb. 11, 1980): 13–20.

60. Erdman Palmore, "Trends in the Relative Status of the Aged," *Social Forces* 50 (1971): 84–91; Erdman Palmore and Kenneth Marston, "Modernization and Status of the Aged," Journal of Gerontology 20. 2 (1974): 205– 210; Cowgill and Holmes, *Aging and Modernization,* p. 20; Irving Rosow, *Social Integration of the Aged* (New York: Free Press, 1967), pp. 8–10; Leo Simmons, *The Role of the Aged in Primitive Societies* (London: Yale University Press, 1945), pp. 9–12.

3. Living Arrangements

1. C. K. Yang, *The Chinese Family in the Communist Revolution* (Cambridge: M.I.T. Press, 1965), pp. 35, 85, 91; C. K. Yang, *A Chinese Village in Early Communist Transition* (Cambridge: M.I.T. Press, 1966), pp. 17, 83–88; Ida Pruitt, *A Daughter of Han* (Stanford: Stanford University Press, 1978), p. 144; Olga Lang, *Chinese Family and Society* (New Haven: Yale University Press, 1946), pp. 230–233.

2. In addition to the secondary sources on pre-1949 life cited in footnote 1, interviews in 1976 with 20 emigrants to Hong Kong who had left Guangzhou, Hunan, and Shandong in the early 1950s made it clear that in times of chaos the elderly were often forced to separate from their children but that in no case did the elderly seek an independent household as an ideal arrangement.

3. *Marriage Law of the People's Republic of China,* trans. in Yang, *The Chinese Family,* pp. 221–226.

4. Yang, *A Chinese Village,* pp. 78, 84; Yang, *The Chinese Family,* pp. 195–196.

5. Yang, *The Chinese Family,* pp. 44, 86–104.

6. *RMRB,* Feb. 25, 1968; Feb. 6, 26, May 14, 1969; Jan. 21, 1970; *GMRB,* Apr. 15, 1970; *Da Gong Bao* (Xiang Gang), Mar. 15, May 5, 1976; *Xin Wen Bao,* Mar. 14, 1965; *Zhong Guo Fu Nu* 2(1964):22–23; 1 (1980):46–48; *Xin Hua* (Guangzhou), Jan. 30, 31, 1969; Aug. 30, 1971.

7. Ho Shuyu, "Sister Red Plum," *CL* 4 (1978):65–83; Fang Nan, "Change of Heart," *CL* 7 (1978):3–28; Wang Wenshih, "Around the Spring Festival," *CL* 6

(1978):3-23; *Li Mei,* ed. Zhang Youming (Beijing: Ren Min Chu Ban She, 1976); *Lian Hua Huan Bao* 3 (1977): 21-26; 6 (1977): 16; *Ren Min Wen Xue* 3 (1977):13-18; 6 (1977): 80-83.

8. The household composition in my two samples was (the percentage of the total sample living with a married son is shown in parentheses):

Area	Married	Unmarried children	children	Spouse	Alone	Other
Hong Kong rural	41%	(37%)	24%	10%	24%	1%
Hong Kong rural (excluding childless)	48%	(43%)	28%	12%	9%	3%
Hong Kong urban	42%	(34%)	38%	7.5%	7%	5.4%
PRC urban	60%	(33%)	31.5%	8.5%	0%	0%

For similar trends by other visitors on official tours, see William Kessen, ed., *Childhood in China* (New Haven: Yale University Press, 1975), p. 18; Ruth Sidel, *Women and Childcare in China* (New York: Hill and Wang, 1972), pp. 104-105; Susan Kinoy, "Growing Old in New China," *New China* (Spring 1975), pp. 18-19; Issac Ascher, *China's Social Policy* (London: Anglo-Chinese Educational Institute, 1976); Jan Myrdal, *Report from a Chinese Village* (New York: Vintage, 1965), pp. 38-44; Terrill, *Flowers on an Iron Tree; Eileen Hsu-Balzar, Richard J. Balzar, and Francis L. K. Hsu, China Day by Day* (New Haven: Yale University Press, 1974).

9. In the Hong Kong rural sample, 4 out of 11 families with 2 or more married sons lived jointly; in the Hong Kong urban sample the figure was 1 out of 10, and in the PRC urban sample 2 out of 14.

10. In the Hong Kong rural samples only 1 percent and 3 percent of elderly lived in households with other than their children; in the Hong Kong urban and PRC urban samples the figure was 5.4 percent and 0 percent respectively. In all of these cases the elderly person lived with a sibling, niece, or nephew rather than an unrelated friend.

11. Cases have been reported where newly married rural couples live only briefly with parents and then split into separate households. In my samples, however, this did not happen among households formed in the 1970s, which may have been partly a regional bias, but was also undoubtedly a reflection of hard times and acute housing shortages. Parish and Whyte, *Village and Family,* p. 211.

12. Li Laoer is a pseudonym for a man described by the same Hong Kong informant who had lived with Li Hoizhong's daughter-in-law. Li Fulan and Zhang Aiguo are pseudonyms for two pensioners I interviewed in their home in 1979 under the auspices of the Chinese Academy of Social Sciences.

13. William L. Parish, Jr., "Socialism and the Chinese Peasant Family," *Journal of Asian Studies* 34.3 (May 1975): 621.

14. The government began to take over privately owned rental properties in 1958, giving former owners fixed amounts of interest over a specified period. In most cities about 10 percent of the homes are owner occupied and 90 percent are rented through a municipal real estate bureau, although percentages vary considerably. In Wuhan, 24 percent of homes are privately owned, whereas in Changsha, the percentage is 10 percent. Robin Thompson, "City Planning in China," *World Development* 3. 7-8 (July/Aug. 1975): 595-606; Peter Cheng, *A Chronology of the PRC* (Totowa: Little Field, Adams, 1972), p. 90; Terrill, *Flowers on an*

Iron Tree, pp. 353–354.

15. David D. Buck, "Urban Development. Beyond the Ta-ching Model," *Contemporary China* 1.6 (Mar. 1977): 48; Thompson, "City Planning in China," pp. 597–599; Judith Bannister, "Mortality, Fertility, and Contraceptive Use in Shanghai," *China Quarterly* 7 (June 1977): 272.

16. Though rents are low, urban housing is a scarce and costly commodity in the eyes of state planners. Such housing costs 40-55 yuan per square meter, with most apartments using 20 square meters, for a total construction outlay of 800-1100 yuan per unit. *Jian Zhu Xue Bao*, (Architecture journal) 2 (1973): 1–6; 1 (1974): 22–32; 2 (1974): 42–45.

17. Zhou Shulian and Lin Senmu, *People's Daily*, Aug. 5, 1980, p.5, trans. in *FBIS*, Aug. 20, 1980, pp. L 15–20; "The Urban Housing Shortage," *BR* 35 (Aug. 31, 1981):28; Li Chengrui and Zhang Zhongji, "Remarkable Improvements in Living Standards," *BR* 17 (Apr. 17, 1982):15–19.

18. *Jian Zhu Xue Bao* 1 (1973):15–17; 2 (1973): 1–6; 1 (1974): 22–26; 2 (1974): 42–45; 6 (1974): 6–25; 5 (1981): 61–63; Thompson, "City Planning in China," p. 599; Terrill, *Flowers on an Iron Tree*, p. 78.

19. Article 90, trans. in Blaustein, *Fundamental Legal Documents*, p. 30.

20. Cheng, *A Chronology of the PRC*, p. 48.

21. Cheng, *A Chronology of the PRC*, p. 83.

22. Revised constitutions appeared in 1975, 1978, and 1982. *The Constitution of the People's Republic of China* (Peking: Foreign Language Press, 1975); *PR* 11 (Mar. 17, 1978):5–14; *BR* 19 (May 10, 1982): 27–47.

23. Among 53 urban households in the Hong Kong sample, 24.5 percent (N=13) had successfully obtained a transfer and 3 others were awaiting official approval. Of the 13 who had been successful, 7 involved a move out of a rural area or small city to a major urban center. Among 74 urban households of the elderly described in the PRC sample, 38 percent (N=28) had successfully obtained a transfer. Of these households, 93 percent involved a permanent move from a rural area or small city to a major urban center. In half of these households (N=13) the move involved a child aged 20-30. Even though urban "educated youth" may be especially easy to transfer since they once were officially registered in the cities and do not really represent a conflict with basic policy, the presence of an ailing or retiring parent is still one of the few valid reasons youths may transfer back to their own city.

24. Deborah Davis-Friedmann, "Welfare Practices in Rural China," *World Development* 6.2 (May 1978): 609–619.

25. Elizabeth Croll, *Feminism and Socialism* (London: Routledge and Kegan Paul, 1978); Norma Diamond, review, *Journal of Asian Studies* 36. 3 (May 1977): 548; Editorial, *RMRB*, Aug. 13, 1979, p. 1; "Zuo hao tuo gong zuo, bao chan er tong shen jian kang" (Do child care work well and guarantee the mental and physical health of the children), *RMRB*, Aug. 18, 1979, p. 1.

26. Among the 24 urban grandmothers of preschoolers interviewed in 1979, 21 had major responsibility for the children.

27. Martin K. Whyte, "Inequality and Stratification in China," *China Quarterly* 64 (Dec. 1975): 684–711; F.W. Crook, "The Commune System in the People's Republic of China," p. 404; Terrill, *Flowers on an Iron Tree*, p. 207.

28. The degree to which siblings complain varies according to age of parents at the time of the children's marriages. When parents are old, disabled, and economically inactive, a younger sibling is happy to leave the natal home and set out on his own. But when parents are vigorous workers in their fifties and early sixties

or the family home is especially large and well furnished, siblings fight over the right to live jointly.

29. In the Hong Kong rural sample 21 percent of the elderly lived in one-generation households, in the Hong Kong urban sample 15 percent, and in the PRC urban sample 8.5 percent. For even lower incidences, see Myrdal, *Report from a Chinese Village*, pp. 38–44; Elizabeth Croll, "Chiang Village," *China Quarterly* 72 (Dec. 1977): 786–814.

30. In the Hong Kong sample 5 families had been able to build an extra house before a son's marriage and 6 had sons working outside the village.

31. In the Hong Kong sample 4 families had experienced difficulties with remarried widows.

32. In the Hong Kong sample 3 families had rejected politically suspect parents.

33. *Marriage Law of the People's Republic of China*, Article 2, trans. in Yang, *The Chinese Family*, pp. 221–226.

34. Parish and Whyte, *Village and Family*, pp. 99–100.

35. In January 1979 the CCP Central Committee changed this policy, stipulating that descendants of rich peasants, landlords, counter-revolutionaries, and bad elements would henceforth have the class status of "commune member" and enjoy "the same rights as other commune members." "Victory for the Policy of Remoulding the Exploiters," *BR* 7 (Feb. 16, 1979): 8–10.

36. In the Hong Kong rural sample there were only two cases of a married daughter and her husband living with the wife's parents, and in neither case did the man change the surname of either himself or his children to that of the wife. This could be because the legal prohibitions on ancestor worship have reduced the symbolic importance of the continuation of the family name, but it may also indicate a regional bias. In 50 households near Yanan in 1962, there was one case of a uxorilocal husband having given his first son the name of his father-in-law and another of a stepson having given his eldest son the surname of his stepfather but retaining his own birth-name for himself. Myrdal, *Report from a Chinese Village*, p. 42.

37. In the PRC sample half of the households shared with a married child were households of the elderly and a married daughter. But 11 of the 14 fathers and 17 of the 20 mothers had no choice. By contrast, among the elderly living with sons, 6 of the 12 fathers and 14 of the 20 mothers had no choice.

38. Even in years when average per capita space increased in urban areas, the likelihood of a newly married couple finding their own apartment grew even smaller. Liu Yirong, "Ying gai zhong shi yen jiou yi shi hu de sheji wen ti" (We must research the problem of one-room apartments), *Jian Zhu Xue Bao* 5 (1981): 61–63.

4. Relations with Children

1. Chu T'ung-tsu, *Law and Society in Traditional China* (Paris: Mouton, 1965), p. 27; Yang, *The Chinese Family*, p. 89; Martin C. Yang, *A Chinese Village* (New York: Columbia University Press, 1965), p. 169.

2. Chu, *Law and Society*, p. 27; Yang, *The Chinese Family*, p. 89; Lang, *Chinese Family and Society*, p. 230.

3. Yang, *The Chinese Family*, pp. 10–17.

4. Delia Davin, *Woman-Work* (Oxford: Oxford University Press, 1976), p. 15; Yang, *The Chinese Family*, p. 16.

5. Tien Lien-yuan, "Something More to Report," *CL* 12 (1974): 66–74; *Xin*

Hua (Guangzhou), Oct. 31, 1969; Chu Yu-tang, "The Call," *CL* 4 (1972): 3–12; Sun Cheng-jiu, "Mother," *CL* 11 (1972): 15–23; *Chuang Yeh* (The Pioneers)(Peking: Ren Min Chu Ban She, 1975), p. 168; "Family Planning in Jutung County (II)," *PR* 15 (Apr. 15, 1968): 26–27; Ho Shu-yu, "Sister Red Plum," *CL* 4 (1978): 65–83; "Family Planning in Jutung County (III)," *PR* 16 (Apr. 21, 1978): 23; Yang, *The Making of a Peasant Doctor;* Yeh Men-ling, "Dan Mei," *Ren Min Wen Xue* 3 (1977): 16; Liu Ching, "Builders of a New Life," *CL* 1 (1978): 4–51.

6. To compare parent-child dyads as objectively as possible, each pair in the Hong Kong sample was scored against a five-item checklist of contacts, all of which were visible to outside observers so that data could be collected from both family and nonfamily members: shared household, exchange of household help on a regular basis, presentation of gifts, shared nursing care or purchase of medicines, and shared child care. Those dyads in which no item was shared or exchanged scored "0" and were defined as dyads of "no exchange." Those that shared one item scored "1" and were defined as dyads of "low exchange." Those that shared two items were scored "2" and defined as dyads of "moderate exchange," while those that shared three or more items were scored "3" or above and defined as dyads of "high exchange." In the Hong Kong rural sample 85 percent of the elderly mothers and 79 percent of the elderly fathers had a score of 3 or higher with at least one child, and only 10 percent of women and 17.6 percent of men scored 0 or 1 with all children. In the Hong Kong urban sample 98 percent of mothers and 82 percent of fathers scored 3 or higher with at least one child. Because the PRC interview situation did not permit extended discussion of parent-child conflict and tension, it was not possible to apply the same measurement of interaction. Support for these conclusions for the PRC respondents came primarily from respondents' self-reports or close observation of a small number of families visited repeatedly in their homes.

7. Two indicators reflect the weaker contact with daughters among rural elderly. First, in reports of significant parent-child dyads in rural families, parent-son dyads outnumbered parent-daughter ones by 133 to 87. Second, parent-daughter dyads were consistently the weakest. For example, in the Hong Kong rural sample 59.5 percent of father-daughter dyads and 48 percent of mother-daughter dyads scored 0 or 1. In contrast, only 9.8 percent of mother-son and 13.5 percent of father-son dyads scored at this low end of the scale.

8. In the sample of 93 rural families, 30 percent of mothers and 34 percent of fathers were significantly dependent on their children. Among dependent mothers, 46 percent turned primarily to a daughter, 54 percent to a son. Among dependent fathers, 59 percent turned primarily to a daughter, 41 percent to a son.

9. In some instances such splitting is also the result of official adjudication. "Lawyers in Beijing," *BR* 23 (June 7, 1982): 15.

10. In the Hong Kong sample the percentage of parent-child dyads scoring 3 or higher was:

Parent	Rural		Urban	
	Son	Daughter	Son	Daughter
Father	63.5%	19%	64%	45%
Mother	77 %	30%	77%	59%

11. Among families with close ties in the Hong Kong rural sample only 9.5 percent of mother-son and 15 percent of father-son dyads had a clearly dependent

parent. For parent-daughter dyads the percentage was higher, 33 percent and 57 percent respectively, a difference largely attributable to the special conditions in the minority of rural families who maintained close parent-daughter relations. In the Hong Kong urban sample 35 percent of mothers and 8.5 percent of fathers were heavily dependent on an adult child for support.

12. Ma Xinwang and Ouyang Xiu are pseudonyms used to protect individuals who did not present themselves to be interviewed. I met them quite by chance and came to know them gradually through a series of daily visits over a period of six weeks. The visits began and ended in the spirit of a casual acquaintanceship. As a result, I did not directly ask questions about income, political experience, or employment record. Instead I watched, they watched, and over the weeks I gradually learned about many vital facets of their lives.

13. Article 13 in the 1950 version and Article 15 in the 1981 draft, trans. in Yang, *The Chinese Family*, pp. 221–226; *BR* 11 (Mar. 16, 1981): 24–27.

14. There are occasional reports of abusive children who have been reprimanded and forced to provide support. "Readers Condemn Unfeeling Sons," *China Reconstructs*, July 1979, pp. 38–39; "On the Home Front," *PR* 44 (Nov. 3, 1978):31; "The Need to Respect the Old," *PR* 15 (Apr. 13, 1979):7–8.

15. Davis-Friedmann, "Welfare Practices," p. 610.

16. Parish and Whyte, *Village and Family*, pp. 180–186; "Problems of Marriage," *BR* 48 (Nov. 30, 1979): 7.

17. Parish and Whyte, *Village and Family*, p. 188.

18. For 1979 the cost to raise an urban child to age 16 was estimated at 6900 yuan. Ouyang Huizun, "Marked Results in China's Most Populous Province," *BR* 46 (Nov. 16, 1979): 22. By comparison, it cost 1600 yuan in rural areas and 4800 yuan in small towns. "Ren kou li lun zuo tan hui," (A discussion of population theory) *RMRB*, June 5, 1979, p. 3.

19. "Events and Trends," *BR* 8 (Feb. 22, 1982): 8; C.K. Lyle, "Planned Birth in Tianjin," *China Quarterly* 83 (Sept. 1980): 551–567.

20. Chen Jinzhong is a pseudonym for a former peasant from Nanhai County, Guangdong whom I interviewed in Hong Kong in 1976.

21. Dorrian Sweetser, "The Effect of Industrialization on Intergenerational Solidarity," *Rural Sociology* 31 (June 1966): 156–170; Meyer F. Nimkoff and Russell Middleton, "Types of Family and Types of Economy," *American Journal of Sociology* 66 (1960): 215–225; Adams, *Kinship in an Urban Setting*, p. 170; Townsend, *The Family Life of Old People*, p. 206; Paul Reis, "The Extended Kinship System," *Journal of Marriage and Family Living* 24 (1962): 333–339.

22. Although not recognized openly by the Chinese government until after 1978, the problem of urban unemployment has been significant since the mid-1960s. *BR* 8 (Feb. 23, 1981): 8–9; 39 (Sept. 28, 1981): 27; Feng Lanrui, "On Factors Affecting China's Labor Employment," *People's Daily*, Nov. 16, 1981, p. 5, trans. in *FBIS*, Nov. 20, 1981, pp K5–6.

23. Davin, *Woman-Work*, p. 187.

24. Davin, *Woman-Work*, p. 189.

25. Changing opportunities in rural areas also strengthen parent-daughter ties. In the Hong Kong sample, among 31 families where parents had both an adult son and adult daughter, 82 percent of the mothers had a polarized relationship favoring their sons when educational and work opportunities for women remained traditional. In contrast, in villages where girls had access to junior high school education and jobs in industry and commerce, only 20 percent of the mothers clearly favored their sons. For fathers the pattern was the same: when

there were no new opportunities for girls, 77 percent of the fathers had polarized relationships favoring their sons, but when there were new opportunities, no father expressed exclusive favoritism.

5. Funerals and Filial Piety

1. Chu, *Law and Society*, pp. 24–27; Yang, *The Chinese Family*, p. 89; C. K. Yang, *Religion in Chinese Society* (Berkeley: University of California Press, 1967), pp. 45–48.

2. From interviews in Hong Kong in 1976 with former urban residents, all of whom had been educated after 1949.

3. New China News Agency (hereafter NCNA), June 21, Dec. 12, 1974, trans. in *China Mainland Press* (hereafter CMP) 74-27 (July 2–5,1974):59–60; 74-52 (Dec. 23, 1974): 16–19; *People's Daily*, June 20, 1974, trans. in *CMP* 74-27 (July 2–5, 1974): 12–14.

4. Mao spoke of the futility of using force in a 1957 essay, "On Correct Handling of Contradictions," and a Mar. 31,1965, *People's Daily essay, trans. in Mao Tsetung, Selected Readings* (Peking: Foreign Languages Press, 1971), pp. 432–479; *Joint Publications Research Service* (hereafter *JPRS*) 29,697 (Apr. 21, 1965): 18–19. On freedom of religion in China, Lu Dingyi noted in 1956 that, while atheism was the preferred "belief," the state generally followed a policy of noninterference, which meant that "atheists don't go to temples or churches, and theists do not make religious propaganda in public places." *China News Analysis* 138 (July 6, 1956): 4.

5. *People's Daily*, Mar. 31, 1965, trans. in *JPRS* 29,697 (Apr. 21, 1965): 18–19.

6. Donald E. MacInnis, *Religious Policy and Practice in Communist China* (New York: Macmillan, 1972), p. 39.

7. Yang, *Religion in Chinese Society*, pp. 392–393; Yang, *The Chinese Family*, pp. 192–93; Parish and Whyte, *Village and Family*, p. 28; Isabel Crook and David Crook, *Ten-Mile Inn* (New York: Pantheon, 1979), p. 107.

8. When former residents living in Hong Kong in 1975 were asked to describe funerals they had observed during the years since land reform and early collectivization, they reported that Daoist and Buddhist priests had disappeared from public view as full-time practitioners in the years immediately after 1949, but their skills were well known and many continued to conduct services. See also *Talks on Smashing Superstitions* (Peking: Chinese Youth Publishing Agency, 1965), trans. in *JPRS* 32,799 (Nov. 10, 1965): 17–29; Ma Han zhang, "Guan yu zong jiao mi xin wen ti" (In regard to the problem of religion and superstitions), *RMRB, Aug. 8, 1963*, p. 5.

9. Yang, *The Chinese Family*, p. 89. Social surveys in Shanghai in 1927–1928 showed that among textile workers with an average monthly income of $32, the average funeral cost $28. Simon Yang and L.K. Tao, *A Study of the Standard of Living of Working Families in Shanghai* (Peiping: Institute of Social Research, 1931). In contrast, another study by John Buck found that the average peasant family in the 1930s spent 3 months' income on a funeral. Parish and Whyte, *Village and Family*, p. 250.

10. Trans. in Blaustein, *Fundamental Legal Documents*, pp. 542–544.

11. MacInnis, *Religious Policy*, pp. 312–322; Zhao Jianmin, "Gai ge sang zang" (Reform funeral customs), *RMRB*, June 17, 1958, p. 4.

12. Article 8 or the 1958 Provisional Regulations of State Council Concerning Retirement of Workers and Staff Members provides a 50–100 yuan lump-sum

payment upon the death of a retired person. For workers who die before retirement, 1953 regulations guaranteed a funeral benefit to their survivors 2–3 times the average monthly wage in the enterprise. Blaustein, *Fundamental Legal Documents*, pp. 542–543, 559; Charles Hoffman, *The Chinese Worker* (Albany: SUNY, 1974), p. 37.

13. Lynn T. White, III, "Workers' Politics in Shanghai," *Journal of Asian Studies* 36. 1 (Nov. 1976): 99–116.

14. *RMRB*, Jan. 26, 1956.

15. *Guang Xi Ri Bao*, Feb. 17, 1956; *Liao Ning Ri Bao*, Nov. 2, 1956; *RMRB*, Sept. 17, 1956; Mar. 11, 1957; *Ji Lin Ri Bao*, Sept. 7, 1956; *Zhou Mo Bao*, (Xiang Gang), Nov. 6, 1956; *Liao Ning Ri Bao*, Jan. 12, 1957; *Xin Jiang Ri Bao*, Mar. 1, 1957; *Nan Jing Ri Bao*, Mar. 15, 1957; *He Bei Ri Bao*, July 1, 1957; *Shen Yang Ri Bao*, Oct. 12, 1957.

16. Richard C. Bush, *Religion in Communist China* (Nashville: Abingdon Press, 1970), pp. 398–400; *China News Analysis* 308 (Jan. 15, 1960): 2; Yang Qi, "Lao tian yeh ke yi xiu yi" (Can they renounce the 'Old Man in Heaven'?), *RMRB*, Oct. 15, 1959, p. 4; Zhao Jianmin, "Gai ge sang zang" (Reform funeral custom), *RMRB*, June 17, 1958; MacInnis, *Religious Policy*, p. 318.

17. Cremation was general policy for the institutionalized elderly. Although these elderly people represented only a minority of the childless destitute and an even smaller percentage of the total elderly population prior to 1959, even they were granted ground burials and some traditional rites. Zhou Chuanzhen, "Ren min gong she jing lao yuan" (Old-age homes in people's communes), *RMRB*, Oct. 23, 1959, p. 4.

18. Myrdal, *Report from a Chinese Village*, p. 11.

19. Bush, *Religion in Communist China*, pp. 415–416; *China News Analysis* 515 (May 8, 1964): 7; 601 (Feb. 25, 1966): 4; Ma, "Guan yu zong jiao" (About the problem of religion and superstition), *RMRB*, Aug. 8, 1963, p. 5.

20. *China News Analysis* 515 (May 8, 1964): 7; "Yi feng yi su hua Qing Ming" (About changing the customs of Qing Ming), *RMRB*, Apr. 10, 1964, p. 2; "Qi fa qun zhong ze jue gai ge sang yi" (Raise the masses' consciousness to reform funeral rites), *RMRB* Apr. 25, 1964, p. 4; Editorial, *RMRB*, Mar. 31, 1965 trans. in *JPRS* 29,697 (Apr. 21, 1965): 18–19; Editorial *RMRB*, June 7, 1964, p. 6.

21. Terrill, *Flowers on an Iron Tree*, pp. 17–18; Chen, *A Year in Upper Felicity*, p. 150; *Jian Zhu Xue Bao* 3 (1975): 13–17.

22. Interviews with former residents of rural Guangdong in Hong Kong in 1976; "Farm Mechanization in Wusih County" (I), *PR* 31 (July 29, 1977): 24–25.

23. This case study came from a Hong Kong man who had lived near the Wus, a pseudonym, between 1968 and 1975.

24. One Labor Bureau cadre in Shijiachuang reported in an interview, May 31, 1979, that 200 yuan was the average cost for funerals in that city. This report coincides with reports of the Hong Kong respondents and with the system of reimbursements outlined in the Labor Insurance Regulations. Blaustein, *Fundamental Legal Documents*, pp. 542–543,559.

25. Fox Butterfield, *New York Times*, Feb. 4, 1978, p. 2; *China Quarterly* 75 (Sept. 1978): 686–687; *China News Analysis* 1121 (June 2, 1978): 6; Ting Yi, "Letters from the People," *PR* 45 (Nov. 10, 1978): 15–17.

26. This case study came from an interview with a close friend and long-time neighbor of the eldest son of Wang Yen, a pseudonym.

27. This case study came from an interview with the wife of a nephew of Li Danhua (a pseudonym) who visited the family four months after her death and

accompanied her husband and son to the cemetery. Li Danhua's younger brother emigrated to the United States in 1947, and in 1979 he visited his sister with his own son and daughter-in-law. I interviewed the daughter-in-law three months after she returned from China.

28. This material comes from an interview in 1976 with a Hong Kong resident who lived in the village of this man between 1958 and 1974. For similar sentiments from an official source, see Chen Shi-xu, "The General and the Small Town," *CL* 6 (1980):3–17.

29. From an interview in Hong Kong in 1976 with a former resident of Guangzhou three months after he left the PRC.

30. Qian Fong, "Qian li yin yuan," (A happy marriage after a thousand mile journey) *Zhong Guo Fu Nu* 9 (1979): 16–20; "Gei ren qi shi, gei ren jiao yu" (Give people inspiration, give people an education), *Zhong Guo Fu Nu* 1 (1980): 46–47; "Zai she hui si bao" (In the cell of society), *Zhong Guo Qing Nian* 5 (1982): 14–15; "Kong ze de hao xue sheng" (The good student of Confucius), *Er Tong Shi Dai* 1 (1981): 26–28.

31. "Gei Ren Qi Shi, Gei Ren Jiao Yu," *Zhong Guo Fu Nu*, pp. 46–47.

32. Xiao Wen, "Policy on Religion," *BR* 51 (Dec. 21, 1979): 15–16; "Zong jiao he feng jian mi xin" (Religion and superstition), *RMRB*, Mar. 15, 1979, p. 4.

33. Xiao Wen, "Policy on Religion," *BR*; Xiao Xian Fu, in *FBIS*, Sept. 21, 1979, pp. L7–8; Beijing Domestic Service, Jan. 31, 1980, trans. in *FBIS*, Feb. 6, 1980, p. L15; Zhou Enlai, "Questions Related to Art and Literature," *CL* 6 (1979): 87.

34. Bush, *Religion in Communist China*, pp. 410–411.

35. Ko Hua, "Comedy at the Fish Market," *CL* 3 (1978): 65.

36. Informal lecture by Sun Yuesheng, June 30, 1979 in Beijing.

6. Intergenerational Conflict

1. *RMRB*, Oct. 29, 1964, p. 6; Sept. 20, 1968, p. 3; Feb. 6, 1969, p. 4; Jan. 8, 1969, p. 3; *China Reconstructs* 18. 1 (Jan. 1969): 30; Sung An-na, "Granny Chin," *CL* 11 (1974): 47–54; *Guang Ming Ri Bao*, Nov. 25, 1974; Jan. 13, 1975, p. 1; Lin Nan, "Storms in a Mountain Village," *CL* 3 (1972): 71–78; *PR* 22 (June 22, 1978): 23–24; Zhai, "Jue Zhan," *Ren Min Wen Xue* 2 (1978): 71–72; Wang Yi, "Jin Se de Jiao," *Ren Min Wen Xue* 2 (1978): 79–86; "Chinese Press Summary," *PR* 36 (Sept. 8, 1979): 20; Qian Fung, "Qian Li Yun Yuan," *Zhong Guo Fu Nu* 9 (1979): 16–21; *Ren Lao Xin Hong* (Shanghai: Ren Min Chu Ban She, 1976), p. 52; *Nu Qing Huo Gong* (Shanghai: Ren Min Chu Ban She, 1976); "The Need to Protect the Old," *PR* 15 (Apr. 13, 1979): 7–8; Li Jing-Ming, "Wode huan yin," (My marriage), *Zhong Guo Fu Nu* 7 (1979): 33–35; "On the Home Front," *PR* 44 (Nov. 3, 1978): 31; Lu Xinhua, "The Wound," in *The Wounded* (Hong Kong: Joint Publishing, 1979), pp. 9–24. The bias in favor of political explanations was especially marked during the Cultural Revolution. Before 1966 most accounts cited the same mundane household problems that respondents described for the 1970s. E.g. *Zhong Guo Fu Nu* 1 (1964): 24–26.

2. The average age of brides in a model Hebei village cited as representative of national trends was 22.5 years for 1967–1980. Kong Yang, "Marriage and Family Relations," *BR* 18 (May 5, 1981): 20. In the Guangdong villages it was 21.1 years for 1968–1974. Parish and Whyte, *Village and Family*, p. 163. In the Hong Kong urban sample the average age of urban brides was 25 years, an age the respondents and also some Chinese publications viewed as appropriate. "Chen Chi-Chung," "Double Happiness," *CL* 3 (1978): 18–33; *PR* 14 (Apr. 7, 1978): 18–20.

3. Since implementation of the one-child family ideal in 1980, there has been an increase in mistreatment of daughters-in-law whose first, and thus only, children are girls. But even before this especially stringent birth control campaign, daughters-in-law who had not yet produced a son were under greater stress than those who had. Christopher Wren, "Old Nemesis Haunts China on Birth Plan," *New York Times*, Aug. 1, 1982, p. A9; *Chinese Medical Journal* 2.3 (May 1976): 165-170; William Shawcross, "Inside a Maoist Courtyard," *South China Morning Post*, Apr. 4. 1976, p. 11; William Parish, "China: Team, Brigade, or Commune?" *Problems of Communism*, Mar./Apr. 1976, p. 61; Seun Yiqiang, *Zhong Guo Fu Nu* 1 (1964): 24-25; "On the Home Front," *PR* 44 (Nov. 3, 1978):31.

4. Song Meihua, a pseudonym, was a neighbor of one of the Hong Kong respondents who lived next door to her and her son for 5 years before escaping to Hong Kong. He had special knowledge of this family because, when the son would leave home to escape the arguments between his wife and his mother, he stayed with the respondent. Luo Erniang, a pseudonym, lived next door to one of the Hong Kong respondents, who knew about her quarrels with her daughter-in-law because her own mother was a confidant of both women. It was to the respondent's house that Hu Shihping came to eat her dinner, and it was to the respondent's mother, who had had four girls before the birth of her only son, that Luo Erniang came for advice.

5. In the Hong Kong rural sample 15 percent (N=17) of elderly parents had irreconcilable differences. In all but one case the consequence was a divided household or refusal to form a joint household despite favorable economic incentives. In the Hong Kong urban sample the figure was 6 percent (N=3). Chinese studies in urban settings report severe conflict in 4-6 percent of urban elderly. Wu Zhengyi, "A Survey of Emotional Status of 403 Unemployed Aged Residents," unpub. paper, Anding Hospital, Beijing, 1980; Yuan Jihui, "Living Conditions of Elderly Retirees in Shanghai," paper prepared for conference on Cross National Studies of Retirement, Bellagio, Italy, June 1981.

6. Parish and Whyte, *Village and Family*, pp. 65, 98-100, 110; "Fundamental Change in China's Class Situation," *BR* 46 (Nov. 16, 1979): 9-13; broadcast of Beijing Xinhua, Aug. 22, 1979, trans. in *FBIS*, Aug. 24, 1979, pp. L5-8; "Policy Toward Descendants of Landlords and Rich Peasants," *BR* 4 (Jan. 26, 1979): 8.

7. Excluding parents who had no adult sons living in China in the Hong Kong rural sample, 5 out of 10 former landlords or rich peasants, 1 out of 12 middle peasants, and 9 out of 57 former poor peasants split with their sons.

8. In the Hong Kong urban sample all three cases of complete breakdown involved parents who were political outcasts.

9. *PR* 36 (Sept. 8, 1967): 20; 22 (June 22, 1978): 23-24; Qian Fung, "Qian Li Yun Yuan," *Zhong Guo Fu Nu* 9 (1979): 16-21; Chang Li-han, "A Chinese Love Story," *China Reconstructs* 28. 1 (Jan. 1979): 10-12.

10. In the Hong Kong rural sample, drawn from an area where traditional taboos were strong, there were 11 remarried widows. In 4 of these cases the remarried parent was abandoned, in 4 the sons stayed close, and in 3 the daughters remained loyal. In the Hong Kong urban sample there were 5 remarried widows, all of whom had good relations with their children. Similarly, Chinese stories set in urban areas reveal remarriage to be acceptable or even desirable, while those set in rural areas show remarriage to be problematic. Yu Guohou, "A Wife and Her Mother-in-law," *China Reconstructs*, Sept. 1979, p. 70; "Power Plant Restored, A Family Reborn," China Reconstructs, Oct. 1980, pp. 9-10; "Gei ren qi shi, gei ren jiao yu," *Zhong Guo Fu Nu* 1 (1980): 46-47; "Bao hu gua fu nu de li yi"

(Protect the interest of widows), *Zhong Guo Fu Nu* 10 (1979): 18–19; "Cao mao bien de feng bo" (The disturbance of the grass hat plait), *Lian Huan Hua Bao* 1/2 (1977): 51.

11. Lin, *The Golden Wing,* p. 160; Maurice Freedman, *Chinese Lineage and Society* (London: Athlone Press, 1966), p. 47; Levy, *The Family Revolution* pp. 132–144; Fei Hsiao-tung, "Peasantry and Gentry," *American Journal of Sociology,* July 1946, p. 4; Dai Yan-hui, "Qing-dai Tai-wan zhi jia-zhi ji jia-chan (Taiwan family system and property in the Ching dynasty), *Taiwan Wen Xian* 3 (1963): 7–10.

12. Kan Wei, "The Whole Country Distributes Cash Retirement Benefits," *Da Gong Bao* (Hong Kong), Feb. 11, 1982, trans. in *FBIS* 29 (Feb. 11, 1982): W4.

13. The sixtieth birthday, which traditionally required elaborate celebration by the entire family, is still observed as a major turning point, but it does not have a clear-cut association with the loss of family headship.

14. *Xin Hua* (Beijing), Sept. 28, 1961; *Xin Hua* (Guangzhou), May 12, 1962; *Zhong Guo Qing Nian Bao,* Oct. 13, 1962, p. 2, trans. in *JPRS* 16,433 (Nov. 30, 1962): 25; *GRRB,* Feb. 7, 1963, trans. in *JPRS* 18,478 (Apr. 1, 1963): 18–21.

15. "Sources for the Retired," *BR* 29 (July 21, 1980): 25–26; *From Youth to Retirement* (Beijing: Beijing Review, 1982), p. 89; "After Retirement," *PR* 22 (June 2, 1978): 20; "Are All These Wastes?" *BR* 8 (Feb. 23, 1979): 24–27; "Lightening the Load of Working Mothers," *China Reconstructs,* Mar. 1980, pp. 19–23.

16. A 1980 study of 294 elderly not living in an institution and not dependent on state aid similarly found that 47 percent participated in no social activity outside the home, and for the remaining 53 percent there was a wide range in the number of hours spent per week in activity outside the family. Wu, "A Survey of Emotional Status." A study of retirees in Shanghai similarly found that despite a variety of organized activities, most elderly were heavily burdened at home and lived too far away for easy use of existing parks. Yuan, "Living Conditions of Elderly Retirees in Shanghai."

17. An early morning exercise group I joined in Beijing in 1979 was notable for the large number of active participants and the complete absence of children. Several elderly regulars explained that this group was just for them and their friends and that during this time they had no household responsibilities.

18. I interviewed both of these women and visited their places of work in June 1979.

7. The Childless Elderly

1. Pruitt, *A Daughter of Han,* p. 110; Yang, *The Chinese Family,* p. 198; James McGough, "Marriage and Adoption in Chinese Society," unpub. Ph.D. diss., Department of Anthropology, Michigan State University, 1975, p. 35; Wolfram Eberhard, "The Upper-Class Family in Traditional China," in *The Family in History,* ed. Charles E. Rosenberg (Philadelphia: University of Pennsylvania Press, 1975), pp. 81–82.

2. Soong Ching-ling, "The China Welfare Institute," *China Reconstructs* 27. 6 (June 1978): 6–10; Dwight Perkins, *China's Modern Economy in Historical Perspective* (Stanford: Stanford University Press, 1975), p. 14; *RMRB,* May 24, 1956; Pruitt, *A Daughter of Han,* pp. 55–65.

3. In 1953 the Chinese population was estimated at 582,603,000; 48.7 percent (283,718,000) were under 29 years of age, and only 11.8 percent (69,081,000) were 50 or older. Aird, "Population Growth in the People's Republic," p. 468. According to informal reports of former residents, the childless appear to make up

no more than 15 percent of urban or rural elderly populations, and most frequently they represent 7-10 percent of the total elderly population. These estimates are confirmed by reports on the rural welfare stipends and by two village
censuses. In a 1962 census 9 percent of the elderly team members (N=3/31), or
1.5 percent (N=3/212) of the entire village, were childless. Myrdal, *Report From
a Chinese Village*, pp. 38–44. In a 1977 census there was not a single childless elderly individual in a team of 27 households. Croll, "Chiang Village," pp. 786–814.
Given the recently lowered child mortality, the vastly improved epidemic control, and the absence of major wars since 1952, it is likely that a range of 0 to 2
percent childless elderly is a more accurate indication of the long-term situation
than either the 1962 census or the 1956–1958 newspaper reports when the legacies
of 30 years of famine and war were much stronger. *Gan Su Ri Bao*, Nov. 10,
1956; *RMRB*, Nov. 15, 1956; *Ching Hai Ri Bao*, Jan. 6, 1957; *Zhe Jiang Ri Bao*,
Oct. 16, 1957; *Zhong Guo Qing Nian Bao*, June 4, 1958; *Da Gong Bao* (Hong
Kong), Sept. 2, 1958; *Gan Su Ri Bao*, Sept. 27, 1958.

4. *Qiong bang zi jing shen fang guang wang* (The qiong bang spirit spread
out) (Beijing: Ren Min Chu Ban She, 1975), pp. 55–61; Crook and Crook, *Ten
Mile Inn*.

5. *Xi Kang Ri Bao*, Jan. 19, 1955; *Da Gong Bao*, Oct. 30, 1955; *RMRB*, Nov.
16, 1955; Feb. 5, 1956; *Xing Hua Ri Bao* (Nanjing), Jan. 20, 1956; *Jie Fang Ri Bao*,
Jan. 30, 1956.

6. *RMRB*, Jan. 26, 1956. In the beginning the administrative burden was
placed entirely on higher stage cooperatives, with production teams providing
the material support. Gradually the burden on the lowest levels was reduced.
First, brigade-level welfare funds took over the funeral and clothing expenses and
in some cases even paid for grain and cash stipends. Since at least 1970 in the most
politically advanced areas there has been an effort to move the level of responsibility one administrative step higher, from brigade to commune.

7. *Ji Lin Ri Bao*, Nov. 26, 1956; *Guang Xi Ri Bao*, Feb. 2, 1956; Feb. 7, 1957;
Tie Lu Gong Ren (Guangzhou), Feb. 28, 1957; *Lu Da Ri Bao*, Oct. 8, 1957; *Zhe
Jiang Ri Bao*, Oct. 16, 1957; *Bao Tou Ri Bao*, Oct. 31, 1957; *Zhong Guo Qing
Nian Bao*, Dec. 1, 1957; *Da Gong Bao*, (Beijing), Jan. 24, 1958; *Su Zhou Da
Cong*, Jan. 30, *Qun Cong Bao* (Sichuan), May 4, 1958; *RMRB*, Nov. 16,
Mar. 18, 1958; *Xin Hua Ri Bao* (Nanjing), Jan. 22, 1956; *Jie Fang Ri Bao* (Shang-
hai), Jan. 30, 1956; *Da Gong Bao* (Hong Kong), Apr. 29, 1956.

8. *RMRB*, June 10, 1958; *Da Gong Bao* (Hong Kong), July 23, Sept. 2, Oct.
25, 1958; *Hong Qi* (ban yueh kan), Aug. 16, 1958.

9. *Xin Hua Nan Bao*, Nov. 25, 1958; *RMRB*, Dec. 19, 1958; Sept. 9, Oct. 23,
1959; *Zhong Guo Qing Nian Bao*, Feb. 7, 1959; *Da Gong Bao* (Hong Kong), July
20, 1959; *Jiang Xi Ri Bao*, Oct. 5, 1959; *Zhong Guo Xin Wen*, Oct. 22, 1958.

10. *RMRB*, Jan. 15, 1959.

11. *RMRB*, June 10, 1958; *Zhong Guo Xin Wen*, Oct. 24, 1958; *Wen Hui Bao*
(Hong Kong), July 23, 1958; *Si Chuan Ri Bao*, Jan. 16, 1959; *Zhong Guo Qing
Nian Bao*, Feb. 4, 1959.

12. *Gong Ren Ri Bao*, Nov. 1, 1960; *Zhong Guo Xin Wen* (Hong Kong), Jan.
10, 1961; Feb. 1, 1962; *Ao Men Ri Bao* (Macao), Jan. 15, 1961; *GRRB*, Feb. 2,
1961; Sept. 25, 1962; *RMRB*, Feb. 12, 1961; *Zhong Guo Fu Nu* 4 (Apr. 1, 1961): 8;
Zhong Guo Qing Nian Bao, Mar. 20, Apr. 1, 1962.

13. According to interviews with officials in charge of welfare work in Hebei
Province in 1979, Pu County had over 300 five-guarantee households out of a
total population of over 380,000, and *Shu Lu County* had over 500 out of a total

population of over 490,000. Pu County planned to build a home for only 20 residents; Shu Lu already had a home for just 25 and planned to restrict the next additional home to former cadres and model workers.

14. In 1978 the average annual income in Nan Yuan from the collective sector was 450 yuan per agricultural worker and 540 yuan per worker in a commune industry. In contrast, the national average wage for state sector workers was 644 yuan and the per capita (not per worker) wage in collective agriculture was 70–72 yuan. BR 46 (Nov. 16, 1979): 17–20; 16 (Apr. 21, 1980): 17; 12 (Mar. 24, 1980).

15. Money for welfare recipients came from the brigade accumulation fund (gong gong ji lei), which was usually divided between a large reserve fund (gong ji jin) to guard against bad years and a welfare fund (gong yi jin) to cover collective entertainment, medical expenses, and education fees as well as aid to the destitute. There was no fund especially maintained for five-guarantee households.

16. In one study over 75 percent of the teams had one or no five-guarantee households. Parish and Whyte, Village and Family, p. 76. In contrast, Tian Jia in a 10-year period housed 27 five-guarantee households in its old-age home and partially supported 10 others outside the home. Although in any one year each team supported an average of only 1 or 2 five-guarantee households, the concentration in a brigade where all teams lived in one village was higher than usual. For example, in nearby Ninth Street Brigade just outside the county seat there was 1 five-guarantee household, and in Hua Xi Brigade in Jiangsu there were 4. In these two brigades the total population was less than half that of Tian Jia, so the ratios were rather close, but because Tian Jia Brigade had an absolutely larger number, the problem of five-guarantee households was experienced there very differently.

17. In 1978 per capita income in Tian Jia was 114 yuan, while the national average was 70–72 yuan.

18. In all four rural communities visited in 1979 there had been a large drop in the number of five-guarantee households in the preceding 5–7 years. The Nan Yuan old-age home went from 90 to 66 residents, Tian Family from 14 to 8, Hua Xi from 5 to 4, and the Ninth Street Brigade from 3 to 1. Similar trends were reported in the official press. Zhong Guo Xin Wen (Guangzhou), Nov. 21, 1972; Da Gong Bao (Hong Kong), Dec. 5, 1972.

19. NCNA (Chengchou), Aug. 15, 1973, trans. in SCMP 73–35. 5445 (Aug. 29, 1973): 53; Xin Hua (Guangzhou), Dec. 27, 1973; July 26, 1974; PR 36 (Sept. 5, 1975): 23; Da Gong Bao (Hong Kong), Apr. 26, 1976, p. 2.

20. The 23 childless elderly from the Hong Kong sample came from 8 different rural communities. The 3 who were overseas Chinese received a direct cash payment of 12–15 yuan per month through the county using provincial funds. The remaining 20 childless elderly lived in 5 different villages and, except for one community where the benefits took the form of subsidized workpoints, received similar monthly benefits of 15–17.5 kilos of grain and 2.5 yuan cash. In two model villages I visited in 1979 benefits were substantially better. At Hua Xi, the 4 five-guarantee households received 17.5 kilos of grain and 5 yuan per month, vegetables daily, eggs weekly, and meat at least once a month. In Ninth Street Brigade the single five-guarantee household was supplied with all her food (the exact amount was impossible to verify) and 8 yuan per month.

21. "The best method [for elderly without children] is, on the basis of one's own scrutinizing, to find a close friend with whom one has special relations [guan xi] to take care of one. The cooperative will give some money, the close friend will care for the person, and the old man or woman will do some housework for the family. Such a policy reduces the number of five-guarantee households, and it

also reduces the cooperative's responsibility and expenditures." *Hu Bei Ri Bao*, Oct. 13, 1956. See also "Spring Shoots," *CL* 10 (1976): 13; Hsing Tung-chi, "The Northern Wilderness Is My Home," *CL* 9 (1976): 84; *Da Gong Bao* (Hong Kong), Mar. 20, 1974; Hung Shan, "Spring Comes to the South," *CL* 5 (1972): 23–28.

22. Among the 23 elderly welfare recipients in the Hong sample, 20 percent of the men (N = 2/10) and over 90 percent of the women (12/13) had special relationships with younger villagers who provided important supplements to their monthly rations. Assuming that isolates are more often institutionalized than those who are socially engaged, the sex ratios in the old-age homes visited in 1979 gave added proof of women's superior coping strategies: at Nan Yuan there were 49 men, 17 women; at Tian Family, 5 men, 3 women; and at the Taihang Mountain home, 13 men, 4 women.

23. Great Uncle Li and "The Useless Old Woman," pseudonyms, were five-guarantee households known to one of my Hong Kong respondents who lived in their village in 1964–1974. As a cadre in charge of gathering family histories during one political campaign in the late 1960s, she was in a good position to learn the history of the older villagers. I interviewed her in 1976, two years after she left China.

24. *RMRB*, May 7, 1950.

25. For workers covered by the Labor Insurance Regulations, benefits for sick leave, disability, funerals, and survivors are all calculated as a proportion of the workers' salary. In addition, most large collective enterprises have a minimum per capita income for households of their employees. When the total family income fails to meet this per capita standard, the workplace subsidizes the family until the minimum level is met. The actual cash amount varies from place to place. In Beijing in the summer of 1979 most large factories set a minimum of 22 yuan for each family member over 16 years of age.

26. Terrill, *Flowers on an Iron Tree*, p. 181. In 1966-1978 the Neighborhood Committees were known as Neighborhood Revolutionary Committees (*Jie Dao Ge Ming Wei Yun Hui*), but the type of cadre and the relative level of authority vis-à-vis other municipal organs were unchanged.

27. In reviewing a request for aid, committee members would conduct an "investigation" into the personal circumstances of the applicant. This necessitated visiting not only the applicant's house but also those of neighbors to attest that the applicant's standard of living had in fact fallen far below subsistence and that the causes of the decline were beyond remedy by the applicant.

28. "On the Home Front," *PR* 16 (Apr. 21, 1978): 30–31; *Xin Min Wan Bao* (Shanghai), Jan. 5, 1966. Hong Kong respondents also heavily stressed the prevalence of voluntary, private arrangements.

29. *Gong Shang Ri Bao*, Aug. 4, 1950.

30. *Wen Hui Bao* (Hong Kong), Aug. 5, 1950.

31. Ezra Vogel, *Canton under Communism* (New York: Harper and Row, 1971), p. 369; *Da Gong Bao* (Hong Kong), May 22, 1952.

32. *Xin Wen Ri Bao* (Shanghai), Feb. 3, 1953; *GRRB*, June 4, 1955.

33. RMRB, Apr. 27, 1954; *Zhong Guo Xin Wen*, Sept. 30, 1955; Feb. 2, 1956; *Hei Long Jiang Ri Bao*, Dec. 8, 1956; *Da Gong Bao* (Tianjin), July 9, 1956.

34. *Jin Bu Ri Bao* (Tianjin), Oct. 27, 1952; *Da Gong Bao* (Hong Kong), May 22, 1952.

35. As of November 1952 the National Labor Insurance Regulations provided for only 14 homes in the entire country. *RMRB*, Jan. 11, 1953.

36. Comparison of the size of the institutionalized population and the dates

at which formal old-age homes were opened shows that larger cities faced a
greater demand for institutional accommodation than did smaller cities, and the
demand was so pressing in 1949-1952 that the policy of returning childless elderly
to their natal villages was inadequate. In early 1952 Guangzhou had 2 homes with
over 270 residents, and by 1956 it had 8 homes with over 2000 residents. The
major cities of Tianjin (Tientsin), Shanghai, and Beijing reported similar rapid
growth. *Nan Fang Ri Bao*, May 22, 1952; *Wen Hui Bao* (Hong Kong), Dec. 4,
1956; *Xin Wen Bao*, July 24, 1956. In contrast, the smaller cities of Changzhou,
Xiamen, Wuzhou, and the Swatow area of Fujian had either no homes specifically
for the aged or small ones with a total city-wide capacity of less than 100 beds.
Xia Men Ri Bao, Aug. 7, 1956; *Gong Ren Bao* (Changzhou), Aug. 9, 1956; *Da
Gong Bao* (Hong Kong), Aug. 29, 1956; *Guang Xi Ri Bao*, Nov. 1, 1956. In 1979
in Changzhou city officials reported that the city did not have an old-age home
because there was no real demand for the service.

37. *Guang Ming Ri Bao*, Sept. 8, 1956; *Nan Fang Ri Bao*, Nov. 25, 1956; *Da
Gong Bao* (Beijing), Jan. 7, 1957.

38. *Guang Ming Ri Bao*, July 24, 1956.

39. *Da Gong Bao* (Hong Kong), Aug. 29, 1956; *Zhong Guo Xin Wen*, Oct.
24, 1956; Apr. 25, 1957; *Guang Xi Ri Bao*, Nov. 1, 1956; *Shen Yang Ri Bao*, Nov.
22, 1956; *Wen Hui Bao* (Hong Kong), Feb. 18, 1957; *Chong Qing Ri Bao*, July 25,
1957.

40. *Liao Ning Ri Bao*, Oct. 5, 1958; *Da Gong Bao* (Hong Kong), Nov. 12 and
29, 1958; *Xia Men Ri Bao*, Dec. 26, 1958.

41. *Lu Da Ri Bao*, Sept. 29, 1958; *Yu Nan Ri Bao*, Oct. 8, 1958; *Zhong Guo
Qing Nian Bao*, Oct. 16, 1958; *Qiao Wu Bao*, Oct. 20, 1958; *Da Gong Bao* (Hong
Kong), Nov. 27, 1958; *GRRB*, Dec. 24, 1958; *Guang Dong Qiao Bao*, Jan. 7,
1959.

42. *Da Gong Bao* (Beijing), Sept. 26, 1959.

43. *Yang Cheng Wan Bao*, Jan. 2, 1965; *Wen Hui Bao* (Hong Kong), Nov.
13, 1963; *Zhong Guo Xin Wen*, Oct. 29, June 19, 1965; *GRRB*, Dec. 26, 1961;
Aug. 17, 1963; Oct. 22, 1964; *Xin Min Wan Bao* (Shanghai), Jan. 13, May 23,
1964.

44. *Zhou Mo Bao* (Hong Kong), Mar. 16, 1972; "On the Home Front," *PR* 16
(Apr. 21, 1978): 30–31; "On the Home Front," *BR* 27 (July 7, 1978): 47; "Social
Welfare Institutions," *BR* 45 (Nov. 9, 1979): 28; Interview with head of Shijia-
chuang municipal old-age home, June 1979.

45. The respondent in this first case study was Yang Meihua, a pseudonym,
Lao Yeh's foster daughter, who was interviewed in 1976 when she was visiting her
elderly parents in Hong Kong. Wu Laoliu, a pseudonym, was interviewed in 1979
at the Shijiachuang home.

8. Old Age under Communism

1. In 1953 life expectancy at birth was 39.8 years for males and 40.8 for females. By 1964, they had risen to 55.5 and 58.7, by 1972 to 61.4 and 63.7, and by
1984 to 64.9 and 64.1. Banister, *China's Changing Population*, p. 116.

2. Walder, "Wage Reform and the Web of Factory Interest," *The China Quarterly* No. 109 (March 1987), p. 23.

3. For good descriptions of the role of class labels, see Chan et al., *Chen Village*, and Gao Yuan, *Born Red*.

4. Carl Riskin, *China's Political Economy*, p. 290.

5. The key legislative change came in October 1984 with *guo fa* #141, when
the State Council permitted rural *hu kou* villagers to move freely to the 60,000 *zhen*
below county level if they could supply their own grain rations. *GWYGB* 1984,
pp. 919–20. A year later the State Council passed new regulations outlining the
procedures for obtaining temporary urban *hu kou* for those over sixteen who
stayed more than three months in a city. *GWYGB* 1985, pp. 908–9.

6. Banister, *China's Changing Population*, pp. 35, 116.

7. In the 1964 census there were 11.5 million three-year-olds and 30.2 million
one-year-olds. *Ibid.*, p. 27.

8. *Ibid.*, pp. 116, 230.

9. *Ibid.*, p. 24; *ZGTJNJ 1988*, pp. 106–7.

10. Between 1953 and 1987 the Chinese population grew 83 percent from 582
million to 1.067 billion. By contrast the population over sixty grew by 132 percent
and that over seventy grew by 142 percent. Percentages are calculated from figures
given in Banister, *China's Changing Population*, p. 24 and *ZGTJNJ 1988*, pp.
105–7.

11. Assuming a two-child TFR, Banister predicts that the population sixty-
five and older would number 71.7 million or 6 percent of the population by 1995,
93.5 million or 7 percent by 2005, and 153.3 million or 11 percent by 2020. *China's
Changing Population*, p. 372.

12. A dependency ratio is the ratio of the number of people between ages 0
and 14 plus the number of those 65 and older compared to the number of those
between ages 15 and 64. Using the population estimates in Banister's *China's
Changing Population*, pp. 25, 27, and 34 for 1953, 1964, and 1982, and those from
ZGTJNJ 1988, p. 107, I calculated these dependency ratios. In countries where few
teenagers work or elderly withdraw from the work force before age 65, such a ratio
understates the level of dependency. However, between 1953 and 1987, these ages
rather accurately represent the ratio in China between economically dependent
and economically active because few Chinese teenagers continued in school past
age 16 and most elderly remained active in the household economy between 60
and 64.

13. In 1953 elderly were 10.6 percent of the dependent population, but by
1964, as a result of the high fertility throughout the 1950s and the very high mortality of the old during the famine that followed the Great Leap Forward, the
elderly as a share declined to 7.8 percent, and even after some gains in life expectancies for the old and sustained declines in birth rates in the 1970s, the old were
still only 15.8 percent of the dependent age groups as of December 1987. Based
on the 1973–75 cancer survey, life expectancy for people between 60 and 64 was
an additional fifteen years, and for those between 70 and 74 an additional ten (Banister, p. 91). Numbers for calculating the percentage of old in the dependent population are those shown in note 12 above.

14. Also, because during the 1950s annual TFRs ranged between 5.5 and 6.5
in both urban and rural areas, most elderly parents in the 1980s had at least three
adult children to provide support. Banister, p. 230.

15. In 1964 the mean age of the city population was 23.9 and for *xian* it was
25.0. By 1985 it was 30 for the cities and 26.1 for *xian*. *Zhong Guo She Hui Tong
Ji Zi Liao 1987*, p. 24.

16. The most extreme case I have found of this trend was Shanghai, where
in 1953 only 3.3 percent of the population was 60 and older while in the nation
as a whole it was 6.6 percent. Tao Liqun, "Guan yu wo guo ren kou lao nian hua
wen ti."

17. The divergence between rural and urban birth rates is documented in this table:

Year	Rural TFR	Urban TFR	Year	Rural TFR	Urban TFR
1950	5.9	5.0	1970	6.3	3.2
1955	6.3	5.6	1975	3.9	1.7
1960	6.5	3.7	1980	2.4	1.1
1965	6.3	3.7	1988	2.6	1.0

Sources: 1950–80, Banister, p. 243. For 1988, *RMRB*, Sept. 20, 1989, p. 5.

18. Walder, *Chinese Neo-Traditionalism*, Ch. 2.

19. Article 93 of the 1954 Constitution, Article 27 of the 1975 Constitution, Article 50 of the 1978 Constitution, and Articles 44 and 45 of the 1982 Constitution all make this promise explicit.

20. Riskin, *China's Political Economy*, p. 290; Reeitsu Kojima, "Agricultural Organization: New Forms, New Contradictions," *The China Quarterly* No. 116 (Dec. 1988), p. 713.

21. See *Guo fa* No. 141, in *GWYGB* 1984, pp. 919–20.

22. For the number of emigrants, *RMRB*, Aug. 14, 1988, p. 8. On composition, *Xin Bao* (Hong Kong) April 16, 1987; Wang Shuxin, "Jing ji ti zhi gai ge"; Zhang Yulin, "Peasant Workers in County Towns," p. 204.

23. Mao Kuangsheng and Zhou Guangfu, "Ren kou nian ling jie gou dui jia ting bian hua de ying xiang" (Influence of age structure on family change), *Ren Kou Yan Jiu*, No. 5 (1988), pp. 8–12.

24. Yang Zongchuan. "Hubei sheng cheng zhen xiang lao nian ren kou xian chuang fen xi" (Analysis of condition of elderly in urban and rural Hubei), *Ren Kou Yan Jiu*, No. 1 (1989), pp. 28–36.

25. *RMRB*, Jan. 10, 1990, p. 6.

26. For a fuller discussion of rural welfare losses in post-Mao years, see Davis, "Chinese Social Welfare."

27. *Zhong Guo She Hui Tong Ji Zi Liao*, p. 120.

28. *RMRB* Oct. 17, 1988, p. 4, Jan. 10, 1990, p. 6.

29. Tian Wen-guang. "Da li tui hang nong cun ji hua sheng yu yang lao bao xian," *Ren Kou Yen Jiu* No. 4 (1988), pp. 56–58.

30. Davis, "Urban Job Mobility."

31. For description and analysis of these shifts, *ibid.*

32. Between 1978 and 1987, employment in the state sector grew by 22 million jobs, while collective and private sectors added 19 million. During the same interval bonuses rose from 2.9 percent of the urban wage, to 14 percent, *ZGTJNJ 1981*, p. 427, and *ZGTJNJ 1988*, pp. 153, 182.

33. By 1987, 34 percent of pensioners were 65 or older, 29 percent between 60 and 64, and 35 percent under age 60. *Zhong Guo Lao Dong Ke Xue*, No. 11 (1988), p. 42. In a 1987 survey of 36,755 rural and urban citizens 60 and over, they found that 56.1 percent of all urban respondents received a pension. *BR*, Nov. 14–20, 1988, pp. 27–28. In 1978 17 percent of pensioners had retired from collective enterprises; by 1980 the number had increased to 22 percent and by December 1985, when only 25 percent of the total urban labor force worked in collectives, 28 percent of urban pensioners came from collective enterprises. For 1978 figures, see *Lao Dong Gong Zi Ren Shi Zhi Du Gai Ge de Yan Jiu yu Tan Dao*, p. 453. For 1980, Chinese National Committee on Aging, *Yan jiu zi liao*, May 28, 1984; for 1985, *BR*, Jan. 19, 1987, p. 21. The growth is also documented in the vast sums spent by collectives in Shanghai, *Shang Hai Tong Ji Nian Jian 1983*, p. 335.

34. In 1986 78 percent of all pensioners lived in the 353 largest cities, which had only 11.5 percent of the total population, and in such inland cities as Changsha, Chengdu, Chongqing, and Guiyang, pensioners equaled between 14 and 20 percent of the work force (*Zhong Guo Cheng Shi Tong Ji Nian Jian 1987*, pp. 1 and 539). Another indicator of this shift is found in looking at Shanghai. At the end of 1978 15 percent of all pensioners in China had lived in Shanghai; by December 1987, Shanghaiese represented only 7 percent of the total. Davis, "Unequal Chances," p. 229 and *BR*, July 18–24, 1988, pp. 28–29.

35. In 1982 *zhih yuan* were 25 percent of the working population, but among women between ages 50 and 74 and men between 60 and 74 (that is, the non-working young old), only 13 percent drew pensions. By 1987 *zhih yuan* were still 25 percent of the total working population, but among women 50–74 and men 60–74, 18.2 percent drew pensions (Guo Wu Yuan Ren Kou Pu Cha Ban Gong Shi, *Zhong Guo 1982 Ren Kou Pu Cha*, Table 19, and *ZGTJNJ 1988*, pp. 106–7, 203.

36. In 1978 there were 3.1 million pensioners and 95.1 million urban employees; in 1987 there were 19.6 and 137.8 million respectively. In 1978 the average pension of 551 *yuan* was 90 percent of the average wage; in 1987 it was 1,263 *yuan* or 89 percent of the average urban wage. Growth for pensions was thus 129 percent, for wages 137 percent. *ZGTJNJ 1988*, pp. 153, 190, and 203.

37. *Zhong Guo Lao Nian* No. 4 (1987), p. 42.

38. This included those who had been at or above the rank of local government head or CCP vice-secretary prior to September 1949, at or above county-level CCP secretary before December 1942, or a revolutionary cadre before July 7, 1937. Interview with representatives from the Hebei Province Ministry of Civil Affairs, Shijiazhuang, May 1979. Also outlined in *Lao Dong Ren Shi Zhi Du Gai Ge*, pp. 505–25.

39. Hong Yong Lee, "The Socialist State, Political Elites, and Reforms in China," ch. 12.

40. Based on articles published in the mid-1980s, it appears that several meetings in 1980 were critical for pushing the new line, including a statement by Ye Jianying at the 11th session of the Fifth NPC, and an August 18 speech by Deng at the party plenum. *Lao Dong Gong Zuo Ren Shi Zhi Du Gai Ge*, p. 509, and Xin Hua News, Feb. 4, 1983, translated in *Survey of World Broadcasts* BII/13–14.

41. "Guo Wu Yuan guan yu lao gan bu tui zhi xiu yang de zhan shih gui ding," (Temporary regulation on retirement of old cadres), *Zhong Guo Fa Lu Nian Jian 1987*, pp. 173–74.

42. Depending on the year in which they joined the revolution, they would receive a pension of between 106 and 116 percent of their last wage, access to special clinics and leisure centers, and generous travel allowances, which varied by rank. Former central level officials got 400 km of free travel by car per month, those of vice-minister rank 300 km, and those of section chief rank 150 km. These perquisites were first instituted on a trial basis in 1984 and generalized to all *li xiu* cadres in February 1986. *Lao Dong Gong Zuo Ren Shi Zhi Du Gai Ge*, p. 509; *Zhong Guo Lao Nian* No. 4 (1986), pp. 44–46.

43. Estimates of the total number of those who qualified varies from 2.1 million to 4.3 million. Central Committee "Decision Concerning Retirement of Elderly Cadres" (translated in *Issues and Studies*, Vol. XX, No. 8 (Aug. 1984, pp. 96–105) notes that the maximum number to qualify will be 2.5 million. *BR* No. 37 (Sept. 12, 1983), p. 6, says there will be 2 million; and *RMRB*, Nov. 9, 1984, p. 4, says 2.13 million, as does *RMRB* of Sept. 21, 1987, p. 4. By contrast, *Zhong Guo Lao Dong Ren Shi Bao*, Aug. 19, 1987, p. 3, estimates that 4.15 million are

eligible. I have assumed that the number in the first document gives the most accurate estimate of what the government originally saw as the scope of privilege.

44. In 1987 non-military *li xiu* cadres averaged yearly pensions of 1,635 *yuan*, and the 100,000 military *li xiu* cadres received an average pension of 2,363 *yuan*. *Zhong Guo Lao Dong Ke Xue* No. 10 (1988), p. 43; *RMRB*, June 27, 1988, p. 4.

45. *Zhong Guo Lao Dong Ren Shi Bao*, Jan. 18, 1989, p. 1, on Aug. 1989 Regulations of the Organization Bureau of the CCP Central Committee and the Ministry of Personnel pushed for full implementation of the end of lifetime appointments.

46. Between 1978 and 1983, *zhih yuan* wages rose 34 percent and prices rose 15 percent. Between 1984 and 1987, inflationary pressures increased. Wages rose 62.8 percent in absolute terms, 26 percent in real terms. In 1988 prices jumped far ahead of wage increases, and by December 1988, 34.9 percent of urban families saw a real decline in per capita purchasing power, with no immediate prospect of improvement in the first six months of 1989. *RMRB*, June 24, 1988, p. 2; *RMRB*, March 1, 1989, p. 2; *South China Morning Post* (Hong Kong), June 18, 1989, p. 1; *RMRB*, July 31, 1989, p. 1; Wei Jiuling, "Gai ge shi nian," p. 25.

47. For a good discussion of elderly over age 70 in Guangzhou, see Ikels, "New Options for Urban Elderly."

48. A 1988 national survey of retirees estimated that 20 percent of all urban pensioners held regular paid jobs, and that in addition to their full pension they drew an average monthly salary of 91 *yuan*. *RMRB*, Oct. 22, 1989, p. 8. Surveys in Tianjin conducted in 1984 found that 27 percent of pensioners were working. Yuan Fang ("The Status and Role of the Chinese Elderly," p. 43). In my surveys in Shanghai in 1987 and Wuhan in 1988, I found that among newly retired women, 60 percent had held paid jobs at some time after retirement, and 40 percent did so at the time of the interview.

49. In 1978 the official urban unemployment rate was 5.3 percent; by 1985 it had fallen to 1.8 percent. By the end of the decade, however, it was rising again; in Dec. 1988 it stood at 2 percent and by fall 1989 it was reported to have doubled to 4 percent. *Zhong Guo She Hui Tong Ji Zi Liao 1987*, p. 35; *RMRB*, Sept. 14, 1989, p. 1; *Ming Bao* (Hong Kong), Nov. 17, 1989, p. 8.

50. In 1978 *zhih yuan* averaged 615 *yuan*; in 1983 it was 1,459 *yuan*. *ZGTJNJ 1987*, p. 799.

51. Wei Jiuling, "Gai ge shi nian," *Zhong Guo Lao Dong Ke Xue*, No. 1 (1989), p. 25; Walder, "Income Distribution in Tianjin," Ch. 6, in *Chinese Society on the Eve of Tiananmen*, edited by Davis and Vogel.

52. In 1978 state employees averaged 644 *yuan*, in 1987, 1546 *yuan* — an increase of 140 percent. Those in collectives averaged 506 *yuan* in 1978 and 1,207 *yuan* in 1987 — an increase of 139 percent. Thus in absolute terms the gap between wages in the two sectors grew. *ZGTJNJ 1988*, p. 190.

53. Wei Jiuling, "Gai ge de shi nian."

54. Walder, "Wage Reform and the Web of Factory Interests," *The China Quarterly*, No. 109 (March 1987), pp. 22–41.

55. Between 1978 and 1988, wages increased 160 percent, bonuses, 800 percent. In December 1988, however, bonuses equaled only 13 percent of monthly pay, while wages still brought in 72 percent. *RMRB*, Feb. 19, 1989, p. 8 and *Chinese Statistics Monthly*, Nov. 1989, p. 47.

56. For an earlier, and in some ways more detailed, discussion of the specific policies that supported the advantages of the old, see Davis, "Unequal Chances, Unequal Outcomes."

57. See Ch. 3, note 8, above.

58. Between 1978 and 1987, rural residents built 8.6 billion square meters of new housing, and increased the share of income spent on housing from 3.2 percent to 14.5 percent. *GWYGB 1988*, p. 178, and *ZGTJNJ 1988*, p. 823.

59. Between 1981 and 1987, there were 1.8 billion square meters of new urban housing. *GWYGB 1988*, p. 178. In 1978, 7.8 percent of capital construction went to housing; in 1981–82 it had risen to 25 percent. Naughton, "The Decline of Central Control," pp. 66–67.

60. In 1978 city families averaged 4.2 square meters of living space, rural families, 8.1 square meters; by 1987 urban families had risen to 8.4 square meters, rural families to 16.0 square meters. *ZGTJNJ 1988*, p. 836.

61. At the beginning of the reform era, rural households had averaged 5.7 members, urban households, 4.2; by 1987 the rural average had fallen to 5.01 and the urban to 3.74. *ZGTJNJ 1988*, pp. 806, 822.

62. Between 1982 and 1987, the number of people in families rose 8.2 percent, from 971 million to 1,051 million, while the number of families rose 12.7 percent, from 220 million to 248 million. *Zhong Guo She Hui Ze Liao 1987*, p. 31, and *ZGTJNJ 1988*, p. 103.

63. *Zhong Guo 1987 Nian 1% Ren Kou Chou Yang Diao Cha*, pp. 506–7; *RMRB*, Aug. 5, 1988, p. 4.

64. Yuan Jihui, *Dang Dai Lao Nian She Hui Xue*, p. 30; *BR*, Nov. 14–20, 1988, p. 27.

65. Yuan Jihui, *Dang Dai Lao Nian She Hui Xue*, p. 159.

66. *Ibid.*

67. Yang Zongchuan. "Hubei sheng cheng zhen xiang lao nian ren kou xian chuang fen xi" (Analysis of condition of elderly in urban and rural Hubei), *Ren Kou Yan Jiu*, No. 1 (1989), pp. 28–36. Zhou Jing, "Wo guo xian dai hua guo cheng zhong nong cun jia ting gui mo" (Family form in the Chinese transition to modernization), *Ren Kou Yan Jiu*, No. 2 (1988), pp. 17–21.

68. In Shanghai, for example, suburban elderly were more apt to live alone than those living in the city proper, and on average rural Shanghai households were smaller and less complex than those in the city. In 1982, 15.5 percent of suburban Shanghai families lived in three-generation households; in the city proper, 25.1 percent lived jointly. Households of six or more members were also almost twice as likely to be in the city (14.2 percent) as in the suburbs (8.1 percent). By 1987 average household size in the city was 3.3; in the suburbs it was 3.2, as opposed to 3.7 and 3.8, respectively, in 1978. Fu Luxia, "Jia ting jie gou," *She hui*, No. 5 (1987), pp. 39–41; *Shanghai She Hui Tong Ji Ze Liao 1980–1983*, p. 11; *Shanghai Tong Ji Nian Jian 1988*, pp. 80, 81.

69. Fu Luxia, "Jia ting jie gou"; Zhang Yulin, "The Shift of Agricultural Surplus Labor"; Gu Jirui, *Jia ting Xiao Fe*, pp. 30–31.

70. Cohen, *House Divided, House United*, p. 225.

71. L. S. Sung, "Property and Family Division," p. 377.

72. Zhou Jing, "Wo guo xian dai."

73. This pattern emerges in most published research by Chinese and in my own interviews after 1980. See Qiu Liping, "Cheng shi gao ning lao ren," pp. 22–26; Bei jing jing ji xue yuan, pp. 15–21; Pan, pp. 260–72; Yuan Jihui, *Cheng shi lao nian sheng huo*, pp. 54–56. In Shanghai (1987), 91 percent of my elderly respondents lived with an adult child; in Wuhan (1988), it was 87 percent.

74. After 1980 there was an expansion of the private housing market, which theoretically could have allowed urban families to realize their housing preferences. But the upsurge was primarily in smaller towns and also was concentrated among families with the lowest incomes. (*RMRB*, Nov. 11, 1988, p. 2, and State

Statistical Bureau 1985, pp. 152–53.) In the public housing market, one major obstacle to rapid increase in housing starts was that rents remained so low that the state lost money on every square meter of new housing it built, and it therefore had clear incentives to stop building new housing until a new rental structure could be devised, which in the inflationary period after 1986 was politically impossible. Gu Jirui, *Jia ting xiao fei; BR*, Nov. 14, 1988, pp. 18–20. For a good overview through mid-1980s, see Yok-shiu F. Lee, "The Urban Housing Problem in China," *The China Quarterly*, No.115 (Sept. 1988), pp. 387–407.

75. The 1982 Constitution, which replaced that of 1978, introduced several additional safeguards against state intervention in private life. However, it did not restore the "freedom to change . . . residence" that had been enshrined in the 1954 Constitution and thus maintained one of the legal impediments to easy or spontaneous changes in household composition. The constitutions are translated in Blaustein, *Fundamental Legal Documents*, pp. 2–33 (for 1954); for 1978, *PR*, March 17, 1978, pp. 5–14; for 1982, *BR*, Dec. 27, 1982, pp. 10–29. Similarly the household (*hu kou*) registration system, which required all urban residents to get police approval for any permanent change of address, remained firmly in place and similarly restricted the freedom of movement that would otherwise have encouraged more frequent changes in household membership. Examples of how the *hu kou* laws shaped urban families were found in a series of articles in a legal education journal directed at informing the urban population of their rights. *Min zu yu fa zhi* No. 10 (1983), p. 17; No. 1 (1984), p. 48; No. 3 (1985), p. 34, and No.12 (1985), p. 47.

76. *Hu bei ri bao*, Jan. 1, 1987, p. 1; *RMRB*, April 29, 1989, p. 1.

77. In the 1983 Chinese survey of families in five cities, researchers found that the percentage of newlyweds living neo-locally fell steadily after 1954, until by 1977–82, the percentage (32.3 percent) just barely exceeded the pre-1937 percentage (30.9 percent). (Y. K. Pan, *Zhong guo cheng shi hun yin yu jia ting*, p. 110.) An additional contrast comes with my respondents who married between 1940 and 1955. In my Shanghai survey, 41 percent of my respondents had lived neo-locally at the time of marriage; among the Wuhan respondents it was 45 percent. Similar levels of dependency also appeared in analysis of the 1981 pretest for the 1982 census in Wuxi, where researchers found that 70 percent of married men between 25 and 29 and 60 percent of those under age 35 were not heads of household. Tian and Lee, "The Chinese Family," pp. 619–20.

78. Using national census data, researchers have estimated that between April 1958 and June 1981, the probability of all grandparents surviving to a child's birth rose from 3 percent to 31 percent, and the probability of no paternal grandparent surviving until a child's fifteenth birthday declined from 85 percent to 54 percent. Tu et al., "Mortality Decline and Chinese Family Structure," *Journal of Gerontology* Vol. 44, No. 4 (July 1989), pp. 162–63.

79. In Whyte's 1987 study in Chengdu, 56 percent of women married between 1933 and 1948 had all four parents at their wedding; among those married between 1977 and 1987, it was 79 percent. Whyte, "Changes in Mate Choice in Chengdu," Table 3.

80. In 1930 it was estimated that at birth, 43 percent of firstborns had at least one paternal grandparent living; by age fifteen the percentage fell to 7 percent. Using the 1982 census it is estimated that 93 percent of firstborns had a paternal grandparent at birth, and 46 percent still had at least one at age 14. Tu, "Mortality Decline and Chinese Family Structure."

81. In 1988 overall TFR was 1.09 in urban areas, 2.67 in rural areas. In 1978 it had been 1.55 and 2.97 respectively (*RMRB*, Sept. 20, 1989, p. 5). In Shanghai

96.3 percent of all births in the city districts were first births (*RMRB*, Jan. 14, 1989, p. 3).

82. In June 1987 I interviewed 100 Shanghai women born between 1925 and 1935. In June 1988 I interviewed 100 of their peers in Wuhan. The Shanghai sample was drawn through a random sample of an entire residential committee; the Wuhan respondents were chosen by the leaders of three Wuhan enterprises: a heavy-machine tool factory, a large textile mill, and a collectively owned department store. Each woman was interviewed for two hours about the current composition of her household and of the household at the time of her marriage; and the occupational history of the respondent, her parents, her in-laws, her spouse, and her adult children. In Shanghai most interviews were conducted in the respondent's home in the presence of a basic-level cadre. In Wuhan the interviews were conducted in the units, but no one was present except myself and the respondent.

83. For a fuller description and analysis of these home interiors, see Davis, "My Mother's House," pp. 88–100.

84. In a 1982–83 urban survey, there was already evidence of this trend; researchers found that of those born between 1923 and 1936, 57.9 percent lived in nuclear households; for those born between 1937 and 1949, it was 76.8 percent; but for those born between 1950 and 1958 it was only 46.5 percent. (*Zhong guo cheng shi jia ting* p. 9). And in one study of patterns of nuclear families in rural areas, there was a similar analysis which concluded by saying that with the arrival of two-children families in rural China, the long-term trend would be toward rising rates of stem households. Zhou Jing, "Wo guo xian dai hua guo cheng."

85. See Walder, *Communist Neo-Traditionalism*, for a full discussion of the ways in which favoritism, particularism, and patron-client loyalties dominated the exercise of power by CCP cadres.

86. Compare, for example, the situation of young men described by Chan et al., *Chen Village*, with those described in Gao, *Born Red*.

87. In a study of Tianjin in 1984, only 8.2 percent of elderly respondents reported poor relations with children. Yuan Fang, "The Status and Role of Chinese Elderly," p. 40; Ikels, "New Options for Urban Elderly"; Yuan Jihui, *Dang Dai Lao Nian She Hui Xue*, pp. 162–66.

88. In Shanghai (1987), of the 65 percent living with a married child, 80 percent lived with a married son; in Wuhan (1989), of the 45 percent living with a married child, 84 percent lived with a married son.

89. By contrast in my 1979 urban sample, among elderly living with a married child, only 55 percent lived with a son. Ch. 3, note 8, above.

90. Honig and Hershatter, *Personal Voices*, pp. 82–97.

91. The percentage of patrilocal homes was still noticeably higher in rural areas. For example, in the only published reference to a Chinese survey I have found that breaks down rural households by degree of patrilocal preference, the patrilocal preference in rural families is overwhelming. Only 0.1 percent of all households included a son-in-law, and 0.1 percent the son of a daughter. By contrast, 28.4 percent had a resident daughter-in-law and 16.2 percent the son of a son. Gu Jirui, *Jia Ting Xiao Fei*, p. 28.

92. In 1978 the average wage for a city worker (*zhih yuan*) was 615 *yuan*; by 1988 it had risen to 1,747 *yuan*. In 1982, one out of 100 city households had a color TV and 0.6 had a refrigerator; by 1988, 43 out of 100 had a color TV and 28 out of 100 a refrigerator, *ZGTJNJ 1989*, pp. 138, 728.

93. This interpretation was given to me explicitly by both newly married children and several of the mothers in my sample.

94. Whyte and Parish, *Urban Life in Contemporary China*, p. 137.

95. In a 20-city survey of urban marriages, average costs in 1985–86 were 5,069 *yuan*, which included 1,000 *yuan* for the wedding and 4,000 *yuan* for presents. Gu Jirui, *Jia Ting Xiao Fei*, p. 343. Based on a 1986 survey in 18 large and medium cities, Chinese researchers estimated that for marriages concluded between 1981 and 1985, a groom's family on average needed between 39 and 50 months to save for the marriage of one child, and the bride's family between 24 and 31 months. Qian Jianghong, "Marriage Related Consumption," *Social Science in China*, No.1 (1988), p. 221.

96. In Shanghai 43 percent of the families had at least one CCP parent; in Wuhan it was 61 percent.

97. Honig and Hershatter, *Personal Voices*, pp. 244–63.

98. Bian Yanjie, "Equal Education and Unequal Outcomes," Table 4.

99. Susan L. Shirk, *Competitive Comrades* (Berkeley: University of California Press, 1982), pp. 52–84; Jonathan Unger, *Education Under Mao* (New York: Columbia University Press, 1982), pp. 164–70.

100. Honig and Hershatter, *Personal Voices*, p. 140.

101. An interesting confirmation of this trend was the finding in a 1986 survey of 835 Shanghai elderly over age 80. Although in general less than 10 percent of any subgroup of the population reported poor family relations, what was especially striking was that routinely the oldest, that is, those over ninety and most financially and physically dependent, reported almost no conflict with their children, and to the extent that there was a group who chafed in their subordinate role in their children's homes, it was those who were physically most independent. That is, the one table that showed dissatisfaction above 10 percent, in this case 12 percent, was in the group that labeled themselves totally able to care for themselves. Shang hai shi lao nian wen ti wei yun wei, *Gao Ling Lao Ren Wen Ti Yan Jiu*, pp. 142–50.

102. For an overview of the changes in property rights as well as a translation and analysis of the 1985 Inheritance Law, see Louis B. Schwartz, "The Inheritance Law of the People's Republic of China," *Harvard Journal of International Law*, Vol. 28, No. 2 (Spring 1987), pp. 433–64.

103. English translation from Schwartz, pp. 457–64; Chinese version in *Zhong Guo Fa Lu Nian Jian 1987*, pp. 259–60.

104. The three journals I found of greatest use were *Fa Zhi Jian She*, published by the Ministry of Justice; *Min Zu yu Fa Zhi*, published by a Shanghai-based association of jurists and legal scholars; and *Zhong Guo Fu Nu*. I also consulted *Ren Min Jing Cha, Zhong Guo Lu Shi, Lu Shi yu Fa Zhi*, but found them not very useful for inheritance issues.

105. In that same year, 16.8 percent of mediations were for marriage disputes, and 15.2 percent involved disputes over housing. *ZGTJNJ 1988*, p. 974.

106. *Ibid.*

107. *Ibid.*, p. 973.

108. In field surveys of urban elderly conducted between 1983 and 1986, the percentage of elderly who reported tense or poor relations with their children never exceeded 10 percent, and in most studies it was between 5 and 6 percent regardless of the income level of the family, the health of the old person, or the education of parents and children. Shang hai shih lao nian wen ti wei yuan wei, pp. 142–150; Yuan Jihui, *Cheng Shi Lao Nian Wen Ti*, Vol. 1, p. 102; Pan Yunkang, *Zhong Guo Cheng Shi Hun Yin Jia Ting*, p. 270; Yuan Fang, "The Status and Role of the Chinese Elderly," p. 40.

109. It is somehow inexact to view the *Bulletin* as creating precedent in the same way that such decisions would in a system of common law as in the United

States. China follows a code system, in which only published statutes, not judicial decisions, carry the weight of law. In China during the 1980s, however, the *Bulletin* in practice did articulate the consensus of the highest levels of the CCP judicial leaders, and it is in that sense that I use precedent here.

110. In a 1986 decision, the Supreme Court upheld a decision of a Dalien city court that step-children must continue to support their divorced step-mother on the grounds that she had raised them — thereby reversing a decision of the Provincial Court, which had asked for instructions (*qing shi*). "Guan yu ji mu yu sheng fu li hun hou," *Zui Gao Ren Min Fa Yuan Gong Bao*, No. 2 (1986), p. 33; In 1986 the Court approved a Fujian Provincial Court which upheld an adopted son's right to inherit on the basis that the father had sent him money when he was a child, and testimony by neighbors that the man had acted as a real son, even though after the adopted father's death, the son returned to his biological parents. "Guan yu mei cheng nian yang ze nu," *Zui Gao Ren Min Fa Yuan Gong Bao* No. 3 (1986), p. 17. In 1987 the Supreme Court decided that an elderly widowed daughter in Hunan could inherit a house that had been her mother's since land reform because the daughter was a legal heir and because she had lived jointly with and cared for the mother for more than thirty years. "Guang yu tu gai shi bu fen que quan," *Zui Gao Ren Min Fa Yuan Gong Bao* No. 2 (1987), p. 19. In 1987, the Court instructed the Guizhou Provincial Court that a married daughter who had left home forty years earlier had no right to her parents' home after the death of her brother in 1983 because her mother had given the house to a brother in 1941, he had registered the house as his property twice, and only after his death did she raise a claim. *Zui Gao Ren Min Fa Yuan Gong Bao* No. 3 (1987), p. 26.

111. Also confirming this reluctance to break with past custom are several accounts in the journal of the Ministry of Justice, *Fa Zhi Jian She*, which support the right of individuals to disinherit statutory heirs, even one who provided care; but in every case the disinherited person is a young woman who can care for herself, and thus the articles all enforce the practice that only needy daughters would get consideration. Thus by supporting the use of a will, the articles actually support the right of males or the male line to priority in the share of family or conjugal property. See *Fa Zhi Jian She* No. 3 (1984), p. 48; No. 4 (1984), pp. 62–63.

112. Article 18 stated that parents and children had non-negotiable obligations (*yi wu*) to support each other when members of either generation could not support themselves; by analogy children were given shares of the parents' property in proportion to the care they gave the parents prior to their death. For examples of the application of this argument, see cases in advice columns, in *Min Zu Yu Fa Zhi*, No. 7 (1983), pp. 19–20, and pp. 46–47; *ibid.*, No. 8 (1983), p. 45; *ibid.*, No. 9 (1983), p. 46; *ibid.*, No. 11 (1983), p. 43; *ibid.*, No. 1 (1984), pp. 29–31.

113. Response from Cheng Li to query about inheritance rights of sons and daughters. *Zhong Guo Fu Nu*, No. 2 (1980), p. 29.

114. Horkheimer, "Authority and the Family," in *Critical Theory*, pp. 47–128.

SELECT BIBLIOGRAPHY

Aird, John. "Population Growth in the People's Republic of China." In *Chinese Economy Post-Mao*, U.S. Congress, Joint Economic Committee. Washington, D.C.: U.S. Government Printing Office, 1978.

———— "Recent Demographic Data from China." In *China under the Four Modernizations*, Part I. U.S. Congress, Joint Economic Committee, Washington, D.C.: U.S. Government Printing Office, 1982.

Banister, Judith. *China's Changing Population*. Stanford, Calif.: Stanford University Press, 1987.

Beauvoir, Simone de. *The Coming of Age*. New York: Warner, 1973.

Bei jing jing ji xue yuan ren kou jing ji yen jiu suo (Demographic economics research office, Beijing College of Economics). "Bei jing shi san ge zhu wei tui xiu zhi gong he 60 sui yi shang lao nian ren qing kuang diao" (Survey of living situation of Beijing retirees 60 and older in three residential neighborhoods), *Ren Kou yu Jing Ji*, No. 5 (1986), pp. 15–21.

Bian Yanjie, "Equal Education and Unequal Outcomes." Paper presented at workshop on "Gender and Inequality in Urban China," Yale University, Jan. 20, 1990.

Blaustein, Albert P. *Fundamental Legal Documents of Communist China*. South Hackensack, N.J.: Rothman, 1962.

Burgess, Ernest W. *Aging in Western Societies*. Chicago: University of Chicago Press, 1960.

Bush, Richard C. *Religion in Communist China*. Nashville, Tenn.: Abingdon, 1970.

Chan, Anita, Richard Madsen, and Jonathan Unger. *Chen Village*. Berkeley: University of California Press, 1984.

Chen, Jack. *A Year in Upper Felicity*. New York: Macmillan, 1973.

Chinn, Dennis L. "Basic Commodity Distribution in the People's Republic of China," *The China Quarterly*, No. 84 (Dec. 1980), pp. 744–54.

Chu, T'ung-tsu. *Law and Society in Traditional China*. Paris: Mouton, 1965.

Cohen, Myron. *House United, House Divided*. New York: Columbia University Press, 1976.

Cowgill, Donald O., and Lowell D. Holmes. *Aging and Modernization*. New York: Appleton-Century-Crofts, 1972.

Crook, Isabel, and David Crook. *Ten Mile Inn*. New York: Pantheon, 1979.

Crook, Frederick C. "The Commune System in the People's Republic of China." In *China: A Reassessment of the Economy*, papers submitted to the U.S. Congress, Joint Economic Committee, July 10, 1975, pp. 394–402.

Davin, Delia. *Woman-Work*. Oxford, Eng.: Oxford University Press, 1976.

Davis, Deborah. "Chinese Social Welfare Policies and Outcomes," *The China Quarterly*, No. 119 (Sept. 1989), pp. 577–97.

——— "My Mother's House." In Perry Link, Richard Madsen, and Paul Pickowicz, eds. *Unofficial China*. Boulder, Col.: Westview, 1989, pp. 88–100.

——— "Unequal Chances, Unequal Outcomes: Pension Reforms and Urban Inequality," *The China Quarterly*, No. 114 (June 1988), pp. 223–42.

——— and Ezra Vogel, eds., *Chinese Society on the Eve of Tiananmen*. Cambridge, Mass.: Harvard University Press, 1990.

Davis-Friedmann, Deborah. "Welfare Practices in Rural China," *World Development*, 6 (1978), pp. 609–19.

Domes, Jurgen. "New Policies in the Communes," *Journal of Asian Studies*, 41, 2 (Feb. 1982): p. 253–67.

Freedman, Maurice. *Chinese Lineage and Society*. London: Athlone, 1966.

Fu Luxia, "Jia ting jie gou," (Family structure), *She hui*, No. 5 (1987), pp. 39–41.

Gao Yuan. *Born Red*. Stanford, Calif.: Stanford University Press, 1987.

Gu Jirui. *Jia Ting Xiao Fei Jing Ji Xue* (Economics of family consumption). Beijing: Zhong guo cai zheng jing ji chu ban she, 1988.

Guo Wu Yuan Ren Kou Pu Cha Ban Gong Shi (State Council Census Office). *Zhong Guo 1982 Nian Ren Kou Pu Cha 10% Chou Yang Zi Liao* (10 percent sample of 1982 Census). Beijing: Zhong guo tong ji chu ban she, 1983.

Hochschild, Arlie. *The Unexpected Community*. Englewood Cliffs, N.J.: Prentice Hall, 1973.

Honig, Emily, and Gail Hershatter. *Personal Voices: Chinese Women in the 1980's*. Stanford, Calif.: Stanford University Press, 1988.

Horkheimer, Max. "Authority and the Family." In *Critical Theory*, trans. Matthew J. O'Connell (New York: Herder & Herder, 1972), pp. 47–128.

Hsu, Francis L. K. "Chinese Kinship and Chinese Behavior." In P. T. Ho and Tang Tsou, eds., *China in Crisis*. Chicago: University of Chicago Press, 1968.

Ikels, Charlotte. "New Options for Urban Elderly." In Davis and Vogel, eds., *Chinese Society on the Eve of Tiananmen*.

Judd, Ellen. "*Niangjia*: Chinese Women and Their Natal Families," *Journal of Asian Studies*, 48, 3 (1989), 525–44.

Keyfitz, Nathan. "Population and Employment in China." Working paper of the International Institute for Applied Systems Analysis A-2361. Laxenburg, Austria, Feb. 1982.

Kojima, Reeitsu. "Agricultural Organization: New Forms, New Contradictions," *The China Quarterly*, No. 116 (Dec. 1988), p. 706–35.

Lao Dong Gong Zhi Ren Shi Zhi Du Gai Ge de Yan Jiu yu Tan Dao (Research and inquiry into the reform of the wage and personnel system). Beijing: Lao dong ren shi chu ban she, 1985.

Lao Nian Wen Ti (Problems of the elderly). Shanghai: Fu Dan da xue chu ban she, 1985.

Lee, Hong Yong. "The Socialist State, Political Elites, and Reforms in China" (book manuscript).

Lee, Yok-shiu F. "The Urban Housing Problem in China," *The China Quarterly*, No. 115 (Sept. 1988), pp. 387–407.

Levy, Marion. *The Family Revolution in Modern China*. New York: Atheneum, 1968.

Lin Yueh-hwa. *The Golden Wing*. London: K. Paul, Trench, & Trubner, 1947.

Lippit, Victor D. *Land Reform and Economic Development*. White Plains, N.Y.: International Arts & Sciences Press, 1974.

Lu Ping. *Yin Hai Zhi Ge* (The song of the silver sea). Shanghai: Ren min mei shu chu ban she, 1978.

MacInnis, Donald. *Religious Policy and Practice in Communist China*. New York: Macmillan, 1972.

Mao Kuangsheng and Zhou Guangfu. "Ren kou nian ling jie gou dui jia ting bian hua de ying xiang" (Influence of age structure on family change), *Ren Kou Yan Jiu*, No. 5 (1988), pp. 8–12.

Myrdal, Jan. *Report from a Chinese Village*. New York: Vintage, 1965.

—— and Gun Kessle. *China: The Revolution Continued*. London: Chatto & Windus, 1971.

Naughton, Barry. "The Decline of Central Control over Investment in Post-Mao China." In D. Michael Lampton, ed., *Policy Implementation in Post-Mao China.*(Berkeley: University California Press, 1987), pp. 51–80.

Pan, Yunkang. *Zhong Guo Cheng Shi Hun Yin Yu Jia Ting* (Chinese urban marriage and family). Jinan: Shandong ren min chu ban she, 1987.

Palmore, Erdman, and Kenneth Marston. "Modernization and Status of the Aged," *Journal of Gerontology*, 29, 2 (1974), 205–10.

Parish, William L. "Socialism and the Chinese Peasant Family," *Journal of Asian Studies*, 34, 3 (May 1975), pp. 613–30.

—— and Martin K. Whyte. *Village and Family in Contemporary China*. Chicago: University of Chicago Press, 1978.

Planning Committee of Fujian Province Revolutionary Committee. *Lao dong gong zi wen jian xuan pien* (Collected documents on wages).

Pruitt, Ida. *A Daughter of Han*. Stanford, Calif.: Stanford University Press, 1967.

Qian Jiang-hong, "Marriage Related Consumption," *Social Science in China* No. 1 (1988), pp. 208–28.

Qiu Liping. "Cheng shi gao ling lao ren jia ting jie gou," (Research on family organization of the very old). In *Gao Ling Lao Ren Wen Ti Yen Jiu* (Research on problems of the very old). Shanghai: Shanghai shi lao nian xue xue hui mi shu, 1987.

Rawski, Thomas G. *Industrialization, Technology, and Employment in the PRC*. Washington, D.C.: World Bank, 1978.

Riskin, Carl. *China's Political Economy*. New York: Oxford University Press, 1987.

Rosow, Irving. *Socialization to Old Age*. Berkeley: University of California Press, 1974.

Schulz, James, and Deborah Davis-Friedmann. *Aging China: Family, Economics, and Government Policies in Transition*. Washington, D.C.: Gerontological Society of America, 1987.

Schurmann, Franz. *Ideology and Organization in Communist China*. Berkeley: University of California Press, 1968.

Schwartz, Louis. "The Inheritance Law of the People's Republic of China," *Harvard Journal of International Law*, 28, 2 (Spring 1987), 433–64.

Selden, Mark. *The People's Republic of China: A Documentary History*. New York: Monthly Review Press, 1979.

Skinner, G. William. "Chinese Peasants and the Closed Community," *Comparative Studies in Society and History*, No. 13 (1971), pp. 270–81.

Shang Hai She Hui Tong Ji Zi Liao 1980–1983 (Shanghai social statistics for 1980–1983). Shanghai: Hua dong shi fan da xue chu ban she, 1988.

Shang hai shih lao nian wen ti wei yuan wei (Shanghai committee on problems of the old). *Gao Ling Lao Ren Wen Ti Yan Jiu* (Research on the problems of the very old). Shanghai, 1987.

Shang Hai Tong Ji Nian Jian 1983 (Shanghai Statistical Yearbook for 1983). Shanghai: Ren min chu ban she, 1984.

Shang Hai Tong Ji Nian Jian 1988 (Shanghai Statistical Yearbook for 1988). Shanghai: Zhong guo tong ji chu ben she, 1988.

State Statistical Bureau of the PRC. *A Survey of Income and Household Conditions in China.* Beijing: New World Press, 1985.

Sung, Lung-sheng. "Property and Family Division." In Emily Ahern and Hill Gates, eds., *The Anthropology of Taiwanese Society.* Stanford, Calif.: Stanford University Press, 1981, pp. 361–78.

Tao Liqun, "Guan yu wo guo ren kou lao nian hua wen ti" (On the subject of population aging in China), *She Hui*, No. 2 (1984), pp. 1–7.

Terrill, Ross. *Flowers on an Iron Tree.* Boston: Little, Brown, 1975.

Tian H. Yuan and Che-fu Lee. "The Chinese Family and Induced Population Transition," *Social Science Quarterly* 69, 3 (Sept. 1988), 605–28.

Tian Wen-guang. "Da li tui hang nong cun ji hua sheng yu yang lao bao xian" (Energetically press for rural planned birth–old age insurance), *Ren Kou Yan Jiu*, No. 4 (1988), pp. 56–58.

Tu, Edward, Jersey Liang, and Shaomin Li. "Mortality Decline and Chinese Family Structure," *Journal of Gerontology,* 44, 4 (July 1989), pp. 157–68.

Walder, Andrew. *Chinese Neo-Traditionalism.* Berkeley: University of California Press, 1986.

———— "Income Distribution in Tianjin." In Davis and Vogel, eds., *Chinese Society on the Eve of Tiananmen.*

———— "Wage Reform and the Web of Factory Interests," *The China Quarterly,* No. 109 (March 1987), pp. 22–41.

Wang Shuxin, "Jing ji ti zhi gai ge zhong de Bei jing shi liu dong ren kou" (The floating population of Beijing during the economic reform era). *Ren Kou yu Jing Ji, no.* 1 (1986), pp. 6–11.

Wei Jiuling, "Gai ge shi nian" (Ten years of reform), *Zhong Guo Lao Dong Ke Xue,* No. 1 (1989), p. 25.

Whyte, Martin. "Changes in Mate Selection in Chengdu." In Davis and Vogel, eds., *Chinese Society on the Eve of Tiananmen.*

———— "Inequality and Stratification in China," *The China Quarterly,* No. 64 (Dec. 1975), pp. 688–89.

———— and William Parish. *Urban Life in Contemporary China.* Chicago: University of Chicago Press, 1984.

Wolf, Margery. *Women and the Family in Rural Taiwan.* Stanford, Calif.: Stanford University Press, 1972.

Yang, C. K. *The Chinese Family in the Communist Revolution.* Cambridge, Mass.: MIT Press, 1965.

———— *Religion in Chinese Society.* Berkeley: University of California Press, 1967.

———— *A Chinese Village in Early Communist Transition.* Cambridge, Mass.: MIT Press, 1966.

Yang, Martin C. *A Chinese Village.* New York: Columbia University Press, 1965.

Yang, Mo. *Zai Yen Xiao de Da Di Shang* (Above the smoldering plain). Tianjin: Ren min mei shu chu ban she, 1978.

Yang, Simon, and L. K. Tao. *A Study of the Standard of Living of Working Families in Shanghai.* Peiping: Institute of Social Research, 1931.

Yang Xiao. *Making of a Peasant Doctor.* Beijing: Foreign Language Press, 1976.

Yang Zongchuan. "Hubei sheng cheng zhen xiang lao nian ren kou xian chuang fen xi" (Analysis of the condition of the elderly in urban and rural Hubei), *Ren Kou Yan Jiu,* No. 1 (1989), pp. 28–36.

Youmans, Grant. *Older Rural Americans.* Lexington: University of Kentucky Press, 1967.

Yuan Fang. "The Status and Role of the Chinese Elderly in Families and Society." In Schulz and Davis-Friedmann, eds., *Aging China,* pp. 36–46.

Yuan Jihui. *Cheng Shi Lao Nian Sheng Huo Yan Jiu* (Research on the urban elderly), vol. 1. Shanghai: Shang hai da xue wen xue yuan, 1985.

———— *Cheng Shi Lao Nian Sheng Huo Yan Jiu* (Research on the urban elderly), vol 2. Suzhou: Shanghai da xue wen xue yuan, 1986.

———— *Dang Dai Lao Nian She Hui Xue* (Contemporary gerontology). Shanghai: Fudan da xue chu ban she, 1989.

Zhang Yulin. "The Shifts of Surplus Agricultural Labor," and "Peasant Workers in County Towns." In Fei Hsiao-tung, *Small Towns in China.* Beijing: New World Press, 1986, pp. 171–210.

Zhong Guo 1987 Nian 1% Ren Kou Chou Yang Diao Cha Zi Liao (Tabulations of China's 1987 1 percent Population Sample Survey). Beijing: Zhong guo tong ju chu ban she, 1988.

Zhong Guo Cheng Shi Tong Ji Nian Jian 1987 (Chinese urban statistical yearbook for 1987). Beijing: Zhong guo jian she chu ban she, 1987.

Zhong Guo Cheng Shi Jia Ting (Chinese urban families). Jinan: Shan dong ren min chu ban she, 1985.

Zhong Guo Fa Lu Nian Jian 1987 (Chinese law yearbook for 1987). Shanghai: Fa lu chu ban she, 1987.

Zhong Guo Jiao Yu Tong Ji Nian Jian 1987 (Chinese education statistical yearbook 1987). Beijing: Guo jia jiao yu wei yuan hui ji hua cai wu zhu bian, 1988.

Zhong Guo Lao Dong Gong Ce Tong Ji Zi Liao 1949–1985 (Chinese labor and wage statistics, 1949–1985). Beijing: Zhong guo tong ji chu ban she, 1987.

Zhong Guo She Hui Tong Ji Zi Liao 1987 (Chinese social statistics for 1987). Beijing: Zhong guo tong ji chu ban she, 1987.

Zhong Guo Tong Ji Nian Jian 1988 (Chinese statistical yearbook for 1988). Beijing: Zhong guo tong ji chu ban she, 1988.

Zhong Guo Tong Ji Zhai Yao 1987 (Excerpts from the 1987 statistical yearbook). Beijing: Zhong guo tong ji chu ban she, 1987.

Zhou Jing, "Wo guo xian dai hua guo cheng zhong nong cun jia ting gui mo" (Family form in the Chinese transition to modernization), *Ren Kou Yan Jiu,* No. 2 (1988), pp. 17–21.

INDEX